tender accents of sound

Spanish in the Chicano Novel in English

Bilingual Press/Editorial Bilingüe

General Editor
   Gary D. Keller

Managing Editor
   Karen S. Van Hooft

Associate Editors
   Ann Waggoner Aken
   Barbara H. Firoozye

Assistant Editor
   Linda St. George Thurston

Editorial Consultant
   Ingrid Muller

Editorial Board
   Juan Goytisolo
   Francisco Jiménez
   Eduardo Rivera
   Mario Vargas Llosa

Address:
Bilingual Review/Press
Hispanic Research Center
Arizona State University
P.O. Box 872702
Tempe, Arizona 85287-2702
(602) 965-3867

tender accents of sound

Spanish in the Chicano Novel in English

Ernst Rudin

Bilingual Press/Editorial Bilingüe
TEMPE, ARIZONA

ISBN 0-927534-52-5

Library of Congress Cataloging-in-Publication Data

Rudin, Ernst.
    Tender accents of sound : Spanish in the Chicano novel in English
    / by Ernst Rudin.
        p.   cm.
    Includes bibliographical references (p.   ) and index.
    ISBN 0-927534-52-5 (paper)
        1. American fiction—Mexican American authors—History and
    criticism. 2. English language—United States—Foreign words and
    phrases—Spanish. 3. Spanish language—United States—Influence on
    English. 4. Languages in contact—United States. 5. Mexican
    Americans in literature. 6. Mexican Americans—Language.
    I. Title.
    PS374.M48R83   1994
    813'.540986872—dc20   94-34228
                                                              CIP

PRINTED IN THE UNITED STATES OF AMERICA

Cover design by Thomas Detrie

Acknowledgments

Major new marketing initiatives have been made possible by the Lila Wallace-Reader's Digest Literary Publishers Marketing Development Program, funded through a grant to the Council of Literary Magazines and Presses.

Contents

English, brought to close quarters with formidable rivals, has won very often, not by mere force of numbers and intransigence, but by the weight of its intrinsic merit. "In riches, good sense and terse convenience (*Reichtum, Vernunft und gedrängter Fuge*)," said the eminent Jakob Grimm nearly a century ago, "no other of the living languages may be put beside it." To which the eminent Otto Jespersen adds: "It seems to me positively and expressively masculine. It is the language of a grown-up man, and has very little childish or feminine about it."

H.L. Mencken

Los mejicanos alegres
también a su usanza salen,
que en quien campa la lealtad,
bien es que el aplauso campe.
Y con las cláusulas tiernas
del mejicano lenguaje,
en un tocotín sonoro,
dicen con voces suaves:
Tla ya timohuica
to tlazo ziuapilli
maca ammo tonantzin,
titechmoilcahuiliz.

Sor Juana Inés de la Cruz

To Luschbauer Mitzi's Marianne Sophie
con fuerte acento

Introduction

The Chicano novel has been approached in manifold ways by the critics. Apart from a great number of articles on individual works, there are various surveys of it, its historical development has been delineated, its sources and themes have been documented, and it has been approached ontologically.[1] At the same time, the multilingual potential of Mexican American literature has often been posited and taken for granted by authors and critics alike, and various articles have been published on the theme. But neither in the field of the Chicano novel nor in the more spectacularly bilingual ones of poetry and theater has there been a book-length analysis on the subject to date.

My study intends to fill part of that gap by analyzing the Spanish-language elements that appear in nineteen Chicano prose narratives in English—seventeen novels and two autobiographies—published between 1967 and 1985. I first recorded all the Spanish entries and other language-related passages that occur in that corpus using the text retrieval program *Text-Base* (Dragonfly Software), classifying them according to various criteria and adding contextual quotes and comments. This textual database then became the basis for my analysis of the uses and literary functions of those Spanish-language entries that, by recurring within the corpus, form significant clusters and make patterns recognizable. My study consists of three parts:

• *Contexts* introduces the theme of English and Spanish in U.S. society and in Chicano literature, presents the texts

---

1   See, for example, the bibliographies by Eger, Tatum, Lomelí/Urioste, and the bibliographic sections in Martínez/Lomelí. See also: Tatum "Contemporary Chicano Prose Fiction" and *Chicano Literature* 102-137, Lattin "Novel," and Tonn; Leal "Historical Perspective" and "Narrativa Chicana," Lomelí "Novel"; Leal/Barrón, Jiménez "Chicano Literature"; Ramón Saldívar "Dialectic of Difference."

of the corpus, and deals with issues that are at the core of bilingualism in the Chicano novel. It analyzes the thematic treatment of Spanish and English in the corpus, introduces the notion of the Chicano author as a translator between cultures, exemplifies this notion by means of Rolando Hinojosa's reelaboration of one of his Spanish novels in English, and shows how the texts of the corpus can reveal their Spanish-speaking setting without using Spanish-language elements.

- *Spanish-Language Entries* presents and classifies the Spanish entries according to their type, to the way in which they are incorporated in the English text, and to four semantic fields. Analysis focuses on the literary function of the Spanish-language entries, especially on the distance between the implied author and a monolingual reader that these foreign language elements may express. The section closes with an assessment of four novels written by Chicanas and published after 1985, which, in various respects, represent a change of paradigm in comparison with the texts of the corpus. The question asked will be whether this change also finds its reflection in the uses and functions of Spanish-language elements.

- *Statistics* presents some of the net results of my text-base work. It lists the Spanish entries divided into semantic fields, shows their frequency, and assesses their use in each of the texts statistically.

It is essential to point out that this is a literary analysis. While the political, historical, sociological, and linguistic aspects—crucial factors of Chicano existence, as the considerable number of publications in all these fields shows—[2] are

---

2   Cf., e.g., *450 Años del Pueblo Chicano / 450 Years of Chicano History in Pictures* and Acuña, on Chicano history; Calvo Buezas and Cockroft on Mexican immigrant workers, Namias *First Generation* or Binder *Anglos* on sociopolitical aspects of culture contact and acculturation. Linguistic, sociolinguistic, and historical linguistic approaches, finally, are present in Blanco, Durán, Fernández-Shaw, Hernández-Chavez, and Ornstein "Sociolinguistics."

present as the framework of my study, my interest lies in the ways in which Chicano narratives *represent* and *express* these aspects. The texts of the corpus are clearly related to the sociopolitical reality of Chicanos in the United States, but I am not primarily interested in finding out *how authentically* they depict that reality. I read them, as Tzvetan Todorov would have it, as *acts*, not as *descriptions* (*Conquête* 59).

Most Chicano authors who write in English know both the Anglo and the Mexican American cultural contexts and both languages. It is therefore not astonishing that their narrators often mediate between the two, adopt or subvert culturally conditioned stereotypes, and translate linguistic and cultural differences for their intended readership. And the Spanish-language elements in their texts constitute one of the most salient and revealing markers of these processes of translation.

Since Spanish entries are not distributed evenly throughout the corpus, some texts will be quoted and commented upon more frequently than others in the pages to follow. Moreover, at some points of my study one or several of the texts will be foregrounded in order to illustrate the usage or the function of a specific stylistic device. The amount of coverage a text receives does not primarily reflect its overall literary quality but stands in relation to the amount, the characteristics, and the diversity of the bilingual strategies it uses. By the same token, literary analysis of a determinate set of features in a large number of texts can reveal the distinctive qualities of each of these texts only in an incidental manner. The examination of "subordinated stylistic unities," to phrase it in Bakhtin's words, has to fall short of doing justice to each "novel as a whole," to the interplay of discourses within each text. "A symphonic (orchestrated) theme" is transposed "on to the piano keyboard" (263). When specific discourses and stylistic devices show an increased presence in a body of texts, however, a literary analysis that focuses on *determinate* discourses in *various* works instead of on the *various* discourses within *one* work provides insights that studies of single texts cannot give—and these insights are all the more significant if the chosen focus is as essential a factor as bilingualism in Mexican American lives and letters.

Typographic Conventions

I have adopted some formal and typographic guidelines: apart from their standard uses, italics are used for some terms that have a specifically defined connotation in this study (e.g., *otherness*, *loanword*, *terms of address*), for Spanish single words or compounds, and, in the chapter on Rolando Hinojosa, for quotations from the Spanish version. In all the other chapters, the use of italics in longer quotations reflects that of the original. Moreover, since many of the texts do not use diacritics in Spanish—and since I did not want to cram quotations with royally academic *sics*—the absence of Spanish accents and tildes will be reflected in quotations but not especially marked. The same goes for the orthographic reflection of *seseo* (the pronunciation of Castilian /θ/ as /s/) in Spanish entries.

Acknowledgments

Some of the arguments presented here have been published previously and are used with the kind permission of the copyright holders. An earlier version of chapter 4 has appeared in *Gender, Self, and Society* (ed. Renate von Bardeleben, Frankfurt am Main: Peter Lang, 1993). Spanish versions of the sections "Bilingualism in Literature" (chapter 2) and "Culinary Terms" (chapter 11) have been published respectively in *Literatura y bilingüismo* (ed. Elvezio Canonica and Ernst Rudin, Kassel: Reichenberger, 1993) and *Versants* 21, 1992.
This book arose out of my doctoral dissertation at the University of Basel, Switzerland. While I am the only one responsible for its shortcomings, its merits are not only mine. I would like to thank, in the first place, my two supervisors,

Professors Hartwig Isernhagen and Pere Ramírez. I still have not found out by just what fun-house mirrors, moirés, and mirages Hartwig Isernhagen manages—without sacrificing competence—to convert the ivory tower into a forum that invites discussion and debate. Pere Ramírez backed me up with his profound knowledge of the Hispanic literatures outside the United States and offered me his keen and helpful comments y su amistad in spite of my ongoing Anglophile adultery. I am grateful to the John F. Kennedy Institute of the Freie Universität Berlin for a scholarship that allowed me to use their marvelous library in 1987. Thank you to Gary Keller, who made it possible for me to publish this book in Mexican America, and to Karen Van Hooft, Ann Aken, and Barbara Firoozye for their editorial guidance. Thanks also, for their support and encouragement, their advice and their comments, to Marcelo Aebi, Erlinda Gonzales-Berry, Ramón Gutiérrez, Otto Heim, Urban Hügin, Karin Isernhagen, Francisco Lomelí, Mariano López, Antonio Márquez, Karin Ramírez, Max Scherrer, Winfried Siemerling, Werner Sollors, Eileen Sommer, Erlene Stetson, Horst Tonn, Gayle Wurst, Anne Zimmermann, and Sibylle Rudin-Bühlmann. A very special thank you, finally, to Kevin McCafferty—always much more than a proofreader.

Contexts

1. The Language of Chicano Literature

When, in the late seventies, Juan Bruce-Novoa asks fourteen Chicano authors whether the Chicano novel has "a particular language or idiom," only Estela Portillo Trambley begins her answer with a rotund affirmation:

> Yes, Chicano literature has a particular language. I believe that the idiom of the Chicano finds its spontaneity in the natural combination of the two languages. Language reflects the human experience, and Chicanos do bridge the two cultures. It is a freedom, a flexibility and a confidence. (*Chicano Authors* 171)

while Tomás Rivera is the only one to start out in the negative:

> No, it has to have the particular idiom of the writer, whatever that idiom is. It doesn't have to be a particular one. No, I don't think so. I don't like any kind of dogmas, and certainly not within a creative effort of people . . . (147f)

The *yes* and the *no* do not express contradiction but rather agreement. Though Rivera understands "language or idiom" as 'personal style' while Portillo is referring more explicitly to English and Spanish, both writers agree that Chicano literature cannot be pinned down to any particular mode of expression —that it is marked by stylistic and linguistic diversity. It is this diversity that makes Rivera answer "no" and Portillo "yes." The other authors interviewed, although some of them may state a personal preference for Spanish, bilingual, or *caló* (Chicano slang) texts,[3] tend to make a case for the bilingual or

---

3   "But, as you know, I prefer Spanish" (54, Hinojosa). "I consider myself a nationalist and write in Spanish" (74, Elizondo). "Spanish suits me best" (88, Méndez). "The bilingual expression of the word is probably the most important" (125, Montoya). "I like to think of Caló as the language of Chicano literature" (209, Zamora).

plurilingual potential of Chicano literature and for leaving the choice of language up to each individual author.[4]

Spanish is not the preferred language in the Chicano novel produced so far. English is the language choice of most novelists. While English may also dominate in Chicano theater and poetry, code switching has nonetheless almost become a trademark of a considerable part of Chicano poetry, as well as of some of the stereotypic characters in the *teatro campesino.* The novel, however, is the genre with the strongest predominance of English. The novels written in Spanish, and even more so the bilingual ones, are numerically in a weak position in comparison to the English ones; they are a "minority literature"[5] within a "minority literature," so to speak. The reason for this imbalance is difficult if not impossible to determine. In any case, the Chicano authors' plea for freedom of artistic expression should not detract from the fact that a writer's decision for one of the two languages, or for any kind of combination of them, does have its consequences. For the writer —always provided that she or he is bilingual and *does* have a choice—it leads not only to a different readership, but also to different channels of publication, to a larger or smaller audience, and hence to larger or smaller royalties. And it affects the North American reader, because the reading does or does

---

4   "Chicano literature is written in Spanish, in English, in Spanish and English, in some of the Pachuco caló, and usually colored by the regionalism which may be due to the author's background" (54, Hinojosa); "in the total sum of Chicano literature, bilingualistic mix, even more than two languages at times, is a trademark too big to ignore" (101, Delgado). "Well it has several. The bilingual expression of the word is probably the most important, but there are all kinds of ways, and it's coming out more and more" (125, Montoya).

5   Various other terms like *ethnic, pluriethnic,* or *multicultural literature* have been used to designate roughly the same phenomenon, which Deleuze and Guattari in their turn call *littérature mineure* (24). Each of these designations has its advantages and its drawbacks; none of them can be used anymore as a neutral and purely descriptive term. Instead of adding a new term with a "clean record," I have opted to use the already existing ones and to indicate their problematic nature with quotation marks.

not require a knowledge of Spanish, Spanglish, or Pachuco slang. Moreover, the two languages themselves have quite different values in the United States and in the world. On a global scale, English is the language of one of the world powers, which in its official rhetoric tends to present itself as the world's number one nation and as a model for the rest of the world to follow. Furthermore, what George Steiner observed in 1975 in *After Babel* has only increased since then:

> [The] entire world-image of mass consumption, of international exchange, of the popular arts, of generational conflict, of technocracy, is permeated by American-English and English citations and speech habits . . . English dominates as a world-language whose reach far exceeds that of Latin in the historical past, and whose efficacy has all but nullified such schemes as Esperanto. (468f)

English has become the *lingua franca* for international politics, business, science, and communications, as well as for the so-called "New Literatures in English." By the same token, the "boom" of Hispanic American literature outside the Spanish-speaking world would be a much lesser phenomenon had the works of Borges, Cortázar, Fuentes, García Márquez, and others not been translated into English. Spanish, on the other hand, which is mainly at home in parts south of the North-South divide, has a different status and especially so in North America. If the cover blurb of Paul Ehrlich's *The Golden Door: International Migration, Mexico, and the United States* makes the sensational claim that:

> Our most potentially disastrous national problem, along with the danger of nuclear war and threats to the environment, is the pressing catastrophe of massive illegal immigration,

the threat perceived may in the first place be an economic one. Nevertheless, it also stigmatizes the Spanish language. From a North American standpoint, Spanish is a language spoken by immigrant workers and in countries that the United States has seldom regarded as nations with equal rights, but rather as its

hinterland; Cuba, Nicaragua, and Panama are examples.
Movements like *English Only, English First,* and *English Plus,*
the November 1986 referendum that declared English to be
California's official language, the ensuing similar referenda in
other states, and the ongoing controversy about bilingual
education further indicate that the relationship between English
and Spanish in the United States is not a neutral one.[6] In
addition, the image of Mexican culture is often negatively connoted in North American society,[7] literature (cf. Márquez
"Discordant Image"; Robinson), and film. Mexican Spanish is
a "lingo" used in Westerns and spaghetti Westerns by dim-
witted *bandidos* with *sombreros* who spout "*vámonos*" and
"*ayayay*" and who try in vain to overwhelm solitary Anglo-
Saxon avengers (cf. Pettit, esp. ch. 9), and the Spanish vernacular of the Southwest is frequently regarded as a slang

---

6   See Arciniega, Mackey and Ornstein, Wiget, Elizabeth Ehrlich; or
    the articles compiled under the heading "America's Official Lan-
    guage?" in the September 1990 issue of the *American Studies News-
    letter* ("Say it in English," Glazer, Hayakawa, "English Plus").
7   "Despite the flow of people across the border, not much information
    about Mexico seems to reach the United States. To most Americans,
    Mexico is an undifferentiated area south of the border—a land of
    'Frito banditos,' mariachi music, tropical resorts, corruption,
    siestas, spicy food, marijuana, and poverty. It also seems a land
    without a history, for the average American is unaware of the epic,
    four-hundred-year struggle of the Mexican peoples to form a nation
    and free themselves from foreign domination. How many Americans
    concerned about illegal Mexican immigration and the Chicano
    minority realize that it is the Anglos who are the more recent immi-
    grants to the Southwest, occupying by right of conquest nearly half
    the territory once recognized as Mexico? Ignorance, prejudice, and
    romanticism blend to form a view of Mexico, Mexicans, and Mexi-
    can history that has little to do with reality, but goes a long way to
    explain why many Americans are fooled by jingoistic presentations
    of the Mexican 'problem'" (Ehrlich 94). Ehrlich's book, although
    undoubtedly written from an Anglo American perspective, is more
    nuanced than its cover blurb, cited above, might suggest.

inferior to Standard Spanish.[8] Finally, the hierarchy of power between the two languages can also manifest itself in an Anglo attitude of censure and ridicule towards the faulty use of English by Chicanos—an attitude that contrasts with the frequently incorrect Spanish used by U.S. administrative offices on official papers, street signs, etc. (cf. Peñalosa 11-12). It remains to be seen to what extent the North American Free Trade Agreement will affect the relationship between the languages and the people of the United States and Mexico.

The North American Southwest is what Mary Louise Pratt has called a *contact zone*, a space "where cultures meet, clash, and grapple with each other, often in contexts of highly asymmetrical relations of power" (34). Language contact between Hispanics and Anglos in this zone is marked by the hierarchy of English over Spanish. The existence of this hierarchy and the predominance of English in Chicano literature do not imply that everything English in that literature is inherently non-Chicano or mainstream—nor do Chicano texts in Spanish

---

8   Peñalosa links this with the issue of bilingual education: "One problem making needed reforms difficult is that, in general, Chicanos do poorly in high school and college Spanish classes because of the devaluation of their vernacular. As a result, at the graduate school level Chicanos are vastly outnumbered by Anglos in Spanish M.A. and Ph.D. programs. Spanish departments thus are typically dominated by non-Chicanos: Anglos, Spaniards, or Latin-Americans interested primarily in literature and generally holding narrowly prescriptive attitudes toward language. Chicano self-determination in the linguistic area might well start in Spanish departments as well as in departments of English and Speech.

It is not the case, however, that barrio Spanish must be taught in the classroom. In most instances Standard Spanish will be taught. What is often lacking is teachers' respect for the local vernacular and enough knowledge of it to lead students toward bidialectalism. In some bilingual programs, Spanish is used for teaching Mexican history and literature, for example, but English for mathematics and the sciences, thus fostering the misleading impression that English is the language of a modern scientific, technological society, but Spanish suitable only for literary, folkloristic, and traditional, 'impractical' purposes. Certainly this is not the type of diglossia that we wish to promote" (10).

represent Chicanos per se more "authentically." Nevertheless, the language choice is significant. "Minority" texts in general and Chicano literature in particular have been defined as intrinsically political, revolutionary, and subversive, as writings against the grain of "mainstream" discourses, codes, and values.[9] A Chicano writer's decision to use the "less powerful" of the two languages can in itself be interpreted as a subversive act, as a reaction against linguistic and cultural hegemony (cf. Gonzales-Berry "Chicano Literature" 22-39). Since Spanish or bilingual texts have no means of infiltrating the Anglophone North American culture, their subversiveness has to remain an empty gesture within that culture. On the other hand, those Chicano authors who do not write in Spanish—the first colonial language of the Southwest—encounter a different dilemma that they share with other writers of "New Literatures in English":

> Whatever their aims, all must use the one distinctive common weapon bequeathed to them by the colonizers; the English language, ironically a chief agent in undermining the colonial edifice. (Thorpe 346)

Franz Kafka has defined the very same dilemma for the Jews in Prague, and with regard to the German language, when he talks of their triple handicap: "the impossibility not to write, the impossibility to write in German, and the impossibility to write otherwise" (letter to Max Brod, June 1921, quoted from Deleuze and Guattari 24, my translation; cf. also Steiner 65, Dasenbrock, Isernhagen *Nationale*).

---

9   "Die Literaturen ethnischer, unterdrückter und marginaler Gruppen nehmen im amerikanischen Kanon und Bewußtsein einen Sonderplatz ein. Auf einer abstrakten Ebene wiederholen diese Literaturen den Kampf um literarische Selbstbestimmung und Unabhängigkeit, der die Geschichte der angloamerikanischen Literatur charakterisierte" (Ostendorf "Einleitung" 1, cf. Deleuze/Guattari 28, Ong 3). "It is thus logical for Chicano literature to be of a revolutionary or social-protest nature" (Leal/Barrón 12, cf. Alurista "Cultural Nationalism" 43, Herms, Adolfo Ortega, Trujillo 132, Ybarra Frausto).

The question of why most Chicano novelists have chosen English as their literary language and of the exact motivation for the language choice in the case of each author and each text will not be my concern here. Whether the authors' language preference is ultimately based on economic motivations, whether they have judged English to be the better "agent in undermining" the mainstream "edifice," or whether their language choice is due to still other reasons is a question that is, on the basis of a textual analysis, impossible to answer. What is clear, nonetheless, is that English has come to dominate the global village and that "the weight of its intrinsic merit," as Mencken would have it in *The American Language* (599), is hardly a major reason for that supremacy.

2. Bilingualism

In Literature

Is there such a thing as *bilingual literature?* Bilingual works are a rare phenomenon indeed in the literatures of the Western world if we treat the prefix *bi-* with a minimum of etymological respect and expect it to indicate two elements of equal or at least comparable weight, format, or scope, as other adjectives that include the prefix—from *biacromial* and *bicycle* to *biweekly* and *bizygomatic*—invariably do. One third of the plays of the fifteenth-century Portuguese writer Gil Vicente (Portuguese and Spanish), Felipe Guamán Poma de Ayala's *First New Chronicle and Good Government* (Peru, 1613, Quechua and Spanish), and some poems of the European Baroque could be mentioned as representatives of this very minor genre. The great majority of works that at first sight may present themselves and are sometimes marketed as bi- or even multilingual literature are cases of "bilingualism in literature" rather than "bilingual literature." José María Arguedas's *El zorro de arriba y el zorro de abajo*, T.S. Eliot's *The Waste Land*, James Joyce's *Ulysses*, and Julián Ríos's *Larva* are monolingual works that employ bilingual techniques: One language is clearly primary and the other one (or the other ones) is (or are), equally clearly, secondary.

While bilingual literature proper is hard to find, literary bilingualism—the use of secondary language elements in monolingual literature—occurs frequently and has many different forms. Leonard Forster's classic *The Poet's Tongues: Multilingualism in Literature* shows this for various European literatures from the Middle Ages to the twentieth century, and Elvezio Canonica's extensive study on the use of bilingual techniques in Lope de Vega's theater, to pick an author whom Forster passes over, demonstrates just how variously a monolingual author can employ secondary language entries.

Before dedicating myself more specifically to bilingualism in Chicano literature, I would like to outline some of the essential factors that cooperate in the contact zone of literature and bilingualism, classifying them into the following seven sections:

1. Contexts
2. Genres
3. Forms
4. Types
5. Semantics
6. Methods
7. Functions

It goes without saying that the use of one secondary language differs from the use of of two or more secondary languages in degree, but not in essence.

1. I take *contexts* to designate on the one hand the sociocultural coordinates that determine the relationship of the languages involved, and on the other hand the relationship of the author with these languages. A bilingual work of literature, or one that makes use of a secondary language, may come out of a bilingual region, with a situation of diglossia or code switching between the two languages. Catalonia, the Southwest of the United States, Switzerland, or certain regions of Peru—maybe the entire world with English as a *lingua franca*—offer, at least theoretically, a favorable context for bilingual experiments. There are, however, various social, political and cultural factors that may interfere with such experiments. Diglossia with a spoken and a written language, a difference of social prestige between the two languages involved, or the fact that monolingual publications may transcend the boundaries of the bilingual region and reach a larger audience are three of the possible reasons why the bilingualism of a society is often not reflected—or hardly reflected—in its literature.

If the use of bilingual techniques in a literary work is not directly related to a bilingual environment, the relationship between the two languages involved tends to be less close and more relaxed, although not necessarily neutral. Here, too, the secondary language, especially if it has international resonance, may be marked by prejudices and stereotypes. Russian as a secondary language in a literary work with a Central European or North American audience will evoke different reactions and associations than Arabian, Chinese, or Swahili. And language stereotypes are frequent in Europe, too, where the linguistic and geographic closeness between the various Germanic and Latin dialects facilitates their interaction in and outside literature.

Apart from social factors, bilingual techniques in literature also involve individual factors. An author who uses a secondary language may live or have grown up in a bilingual region, may reflect an individual bilingualism, or her or his use of bilingual techniques may lack any direct autobiographical link. The novel *Rayuela* by the Argentinian author Julio Cortázar, for example, incorporates secondary languages in which its author was fluent (French and English), others of which he had a more passive knowledge (German and Italian), and still others in which he was not versed (Finnish, Japanese, Burmese). Finally, *contexts* includes the motives that impel an author to use a particular secondary language (economic, aesthetic, sentimental) and the connections that may exist between the social and the individual contexts.

2. Although Forster's and other studies of literary bilingualism do without them, considerations of *genre* are essential. Thus, theater can rely on nonverbal means that may make the comprehension of secondary language elements easier. Readers of a poem or a novel, on the other hand, can reread a word, a verse, or a page, or look it up in a dictionary—actions that are hardly practicable during a theater performance. The primacy of rhythm and meter in poetry

or the abundance of different discourses available for the novel are other generic factors affecting the use of secondary language elements.

3. *Forms.* Secondary language elements may take the form of isolated words, phrases, or entire paragraphs and chapters. Their orthography may be left unchanged or may be adapted to the primary language. An author may juxtapose them to the discourses in the primary language or integrate them into them. They may occur—in the case of the novel—only in direct speech passages or also be used by the narrator. Apart from these explicit secondary language elements, the primary language can also be affected by a secondary language in more covert ways, on the morphosyntactic and stylistic levels.

4. The term *types* denotes the degree to which, and the reason why, secondary language entries may already be familiar to a monolingual reader of the primary language. Not all secondary language words are hermetic. Their degree of familiarity depends on the contextual factors mentioned above and on the linguistic distance between the two languages. In addition, some of them may be already known as loanwords, or etymologically related terms may exist in the primary language that facilitate their understanding. By the same token, a considerable number of the secondary language elements in literature are well-known formulas. Expressions like *bonjour, sayonara,* and *señorita*—or *no comment* and *fifty-fifty* if English happens to be the secondary language—are more easily recognizable than cultured, technical, or slang expressions in the primary language.

5. Secondary language entries in a literary work can represent the entire gamut of semantic possibilities or restrict themselves to one or a few *semantic* fields. The *semantic* aspects of secondary language entries tend to be closely related to their *function*.

6. *Methods* signifies the degree of translation of secondary language elements, which may be left without translation

or translated partially or entirely. *Types, semantics,* and *methods* will be analyzed more comprehensively in the respective chapters that follow.

7. Elvezio Canonica distinguishes five *functions* for the secondary language elements in the theater of Lope de Vega: humor, realism, evocation, satire, and narrative. I would propose to expand this list and to structure it slightly in order to make it applicable to other authors, genres, and epochs. I suggest giving priority to the realistic function —to the distinction, in other words, between those uses of a secondary language that have a mimetic function, and those that do not and which—in the absence of a better term—we could call "artificial." There are various kinds of mimetic uses: the secondary language can mark the voice of a stranger, or it may reflect the fact that the literary work is set in a region where another language is spoken than the one in which the book is written. This is the kind of mimesis that is behind the Hispanicisms in Washington Irving's *Alhambra* or the insertions of Galician vocabulary in Camilo José Cela's *Mazurca para dos muertos.* A third possibility could be exemplified by Cela's novel *Cristo versus Arizona* or by some of Luis Valdez's *actos* for the *Teatro campesino,* where *both* languages employed reflect a situation of bilingualism, in this case that of English and Spanish in the Southwest of the United States.

Mimesis, which more often than not adds local color to a literary work, constitutes the bigger share by far of the uses of secondary languages in Western literature. Bilingual techniques without a realistic function are much rarer. They are either purely arbitrary or consist of literary quotations in a secondary language. Cortázar's *Un tal Lucas* and James Joyce's *Ulysses* offer examples of both modalities. *Artificial* uses also include invented languages from macaronic Latin to the nonsense talk of a policeman in Fernando Arrabal's *Triciclo* (203f). In all, the *artificial* use of secondary languages tends to be at home in experimental literature, and it is these two poles, the literary avant-garde and local color, that frame the uses of secondary languages in literature. The other functions mentioned by Canonica can appear in the context of mimetic as well as *artificial* bilingualism: humor, evocation—which operates between identification or sentimental intensification and refusal—, satire, and narrative. I would add seven more functions to the list: sound, characterization, euphemism, insider pun, parody, suspense, and symbolism. These categories are by no means mutually exclusive; most secondary language entries correspond to two or more of them.

In Chicano Society and Chicano Literature

Chicano literature may well be—together with other Hispanic literatures in the United States—the most fruitful area for the study of bilingual literary techniques in our century. Many Mexican American literary works use bilingual strategies to a greater or lesser extent and a few of them are authentically bilingual. But Chicano literature is also bilingual in other respects. The denomination *bilingual literature* encompasses an ampler body of works if we apply the term *literature* to the entire literary production of a bilingual region or country. And in this sense Chicano literature as a whole is bilingual, although fully bilingual literary texts are rather rare in it. In addition, it shows a more profound interplay between the languages involved than, for example, the literatures of Peru, Switzerland, or Catalonia. Furthermore, the production of some Chicano authors is bilingual because they have published works in English as well as works in Spanish. Rolando Hinojosa has translated some of his own bilingual or Spanish-language novels into English, which makes for yet another case of literary bilingualism. My study will take into consideration these broader definitions of *bilingual literature* at least in part, although it focuses primarily on bilingual techniques *within* texts—on *intratextual* rather than on *intertextual* bilingualism. The bilingual *context*—in the sense sketched out above—of Chicano literature is very notably present in the critical evaluation of Chicano literary bilingualism. Linguistic analyses of English-Spanish code switching often take into account literary bilingualism, and literary analyses, in their turn, tend to relate literary bilingualism to code switching in Chicano society. The main reason for this is certainly the high degree of code switching in certain sectors of Chicano society that goes hand in hand with the relatively high degree of bilingual devices in Chicano literature. The fact that the increasing interest of linguists in English-Spanish code switching coincided with an increase in the publication and study of U.S. Hispanic literatures—which offer themselves as a corpus for analysis—may be an additional reason for this overlap. In their *linguistic* studies of Spanish-English language switching in the United States, both Lipski and Penfield/Ornstein include a section on Chicano (or Hispanic) literary bilingualism that is governed by a linguistic perspective. The sociolinguistic background, on the other hand, is prominently present in some of the studies of literary bilingualism (Keller, Valdés). Questions as to the accuracy of literary code switches in comparison to community code switches or the usefulness of literary code switches for a grammar of English-Spanish code switching are raised by both Valdés and Keller and taken up by Lipski. Although the three critics agree, to differing degrees, on the independence of literature in such matters, Chicano literary bilingualism appears in their studies as strongly conditioned by bilingualism in Chicano society—almost as if literature were a subdivision of, or an appendix to, linguistics. This is more clearly so in the cases of Lipski and Valdés, who take the sociolinguist's stance, whereas Keller's position is that of the literary critic.

Bilingual Chicano reality may motivate a writer to use both English and Spanish in her or his work, be it in the form of a fully bilingual text, or with one language primary and the other secondary. Moreover, it may be the function of bilingual devices in Chicano literature to reflect code switching in Chicano society; as a matter of fact, mimetic uses overwhelmingly prevail over *artificial* ones in the Chicano narrative works published so far and are frequent in poetry and theater, too. But literary mimesis is not equivalent to a linguistically faithful copy of spontaneous utterances. At least since corpora of spoken language have become available, we know that literary language, including realist discourses, is a far shot from spoken language. Gary Keller, while stressing the issue of "vernacular authenticity" in his discussion of bilingual techniques in Montoya's classic "El Louie," affirms at the same time that bilingual literature "does not have to reflect the community's bilinguality nor even be semantically or syntactically acceptable in the ordinary sense" (284). In bilingual Chicano poems that are less realism-oriented than "El Louie," the distance to spontaneous utterances is clear, as the first half of a poem from Alurista's *Spik in Glyph* may illustrate:

get

get back two
  that thee para
      dox, dos? two? to?
      of i love u
 hear, i lov u
      too, tu?
      back get thee
      that dox
      para el
      mundo, 'til
cain't keep a won
      der
      in
      try me
      tri mee, again
      a gain
trai me aga
in
u.s. . . a
      u come
back two, also
      . . . mi, my?!

```
          tank u four
          feeling so
                 loonheli, blu
          u, too?  somedai
                 uorri
          pa'qué
                 chood u
          let yo'self uorri
                 crazy
                 cry in, cry in
          fo'lovin'u!
                 simón
          a'nque 'taba ciego
                 el
          kris
                 ti
                 a, no!
                 ano tá!
          pos uorri not, knot? naught?
          pos a des
                 anudar, a des
          ad es alambrar!
          a, nó, amó? . . . a quién?
          ther
          r
          man, u know
          nou, pos simón
          wee
          both had enough
          an'it ain't
          loosin'u
          that got me cry
          in
          . . . . (60-61)
```

The poem contains Pachuco slang (*simón*), regional Spanish (*pos, a'nque 'taba*), and English influenced by Spanish phonology (*uorri, tank*). Some of its elements reflect, in other words, Chicano speech on the lexical and phonological levels. But the mimesis on these two levels does not extend itself to the syntactic level, to the discourse as a whole, as a look at the passages in English—or at any one of the many monolingual poems in *Spik in Glyph*—confirms. Like other poems by Alurista, "get" takes up song fragments—from "Get Back" by the

Beatles to "A desalambrar" by Daniel Viglietti. Such intertextual loans may reflect Chicano experience on the sociocultural level, but not necessarily on the linguistic level. They can even introduce nonstandard elements from other sources than Chicano speech, for example *ain't* and *cain't*. The main principles that govern the development of "get" are homonymy, the repetition of phonic patterns, and the dismembering of words into syllables. This procedure is slightly reminiscent of an *albur* wordplay and has in this respect a mimetic function, but at the same time it alienates the poem from spontaneous speech, an alienation that is further enhanced by the layout of the poem and by those orthographic characteristics that cannot be reproduced in spoken language.

In *Linguistic Aspects*, John Lipski uses *Spik in Glyph* as part of his corpus for a survey of the "Linguistic Constraints on Literary Code Switching." He compares the frequency of different intrasentential shift-types in Chicano literature and speech. The other poets who are represented with an entire collection in this survey are Tato Laviera, Miguel Algarín, and Evangelina Vigil. "In addition, 25 poems by Mexican American and Puerto Rican American writers were selected from the issues of the *Revista Chicano-Riqueña,* with the only criterion for selection being the inclusion of a significant amount of intrasentential code shifting." If we take "get" to be in some measure a representative sample of this corpus—and since Lipski does not restrict his selection to mimetic discourses, it may well be— his conclusion that ". . . the literary values are significantly different from those representing spontaneous discourse" (79-80), is hardly surprising.[10]

---

10 Lipski also compares code switching in poetry and prose, concluding that bilingualism in prose is closer to spontaneous utterances. His source material for prose is a bit slim, however, because it only consists of Hinojosa's novel *Mi querido Rafa.* We can hardly fault Lipski for that, though: Cota-Cárdenas's *Puppet* was published the same year as Lipski's book, and Morales's *Reto en el paraíso,* although bilingual, is based on the juxtaposition of entire passages, not on intrasentential switches.

Chicano literature is, as is any literature, nurtured by the literary traditions that preceded it, surround it, and also—not least—by the mainstream that it often writes against. These *literary* inheritances, including their—however scarce—use of bilingual techniques, tend to impose themselves upon the unquestionable influences from Chicano *speech*. Bilingual Chicano speech, in other words, has undoubtedly triggered the use of bilingual devices in Mexican American literature, but these devices are governed by literary conventions rather than by the laws that control spontaneous utterances. Chicano literature in no way represents a suitable corpus for a detailed analysis of the underlying laws that govern spontaneous code switching. I therefore agree with Lipski in

> assigning literary examples of code switching to a position subordinate to or at least secondary to spontaneous utterances, in writing theoretical grammars. It is only by extrapolating from established corpora of spontaneously produced utterances that linguistic criteria applicable to literature may be derived: to proceed in the opposite direction is to put the cart before the horse. (*Linguistic Aspects* 75)

John Lipski and I are not on the same turf. He approaches literary bilingualism from a sociolinguist's perspective; I am above all interested in its *literary* functions—the functions that it may have within its *literary* context. That Chicano literature can be related to sociocultural aspects is obvious. I am not trying to say that Chicano literature is without any connections to Chicano society; I only doubt that the code switches that are found in Chicano literature are a valid source material to "determine," as Lipski puts it, "the degree of integration in the writer's bilingual grammars" (78), or to "better understand . . . Chicano language as it is communicated in society" (Keller "How Chicano Authors" 172); and their validity is especially low, if they are not previously filtered through literary parameters. On the other hand, Lipski's study is not without interest for analysis of literary bilingualism from a literary point of view. In his discussion of *foregrounding*—a notion Keller introduced into the study of bilingualism in Chicano literature ("Literary Stratagems" 283)—Lipski divides bilingual texts into three categories:

> . . . Type I is the monolingual text, perhaps with a handful of L_2 words thrown in for flavor. . . .
> Type II bilingual literature exhibits intersentential code switches, where entire lines of poetry or entire sentences of prose are produced in a single language, with switches occurring at principal phrase or sentence boundaries. . . .
> Type III bilingual literature exhibits intrasentential code switches, typical of individuals who have learned and/or used both languages approximately in similar or identical contexts.
> . . .
> In each type of text, the role of foregrounding is different. In type I, there is no real L_2 discourse, but merely insertion of individual items, for a variety of effects. The impression is that of a superposition of isolated elements. In type II, two complete sets of logical propositions are offered, and a switch of language automatically entails a shift of domain of discourse. In type III, a more or less balanced bilingual grammar is presupposed, with the extent of balance being reflected by the relative proportion of discourse in each language. While it may be possible to apply the same criteria as in type II to this type of language switching, the prime feature being foregrounded is the fact of bilingualism . . . (78)

The distinction between sporadic lexical items in a secondary language, intersentential and intrasentential bilingual devices, and the different ways in which the two languages interact in each of these types is very useful for the discussion of bilingual literature. Nevertheless, it seems preferable to apply these three types—which in my summary above would form part of the category *forms*—not to entire texts, but to single instances of literary bilingualism. Many Mexican American poems, plays, or novels may stick to one of these categories throughout, but many others do not. Miguel Méndez's novel in Spanish *Peregrinos de Aztlán*, for example, or *Letters to Louise,* Abelardo Delgado's novel in English, can both be ascribed to type I, but they also include instances of types II and III as we shall see in the case of *Letters to Louise*. In Chicano theater, the different types pointed out by Lipski may serve for characterization within one piece. Thus, the parents in Luis Valdez's *acto* "Soldado raso" use a type I discourse, whereas Johnny and La Muerte use mainly type II (*Early Works* 121-133). Some of the longer pieces in Ricardo Sánchez's *Amsterdam cantos* could be mentioned as poems which do not correspond to one type only.

Gary Keller's classification of literary code switches differs from that of Lipski:

> . . . one group of Chicano code switches are achieved in the interests of a fiction of mimesis, where literature aspires to become the microcosm and mirror of the social macrocosm. In these instances where the literary text embraces the aesthetic philosophy of realism or naturalism, the code-switch is fashioned to reflect, like a mirror, the phenomenon as it occurs in Chicano society. The second group of code-switches, while achieved with the assumption that the Chicano reader will understand them because the reader is familiar with the phenomenon in common speech, is intended to obey a more purely literary canon. These literary code-switches in a formal sense are instruments in the pursuit of such goals as irony, characterization, cross-cultural comparisons, rhetorical devices, double entendres, puns, and so on. Clearly the two groups of code-switches are not mutually exclusive. Indeed, they could be reduced to one group, for even the code-switch that is undertaken as a reflection of Chicano society obeys the literary purpose of being a realistic reflection of that society. However, it is useful to separate code-switches into these two groups because those that reflect social usage have been utilized to a significant extent by sociolinguists for the purpose of better understanding Chicano language as it is communicated in society, while the purely literary code-switches are not easily incorporated into a data base that is useful for Chicano sociolinguistics. ("How Chicano Authors" 172)

I have already pointed out that I doubt the suitability of literary code switches in general for sociolinguistic analyses. But even if we leave sociolinguistic considerations aside and concentrate on the literary functions of code switches, Keller's distinction between mimetic and literary code switches remains relevant. In a similar distinction above, I have preferred the term *artificial* over *literary*, mainly because the latter could lead to the false impression that mimetic switches are not literary, an impression which Keller forestalls by stressing that "even the

code-switch that is undertaken as a reflection of Chicano society obeys the *literary* purpose of being a realistic reflection of
that society" (my emphasis). My categorization differs from
Keller's in that functions like *irony* and *characterization* are
not restricted to *artificial* uses of secondary language entries,
but can occur in mimetic discourses as well.

Let me, before I turn to the Chicano novel in English, lin-
ger one personal moment longer with fully bilingual Chicano
texts, with what Lipski calls *type III texts*. "It is in such texts"
—he says—"that the high degree of bilingual integration becomes most apparent, and the texts, while perhaps readable by
a wide range of bilingual individuals, are truly representative
of only a relatively small segment of the national population"
(78). Whereas the opposition between "perhaps readable" and
"truly representative" is a very hazy concept, the issue that
Lipski is addressing is clear nonetheless. He brings it up again
some lines later when he talks of "the existence of a linguistic
in-group where mere knowledge of two languages is not suffi-
cient to share the bilingual grammar, constructed of a finely
integrated blend of the two languages" (78f). Lipski is right,
of course, in pointing out that Chicanos who are familiar with
societal code switching will have easier access to code switching in Chicano literature. They will most likely know Pachuco
terms and they are better prepared to grasp bilingual puns and
double-entendres. But none of this is *per se* an obstacle for
non-Chicano readers to approach bilingual Chicano literature.
In a seminar on the Chicano novel which I taught at the University of Basel, Switzerland, in 1987, I suggested that some
students who knew both English and Spanish work on *Puppet*
(1985), by María Cota-Cárdenas, a type II bilingual novel that
includes long passages of type I discourse, as well as many
instances of type III discourse. None of my students had ever
lived for a long period among Mexican Americans, nor had I,
and we needed the help of specialized dictionaries to find our
way through the work, to grasp the puns, the insider jokes, the
subtleties. Our reading was no doubt different from that of a
Mexican American; we must have missed some of the details

in the context of code switching, details that a scholar of Mexican American descent or who had lived among Mexican Americans could have pointed out to us. Moreover, the text works differently for non-Chicano Europeans on the level of evocation and identification. But since *Puppet* is not only possibly the most fully bilingual Chicano novel, but also an excellent novel with many layers, and since the author does not code-switch for the sake of code switching alone, our reading was very rewarding. By the same token, while code switching may not have exactly facilitated our reading process, our experience was not that unique. Most readers have to translate the majority of the literature they are reading, even that written in their own language. Most readers have to endure the hardships of travelling to the vocabulary, the discourses, the themes and values of another time or space: to Milton, Dickens, and Owen; to Wheatley, Hawthorne, and Williams; to Keri Hulme, Maxine Hong Kingston, and María Cota-Cárdenas.

In the Chicano Novel?

> . . . the games
> como en el teatro played
>   by shakespeare
> he knew
>   and his tizoc
> serenaded tonantzín
>   con lunas (Alurista, "my sister," poem twenty-eight of
> *Floricanto*)

I use six languages: Black English, Anglo English, Mexican Spanish, Chicano Spanish, Nahuatl, and Maya. So I really don't think there is a particular language in Chicano literature. We cover this full range in Chicano literature, the full range of colors, the full rainbow. *All of the sarape. It is one great sauce and that makes it all the tastier, don't you think?* That shows our versatility and multidimensional view of the world. That makes us stronger, a broadly based, more universal people. And as writers, that puts us in a completely different category in the history of world literature. (Alurista in Bruce-Novoa *Chicano Authors* 272)

Before we can embark on the project of analyzing bilingual strategies in Chicano novels written in English, we have to deal with two other questions. For one thing: does Chicano literature not draw from a multilingual background rather than from a bilingual one? Should an analysis of foreign language elements in Chicano texts not also include native Mexican languages and Pachuco slang? For another: does Chicano prose in English offer enough evidence of bilingual (or multilingual) strategies to make an analysis worthwhile?

Many Chicano novels include native American words, personages, and cultural elements that on the thematic level constitute an important component of Chicano heritage, myth, and mythology: "we do have roots in our Mexican past, our Aztec ancestry" (Acosta *Buffalo* 198; cf. Bus). The gesture of retracing Chicano identity to indigenous cultures and to the mythical homeland of *Aztlán*—a gesture that was used in the Chicano movement of the sixties (see Robinson 308)—is a recurrent feature in Chicano narrative.[11] Moreover, Chicano novels may show the opposition between those characters who regard Native Indian culture as part of the Chicano identity,[12] and those who reject it as inferior and stress the Spanish heritage.[13] The two viewpoints may be presented as part of a generational

---

11 Cf. the journal *Aztlán* and the titles *Aztlán* (Valdez), *floricanto en aztlán* (Alurista), *Heart of Aztlán* (Anaya), and *Peregrinos de Aztlán* (Méndez). Cf. also Delgado *Louise* 16f, 26, 50, etc., Acosta *Cockroach* 161, 210, 249, and Gonzales-Berry "Chicano Literature" 9.

12 See Candelaria *Alhambra* 78; Galarza 4; Acosta *Cockroach* 219; Villarreal *Horseman* 84; Rodriguez 115; García *Leaving Home* 41, 94; Delgado *Louise* 16, 18; Barrio 49, 219; Anaya *Ultima* 39, 42.

13 "He liked the superiority he showed by calling Rattler a Mexican, meaning a guy browned by Indian blood and not of pure Spanish descent like themselves" (Salas *Tattoo* 192). ". . . family members were taught that only the Spanish side of their heritage was worth honoring and preserving; the Indian in them was pagan, servile, instinctive rather than intellectual, and was to be suppressed, its existence denied" (Islas 142, cf. 127, 141). See also Acosta *Buffalo* 86, 101; Candelaria *Alhambra* 9, 106, 168, etc.; Candelaria *Inheritance* 16; Garcia *Leaving Home* 26, 40f; Rios 5, 51.

conflict in which a younger generation identifies more readily with native values and traditions than their parents (Candelaria *Alhambra* and Islas *Rain God* 27, 142). Moreover, the global stereotypes of the impassive and stoic, or primitive and savage Indian are also amply represented,[14] and dark complexioned Chicanos are often, and often pejoratively, called Indians.[15] On the linguistic level, matters are different. Native languages have too marginal an appearance in the Chicano novel to offer a functional basis for analysis. Alurista's insistence on the multilingual character of Chicano literature in the quotation which opens this section, while already more rhetorical than descriptive in regard to Chicano poetry, including his own, can be applied even less to Chicano prose. Although all the six languages mentioned by him can be found in the Chicano novel, it builds its discourse on either English or Spanish, or on English *and* Spanish in the few bilingual novels. The terms *English* and *Spanish* are of course not confined to Re-

---

14 "And the peasantry . . . looked upon them with awe. They had eyes and noses and mouths, these people, but they had no faces, for there was not a sign of emotion to them. They showed neither joy nor fear nor humor nor surliness. And the legend about them was well known—they had no fear of death—the bravest men in México, it was said—and one could kill ten thousand of them and the last one would stoically come forward to die. This was the legend, and this made the peones marvel—and also, because the rebels, even the most backward and illiterate of them, were Christians, they marveled, for these Yaquis were heathen—they were savages and were unable even to speak the Christian tongue" (Villarreal *Horseman* 311, cf. 101, 109, 137, 169, 245, etc.). "How silent she had been even when she talked—silent like those pyramids he had finally seen in Teotihuacan built to pay tribute to the sun and the moon" (Islas 27); "a knowledge more ancient than the first Inca, than the first Tarahumara" (Arias 79); "his stony Mexican eyes lied" (Salas *Tattoo* 318, cf. 61); "in the women that docility that came from the Indian ancestors" (Candelaria *Alhambra* 62; cf. 32f, 50, 99, 161); "the meanest Mexicans in all Mexico, *los tarascans*" (sic, Acosta *Buffalo* 188). See also Acosta *Cockroach* 66, 173; Garcia *Leaving Home* 240; Delgado *Louise* 16, 26; Barrio 89, 178; Anaya *Tortuga* 45, 74; Rios 1, 132f).

15 See Candelaria *Alhambra* 33, 93, 144; Barrio 175; Islas *Rain God* 119, 127; Rodriguez 115; Villarreal *Horseman* 84.

ceived Standard English and Royal Academy Spanish but also include the different monolingual dialects and sociolects of both languages.

Pachuco, caló, and Spanglish, which Alurista may include in the term *Chicano Spanish*, are exploited to some extent in the Spanish-language novels by Méndez (*Peregrinos de Aztlán* and *El sueño de Santa María de las Piedras*) and Elizondo (*Muerte en una estrella*), and in Cota-Cárdenas's bilingual novel *Puppet*. In the Chicano novel in English, Pachucos come up sporadically as a theme (Islas *Rain God* 118; Salas *Tattoo* 19, 23, 34, 129f), but their language is hardly reflected. Pachuco slang and hybrids do not in any way offer themselves as a third basic language element beside Spanish and English. And whereas Pachuco slang manifests itself in a couple of Chicano novels as a fully functional language at least momentarily, there is not a trace of native language syntax, not a single verb. Unless one includes age-old loanwords from indigenous Central American languages, like *cacique*, *serape*, or *huaraches*, Native American entries are limited to names, be they toponyms,[16] names of plants,[17] of tribes,[18] of deities,[19] or personal names.[20]

---

16 *Chimayo* (Candelaria *Alhambra* 73); *México*, *Mexico*, or *Méjico* (extremely frequent); Tenochtitlán (Arias 32, Barrio 48, 135). Indian place-names abound especially in Arias's *Tamazunchale*: Apurímac River (32), Huancayo (32), Machu Pichu (35), Panindícuaro (102), Popocatépetl (90), Teocaltiche (90, 102), Río Moctezuma (102).

17 *Maguey* (Arias 106, Villarreal *Horseman* 114); *oshá* (Anaya *Ultima* 37); *yucca* (ibid. 77, 217, 244; Islas 179).

18 Tribe names appear mainly in the context of tracing back Chicano identity. The *Aztecs* dominate overwhelmingly (Acosta *Buffalo* 139, 160, 170, etc.; Acosta *Cockroach* 34, 159; Arias 82; Barrio 48, 89, 178, etc.; Candelaria *Alhambra* 43; Delgado *Louise* 18, 29; Garcia *Leaving Home* 240; Rodriguez 5; Villarreal *Horseman* 337, 348); other tribe names mentioned are *Inca* (Arias 79), *Maya* (Barrio 212, Delgado 17); *Tarahumara* (Arias 31, 79, Villarreal *Horseman* 310f), and *Tarascan* (Acosta *Buffalo* 188).

19 *Tlaloc* (Candelaria *Alhambra* 31f, Villarreal *Clemente Chacón* 153); *Huitzilopotchtli* (Acosta *Cockroach* 33, 48, 256, etc.).

20 *Xóchitl* (Villarreal *Horseman* 5f); *Moctezuma* (Acosta *Buffalo* 101, Candelaria *Alhambra* 34, Garcia *Leaving Home* 207).

Chicano literature clearly uses Spanish and English as its two main languages. It draws on a bilingual background rather than on a multilingual one. But there remains a final question to be answered: does the Chicano novel in English include enough Spanish language elements to justify their analysis? The conglomerate of English and Spanish that sometimes includes elements of native languages, and that has almost become a distinguishing feature of Chicano poetry, is rare in Chicano prose fiction. It is not astonishing therefore that Keller relies mainly upon Chicano *poetry* to exemplify bilingual literary techniques: "code-switching in fact is far more evident in Chicano poetry than it is in prose" ("How Chicano Authors" 171). Most Chicano novels could be discarded from this study, as they were discarded from Keller's:

> Contrary to the assumption of some critics who really do not know Chicano literature well, not all of our literature switches between Spanish and English. Many excellent Chicano works have been written either wholly in English or wholly in Spanish, but these will not be referred to here because the focus of this paper is exclusively on those works that are bilingual. (171)

The focus of my study will be exclusively on those works which are *not* bilingual. Analysis of bilingual techniques in Chicano novels might justifiably concentrate on the few genuinely bilingual novels that rely heavily on code switching discourses. However, a closer look at the Chicano novels in *English* shows that almost all of them include Spanish language elements and that they are, generally speaking; about as "monolingual" or "bilingual" as Hemingway's *For Whom the Bell Tolls*, which Gary Keller uses as the main means for comparison with bilingual Chicano poetry in an earlier version of the article just quoted ("Literary Stratagems" 285, 290). They may not make extensive use of intensive code switching, but, like Hemingway's novel, they employ stylistic devices which reflect or highlight the non-English or bilingual background of their setting. These devices range, in the case of the Chicano texts, from code switching passages to the use of Spanish words and loanwords and to the quotation of entire Mexican songs or poems, and from English phrases with a Spanish sentence structure to implicit and explicit comments on the often bilingual character of Chicano existence. Spanish, which is, in contrast to Indian or hybrid languages, the basic language of various novels, and one of the two primary elements in a few bilingual novels, appears often enough in the novels in English, too, for patterns to become evident in the usage and interplay of the two languages.

In a text that builds its discourse on code switching, the reader, after having read the first couple of pages, will take language switches as the norm, will expect them to occur. She or he may ask the question why a given phrase or passage is rendered in one or the other of the two languages, but switching between the two languages has become the norm and as such no longer constitutes a foregrounding. In a text that relies on one vehicular language, on the other hand, switches to a secondary language are much rarer and therefore take the reader more by surprise. They may constitute, precisely because of their scarcity, a more radical foregrounding.

"It is not coincidental," according to Lipski,

> that the type III texts, which have also attracted the attention of linguists and psychologists when found in spontaneous speech, provide the richest and most rewarding terrain for literary analysis. (*Linguistic Aspects* 79)

The problem with type III texts is that they are rare and especially so as far as the Chicano narrative is concerned. But while Mexican American novels in English include relatively few instances of full-fledged code switching, they rely on bilingual mechanisms that have a long tradition in the literatures of the Western World and that are well worth analyzing.

3. The Chicano Novel in English, 1967-1985

Seventeen novels, a good sample of Chicano novel production in English between 1967 and 1985, and two autobiographies constitute the textual background for my analysis of the uses and the functions of Spanish language elements in the Chicano novel in English. The corpus consists of the following texts, ordered according to the short form that will be used in referring to them (see bibliography for full reference):

Alhambra: Candelaria, N. *Memories of the Alhambra* (1977)
Barrio Boy: Galarza, E. *Barrio Boy* (1971)
Buffalo: Acosta, O.Z. *Autobiography of a Brown Buffalo* (1972)
Clemente: Villarreal, J.A. *Clemente Chacon* (1984)
Cockroach: Acosta, O.Z. *Revolt of the Cockroach People* (1973)
Horseman: Villarreal, J.A. *Fifth Horseman* (1974)
Hunger: Rodriguez, R. *Hunger of Memory* (1982)
Leaving Home: Garcia, L. *Leaving Home* (1985)
Louise: Delgado, A. *Letters to Louise* (1982)
Mango Street: Cisneros, S. *House On Mango Street* (1985)
Plum Pickers: Barrio, R. *Plum Plum Pickers* (1969)
Rain God: Islas, A. *Rain God* (1984)
Rites: Hinojosa, R. *Rites and Witnesses* (1982)
Tamazunchale: Arias, R. *Road to Tamazunchale* (1975)
Tattoo: Salas. F. *Tattoo* (1967)
Tortuga: Anaya, R. *Tortuga* (1979)
Ultima: Anaya, R. *Bless Me Ultima* (1972)
Valley: Hinojosa, R. *Valley* (1983)
Victuum: Rios, I. *Victuum* (1976)

Is it at all possible to treat close to twenty texts written by fifteen authors and in different genres[21] as if they were one

---

21 *Novel* will be used as a generic term for all the texts in the corpus though the latter includes two autobiographies. *Barrio Boy* and *Hunger* have been incorporated because they are thematically and in their use of Spanish elements well in line with the novels, which, moreover, tend to include autobiographical elements. Márquez ("Richard Rodriguez" 131ff.) and Isernhagen ("Anthropological Narrative" 221), among others, have stressed the fictional and literary character of autobiographies. Tonn, in his comprehensive study on contemporary Chicano narrative, also brings together the two

homogeneous textual body on the sole basis that they all have appeared in the same period, in the same country, and happen to be linked by the Mexican American descent of their authors and by the denomination "Chicano novel"? Are there any inherently textual characteristics that they have in common?

All the texts are prose pieces and in all of them the protagonist—or at least one of the protagonists if there is more than one central character—is a Mexican American.[22] Otherwise, there is no relevant thematic or stylistic characteristic that is present in the *entirety* of the corpus. Francisco Lomelí confirms this view in his study on the Chicano novel from 1970 to 1979:

> Upon reviewing the novels produced during this ten year span, the only verifiable constant is the ethnicity of the authors. Beyond ethnicity it is difficult to find common unifying elements for Chicano or non-Chicano experience from which emerge sometimes contradictory perspectives. We find, above all, clear evidence of multiplicity of scope and diversity of subject matter. Even the use of language demonstrates the degree of variation that exists from one author to the next. (Lomelí "Novel" 33)

The corpus does not consist of texts that structurally, stylistically, thematically, and ideologically all conform to the same pattern. However, the literature of no group or period shows such perfect uniformity. A literary genre is defined by the recurrence of certain features and by their statistical prevalence rather than by their uninterrupted and unvarying presence (cf. Beddow, Swales).

---

genres by focusing his detailed analysis on two novels (*Cockroach* and *Ultima*) and one autobiography (*Barrio Boy*).

22   Tonn doubts this for *Tattoo*: "Aaron d'Aragon, der Protagonist in Salas's erstem Roman *Tattoo the Wicked Cross*, ist auf der Grundlage des Textes nicht einmal eindeutig als Charakter spanisch-mexikanischer Herkunft zu identifizieren" (40). The text, however, is clear on this: "Aaron believed he meant what he said, and he liked the superiority he showed by calling Rattler a Mexican, meaning a guy browned by Indian blood and not of pure Spanish descent like themselves" (192f).

Similarities, parallels, and analogies abound in the corpus.
If one takes the texts incorporated here to be representative of
the Chicano novel in English of the seventies and early eighties and if one assumes those characteristics that recur in the
majority of the texts to be significant for an assessment of the
group, a stereotypical Chicano novel of the period analyzed
would have the following features: the narrative voice assumes
a stable point of view that coincides with, or runs parallel to,
the perspective of the protagonist;[23] experimental narrative
techniques are rare;[24] the narrative does not use an artificial,
imaginary, or fantastic setting, but is set in a realistic time and
place, in a Chicano village or barrio and in the twentieth century;[25] the Mexican revolution is mentioned,[26] and elements of
contemporary Chicano history are introduced as well as American history and world history;[27] the Mexican immigrant experience is present in most novels;[28] all American presidents

---

23 This is true for the third-person narrators in *Alhambra, Clemente,
Horseman, Ultima,* and *Valley.* First-person narrators are used in
Buffalo, Cockroach, Tortuga, Mango Street, Victuum, in the autobiographies *Barrio Boy* and *Hunger,* and in the epistolary novel *Louise.*

24 Even *Plum Pickers,* the most "experimental" of the texts in the
corpus, is traditional prose in comparison to the texts of any of the
literary avant-gardes of our century.

25 Exceptions: *Horseman,* which is set in Mexico and partly in the
nineteenth century, and *Barrio Boy,* set for a considerable portion of
the book in Mexico.

26 It is at the core of *Horseman* and *Barrio Boy* and appears in *Alhambra* (31, 42), *Plum Pickers* (34, 53, 134), *Clemente* (51), *Cockroach*
(40, 86, 128 etc.) and *Valley* (28-31).

27 Hector Calderón comments on the relation between history and
Chicano fiction as follows: "Part of the emancipatory and utopian
moment of the late '60s and early '70s was the need for individual
scholars and institutional research centers to begin to rewrite the history of the Southwest from a Chicano perspective. Equally important, I believe, has been the imaginative reenactment of historical
events in recent Chicano narratives" ("History as Subtext" 1).

28 The immigrant experience is the central theme in *Plum Pickers* and
Barrio Boy and comes up, e.g., in *Buffalo* (29, 77), *Tamazunchale*
(74ff), *Mango Street* (74), *Victuum* (183, 232), *Leaving Home* (26),
Louise (35), and *Horseman* (367).

from Hoover to Reagan are mentioned[29] and so are the wars in which the United States was involved in this century (with the obvious exception of Operation Desert Storm) and in which many Mexican Americans fought and died as foot soldiers.[30]

The main character is a male Chicano who shows autobiographical traits of the author[31] and is presented as an exemplary figure.[32] The novel is a portrait of an artist who grows up

---

29 American presidents mentioned: Hoover (*Victuum* 102), Roosevelt (*Buffalo* 76; *Leaving Home* 91, 161, 174, etc., *Victuum* 232), Truman (*Leaving Home* 248, *Victuum* 273), Eisenhower (*Cockroach* 225), Kennedy (*Buffalo* 197; *Victuum* 293f, 318; *Cockroach* 54, 250), Johnson (*Buffalo* 20, 28, 197), Nixon (*Buffalo* 163, 165; *Cockroach*; *Victuum* 317), Ford (*Louise* 34, 114), Carter (*Louise* 32, 34, 36, etc.), Reagan (as governor or presidential candidate in *Buffalo* 28, 100; *Cockroach* 176f; *Louise* 34).

30 World War I (*Alhambra* 29; *Leaving Home* 8, 35, 118, etc.), World War II (*Ultima* 3, 29, 46, etc.; *Tamazunchale* 110; *Alhambra* 136f; *Louise* 44, 82; *Leaving Home* 118, 161, 174, etc.; *Rain God* 3; *Victuum* 229f, 237, 250ff, etc.; *Clemente* 106; *Valley* 43), Korea (*Buffalo* 142; *Louise* 90; *Clemente* 106; *Valley* 49, 53; *Rites*: a major setting and theme), Vietnam (*Cockroach* 13, 25, 70, etc.; *Rain God* 45; *Victuum* 295; *Hunger* 162ff).

31 In addition to the autobiographies (*Barrio Boy, Hunger*) and alleged autobiographies (*Buffalo, Cockroach, Louise*), this can at least be assumed for *Alhambra, Rain God, Rites, Ultima, Valley, Victuum*.

32 "Once in every century there comes a man who is chosen to speak for his people. Moses, Mao and Martin are examples. Who's to say that I am not such a man" (*Buffalo* 198). "If I had been able to write I could have easily been a Chicano Karl Marx, Mao, Cervantes or Shakespeare" (*Louise* 27). "What brought me and my family to the United States from Mexico also brought hundreds of thousands of others like us. In many ways the experiences of a multitude of boys like myself, migrating from countless villages like Jalcocotán and starting life anew in *barrios* like the one in Sacramento, must have been similar" (*Barrio Boy* 1). "But I write of one life only. My own. If my story is true, I trust it will resonate with significance for other lives. Finally, my history deserves public notice as no more than this: a parable for the life of its reader. Here is the life of a middle-class man" (*Hunger* 7). "There was no Heraclio Inés, as there were tens of thousands of Heraclio Ineses who died for a right they believed was theirs. . . . This is of the peon, who exists yet today. This is of the slave anywhere, any time." (*Horseman* introductory note; Villarreal's introductory statement stands in stark contrast to the rest of his novel. In "*Fifth Horseman*," I try to show why the protagonist of Villarreal's novel cannot serve at all as a model of the peón nor of the oppressed in general, as the author pretends.)

in a family in which traditional Mexican-Hispanic customs and values dominate.[33] Different members of the protagonist's family tend to embody different elements of a traditional Chicano way of life. Machismo can be represented by the father or the brothers of the protagonist (*Alhambra, Rain God, Ultima, Victuum*), or by the protagonist himself (*Buffalo, Horseman*); catholic religiousness and Mexican cooking appear through the mother of the protagonist; and in various novels, Mexican (American) folklore, healer wisdom, and magic find their expression in the grandmother or another elderly female family member who is a good storyteller.[34]

The hero undergoes a cycle of initiations that alienate him from his family and its values and that include, besides the initiations conventional in a *Bildungsroman*—sexual initiation, confrontation with death, fights with classmates[35]—the confrontation with another culture and another language.[36] The exposure to English in school comes as a shock, and initially the protagonist feels ill at ease in the classroom.[37] Soon, how-

---

33 This is true at least for *Alhambra, Barrio Boy, Buffalo, Clemente, Hunger, Louise, Mango Street, Rain God, Ultima, Victuum,* and *Valley,* though not to the same extent in all these novels.

34 *Barrio Boy* 43; *Hunger* 37; *Louise* 27, 94; *Rain God* 161; *Ultima* 115. See also Romero *Nambé—Year One.* Cf. Binder "Mothers" for the same phenomenon in poetry.

35 *Buffalo* 92; *Ultima* 34; *Alhambra* 80; *Rain God* 96; *Louise* 46, 56.

36 Lyon states that "much of contemporary Chicano prose creates a child or adolescent as protagonist, narrator, or focus character and examines problems typical to that age: how to get along with society, how to harmonize one's past with his present and future, how to become an individual without totally rejecting family and friends, and how to harmonize one's interior feelings with the exterior world. In this search for identity, the concept of 'loss of innocence,' typical to many adolescents in real life, becomes a basic theme for Chicano fiction" (255). Under the heading of "Loss of Innocence" he brings together the three categories: "(1) loss or rejection of religious belief, (2) exposure to the cruelties of the adult and Anglo world, and (3) experimentation with sex, drugs, and alcohol" (256). He stresses the protagonists' "initiation and full integration into manhood and society" but largely neglects acculturation.

37 *Buffalo* 186, *Ultima* 10, *Rain God* 119, *Mango Street* 13, *Leaving Home* 29, *Hunger* 11ff, *Alhambra* 35, *Victuum* 154.

ever, he starts to like the English language, becomes a dedicated student, the teacher's favorite even, and often goes on to a college and university career rewarded with scholarships.[38]

In affinity with the personal experience of most Chicano authors (cf. Bruce-Novoa *Authors*), the themes of language conflict and of giving up Spanish for English are thematic constants in the texts and part of the more general constant of culture conflict and acculturation. Cultural conflict, the search for one's "true" roots, one's identity, and the step from a Hispanic environment into an Anglo-Saxon one, are among the most frequently recurring features of the corpus.[39]

Not all the Chicano novels written in the period analyzed here are in English. As pointed out earlier, there also exists a Chicano novel production in Spanish, though with a considerably smaller and decreasing output, and with growing difficulties to publish in the United States, at least as far as the period covered here is concerned. Only four of the eleven novels in Spanish included in the bibliography appeared after 1980, two of them in Mexico (Elizondo, 1984; Méndez *El sueño*, 1986). Hinojosa's *Claros varones*, 1986, and *Los amigos de Becky*, 1991, were published in bilingual editions in the United States. The remaining seven novels were published in the seventies, mainly in the United States.[40] It is also in the early eighties that Rolando Hinojosa, one of the most prolific Chicano writ-

---

38 *Alhambra* 27, 35, 87; *Barrio Boy* 210; *Louise* 67; *Rain God* 4f, 77; *Victuum* 236; *Valley*; *Hunger* in its entirety.

39 *Buffalo, Cockroach, Ultima, Alhambra, Louise, Leaving Home, Victuum, Clemente*. The features described are not exclusive to Chicano literature but appear in other Hispanic North American literature as well (cf. Marta Sánchez).

40 Brito *El diablo en Texas*, Hinojosa *Estampas del Valle*, Méndez *Peregrinos de Aztlán*, and Rivera *"...y no se lo tragó la tierra"* were published in the United States (Hinojosa's and Rivera's texts in bilingual editions); Alejandro Morales's two novels *Caras viejas y vino nuevo* and *La verdad sin voz* in Mexico. *Hinojosa's Klail City y sus alrededores* appeared first in Cuba (1976) and was reissued in the United States as a bilingual edition under the title *Generaciones y semblanzas* (1977).

ers, changes from Spanish as his main literary language to English. Before switching languages, he writes *Querido Rafa*, a bilingual novel, published in Texas (1981). Interestingly enough, two other bilingual novels go to press in the United States in the mid-eighties: Morales's *Reto en el paraíso* (1983), and Cota-Cárdenas's *Puppet* (1985). A comparison of the texts of the corpus with these bilingual texts or with the Spanish Chicano novels of the same period shows that the latter use a more aggressive and politically outspoken language and are more inclined to experimental literary discourses (cf. Rodríguez del Pino 3). In the case of the bilingual works, the refusal of the author to rely on one discursive language is in itself an experimental element. In the non-English texts, moreover, the culture conflict experienced by the protagonist less often leads to acculturation, but can end with a violent clash and even with the death of the protagonist (Cota-Cárdenas, Elizondo, Morales *Caras viejas*). In the novels in English, on the other hand, the (author-narrator-)protagonists cease at the end of the text to belong to the world, the society, and the value system that surrounded them at its beginning, and they reconstruct their former cultural self for an Anglo American audience whose culture has now become theirs.

The generalization of the texts of the corpus has to be followed by particularization and differentiation. *Ultima* is the text that corresponds most faithfully to the stereotypical and hypothetical Chicano novel as it has just been outlined; the other texts come more (*Alhambra, Hunger, Louise*) or less (*Rites, Tamazunchale, Tortuga*) close to it. Exceptions can be found for all the traits mentioned, and if similarities between the texts abound, so do differences. The corpus can be subdivided geographically as well as chronologically. While in a few texts the regional setting is of secondary importance (*Louise, Mango Street*), it is essential to Acosta's, Anaya's, and Hinojosa's novels that they are set in California, New Mexico, and Texas respectively. Furthermore, the contemporary Chicano novel has undergone a development in the first twenty years of its existence, a development marked by diversification, depoliticization, and the movement away from an "ethno-graphic"[41] presentation of Chicano culture and from the quest for cultural identity. This development is not exclusive to Chicano literature, but seems to have taken place within other Hispanic groups and other arts as well, as two chapter titles in the recently published *Handbook of Hispanic Cultures in the United States* indicate (Kanellos). The chapter on U.S.-Puerto Rican literature is entitled "From Ethnicity to Multicultur-alism," the one on Latino art "From Barrio to Mainstream." In the Chicano novel, to come back to the genre I am interest-ed in here, the treatment of some themes has even been re-versed. The virile and patriarchal Mexican male, for example, a stereotypical figure pinned down maybe too narrowly by Octavio Paz in *El laberinto de la soledad* (32), and quite prominent in the earlier novels, gives way to male figures that do not fit the cliché, but reverse or subvert it in different ways—homosexuals, impotent, bedridden, or old and physical-ly run-down male protagonists.[42] This gesture of negation of a stereotype runs parallel to an increase in the presence of female novelists and protagonists, a process which has con-firmed itself in the novel production after 1985, as we shall see in chapter 12.

Besides the differences between groups of texts, such as the groups just mentioned or autobiographies and historical novels, each text has its individual character. In the case of those authors who are represented by more than one novel, for example, the first to be published fits the stereotype best, is the most autobiographic work and the one that concentrates

---

41 The adjective *ethnographic*, as I use it here and in the following, denotes discourses that concentrate on presenting a culture in a des-criptive and explanatory manner.
42 The still young narrator figure of *Rain God*, Miguel Chico, after an operation has to wear a catheter for the rest of his life, and Felix, another central character of the novel, is homosexual. Adolfo, the protagonist of *Leaving Home*, can hardly "get it up" anymore be-cause he is too old, and in *Tamazunchale* old and decrepit Fausto is confined to his bed and his fantasies most of the time.

most strongly on the depiction of the protagonist's Hispanic childhood and on his acculturation, while the later works by the same author bring in new themes.[43] The language question, the tension between English and Spanish, appears in most texts; its importance, the position it takes, and the way in which it is treated vary greatly, however. Language is at the core of *Hunger* and marginal in *Tattoo*. *Horseman* and *Rain God* both foreground Spanish in an English text through stylistic means but in very different manners. In addition, *Rain God* thematizes the language question. *Hunger*, an autobiography and not a novel, treats it thematically and essayistically rather than stylistically. Finally, differences exist in many other areas. *Plum Pickers*, for example, uses more satirical discourses on average than the other texts, *Mango Street* more poetical ones; Acosta's novels are more politically outspoken, and Villarreal's are more cynical. Individual differences between works will be commented on time and again on the following pages, albeit randomly. Martínez/Lomelí and Tonn provide more systematic and more thorough information on the characteristics of most of the texts contained in the corpus (cf. also Bruce-Novoa *Authors*). Those characteristics that are directly linked to the use of Spanish language entries will be summarized in chapter 16.

The corpus does not cover all the texts in English that have appeared between 1967 and 1985 under the heading of "Chicano novel." For one thing, it excludes the *literatura chicanesca*, texts set in a Chicano context but written by non-Chicanos (cf. Márquez *Literatura Chicanesca*). For another, Floyd Salas is only present with *Tattoo the Wicked Cross* and not with his other novels (*What Now My Love*, 1969, and *Lay My Body on the Line*, 1978), because Spanish is virtually nonexistent in his work. For the same reason, John Rechy has been left out entirely. Anaya's *Heart of Aztlán*, as well as Hinojosa's *Dear*

---

43   This is true for the two novels by Acosta and also for the novelistic production of Anaya, Candelaria, Hinojosa, and Villarreal, only some of whose works are included in the corpus.

Rafe and *Partners in Crime* have not been considered, since I decided to include two texts per author at most. By the same token, Nash Candelaria's *Memories of the Alhambra* is included, but not so the two novels that complete his saga of the Rafa clan (*Not by the Sword*, 1982; *Inheritance of Strangers*, 1985). Other novels that could have been included but were not are *Nambé—Year One* by Orlando Romero (1976), *Below the Summit* by Joseph Torres-Metzgar (1976), *there are no madmen here* by Gina Valdés (1981), *Chicano* by Richard Vasquez (1970) and *Macho!* by Edmund Villaseñor (1973). I regret these omissions inasfar as each one of these works could have added its individual voice as well as new instances of the use of Spanish. At the same time, however, including them would have made my analysis bulky and repetitive without affecting its conclusions in any significant way.

4. Language as a Theme: Hard English and Soft Spanish

> Tia Cuca was more romantic about language. "Italian is the language of music," she said to the children in her lovely contralto voice. "French is the language of manners, English is the language of business, and Spanish—don't forget, children—is the language of love and romance." The only poetry she thought worth reading was that written in Spanish, "because it sings!" (*Rain God* 142)

Tía Cuca's fourfold definition is an exception. Language, a theme in all the texts—in *Clemente, Hunger, Barrio Boy*, or *Rites*, for example to a greater extent, and in *Tattoo* or *Tortuga* to a lesser extent (see 16.6)—means in most cases either *Spanish* or *English*, or *Spanish vs. English*. The terms *Chinese, French, German, Italian*, and *Japanese* appear repeatedly, too, but hardly ever connote language.[44]

The treatment of Spanish and English has one essential feature in common with Tía Cuca's approach: the separation of the two languages according to their functions. It is rare to find the words *English* and *Spanish* together in phrases like:

> In one afternoon he could sell . . . at least a half a dozen cookbooks in Spanish or in English. (*Tamazunchale* 29)

---

44 *Chinese* always designates the Chinese people (*Horseman* 262, 314; *Louise* 42; *Tamazunchale* 89). The same is true for *Italian* (*Cockroach* 31; *Louise* 45), *German* (*Alhambra* 20; *Cockroach* 28; *Leaving Home* 35; *Louise* 43, 44; *Victuum* 153), and *Japanese*, which moreover is restricted to the context of the Second World War (*Leaving Home* 165, 177, 191, 201; *Louise* 82; *Ultima* 30, 46; *Victuum* 250, 273). *French* denotes "the French" (*Leaving Home* 215), "the French occupation" (*Horseman* 19), and the language (*Rites* 16), and is also used in connection with earthly pleasures: "French bread" (*Victuum* 255), "French dessert" (*Rain God* 120), "French kiss" (*Cockroach* 31).

> . . . he wrote down all the names of Tía Cuca's cats that he could remember and then began making up riddles about them in Spanish and English. (*Rain God* 150, cf. 123)

> . . . whatever I read, in Spanish and English. (*Barrio Boy* 250)

> Words in English and Spanish rattle their tin cups on the cell bars of my brain, like rioting prisoners. Words that all at once want to scare, to change, to warn, and to form poem-prayer-song. (*Louise* 11, cf. 106)

> Spanish is the language of our conquerors. English is the language of our conquerors. (*Buffalo* 198, cf. 132)

In contrast to these phrases, which give English and Spanish the same potential and qualities, the theme of language appears in the corpus mainly in the form of a dichotomous treatment of English and Spanish. The divergent functions that are attributed to the two languages correspond in essence to Tía Cuca's view that "English is the language of business," while Spanish "is the language of love and romance."

Hunger is the text that comments on language most thoroughly and most explicitly:

> This autobiography, moreover, is a book about language. I write about poetry; the new Roman Catholic liturgy; learning to read; writing; political terminology. Language has been the great subject of my life. In college and graduate school, I was registered as an "English major." But well before then, from my first day of school, I was a student of language. Obsessed by the way it determined my public identity. The way it permits me here to describe myself, writing . . . (7)

The author-narrator-protagonist Richard Rodriguez contends that his "essays impersonating an autobiography" do not depict "the typical Hispanic-American life," but that "of a middle-class man" (7). His language education leads him to argue against bilingual education. Other narrators tend to favor bilingual education, if they pronounce at all on the issue:

> Are we such a threat just because we have demanded a compliance with the Treaty of Guadalupe Hidalgo, which provided

for a bilingual society? Is there something wrong with speaking Spanish in our schools? (*Cockroach* 60)

Rodriguez has been attacked for being an elitist and a renegade (*Hunger* 148, cf. Márquez "Richard Rodriguez" 131-133, Cazemajou 151-152). And Hector Calderón argues that Arturo Islas's *Rain God*, one of the other texts of our corpus, "should be read as a response to *Hunger of Memory*" ("Rain God" 70). But while Rodriguez's political *standpoint* and the *conclusions* he draws from his language education differ from the attitude that is generally manifested in Chicano letters of the period, his *characterization* of Spanish and English shows more parallels with the other texts than disparities. In spite of the different ideological subtexts, the account of Rodriguez's upbringing, of his early childhood especially, and the *role* he gives language in it, is similar to the treatment of these issues in the rest of the corpus.

The main distinction Rodriguez draws between Spanish and English is between their respective functions as a private and a public language:

> I shared with my family a language that was startlingly different from that used in the great city around us.
>   For me there were none of the gradations between public and private society so normal to a maturing child. Outside the house was public society; inside the house was private. (16)

The distinction between *private* and *public* is quite close to Tía Cuca's *love* vs. *business* differentiation, and it also presents itself in other novels:

> All of the older people spoke only in Spanish, and I myself understood only Spanish. It was only after one went to school that one learned English. (*Ultima* 9)

> Albuquerque High School . . . A strange place. Almost a foreign land that he visited every week day with fear and apprehension. Be polite. Smile. Always say yes to the Anglo teachers. Hide what you really feel. Then home again at the end of the day, carrying the verbal passport—the shift to the Spanish language— that was his readmission to Los Rafas. (*Alhambra* 35)

> "Listen to your teachers at school," Mama Chona told them in Spanish, "and learn to speak English the way they do. I speak it with an accent, so you must not imitate me. I will teach you how to speak Spanish properly for the family occasions."
> (*Rain God* 141)

Rodriguez argues that Spanish is not intrinsically more private than English:

> Because I wrongly imagined that English was intrinsically a public language and Spanish an intrinsically private one, I easily noted the difference between classroom language and the language of home. (20)
>
> *Intimacy is not created by a particular language; it is created by intimates.* (32)

Nevertheless, Spanish signifies the togetherness and the shelter of the family during his early childhood which he describes in affective terms. English, on the other hand, has become his professional and public language. The protagonist only attains his public North American identity after his family members have forced themselves to switch from Spanish to English at home, a change that results in a loss of communication and intimacy within the family. Rodriguez deplores this loss and feels guilty towards his parents, but sees the switch to English at home as a necessary step towards creating his public identity in an anglophone society (3-40).

The circumstances, events, and attitudes that characterize Richard Rodriguez's story about his move from Spanish to English as his main language are recurring motives in the corpus. Though most texts are novels, those recurring motives can be read as constituting a collective autobiography of Chicano acculturation. The protagonists as children speak only Spanish at home and have to start learning English at school (see 34-35 above). The acquisition of English goes hand in hand in most cases with forgetting or repressing Spanish partially if not completely: "As I grew fluent in English, I no longer could speak Spanish with confidence. . . . A powerful guilt blocked my spoken words" (*Hunger* 28). Generational conflicts may ensue, in which elder family members or Mexican relatives, although proud of the younger generation's achievement in the English-speaking North American society, are ashamed that the younger members of their family no longer speak proper Spanish (*Alhambra* 94, *Hunger* 29, *Mango Street* 74, *Rain God* 142, *Ultima* 50); while the younger generation—in most cases the generation of the protagonist—may be ashamed of their own lack of Spanish (*Alhambra* 179), but are more so of their progenitors' accented and faulty English (*Rain God* 119, cf. *Hunger* 53).

The switch from Spanish to English not only marks a division in the life of most protagonists; the two languages also bring about divisions between characters. Language is seldom treated as lightheartedly as among the poker player party in *Rain God*, who distort and mix English and Spanish and fool around with them by speaking English with a Mexican accent, anglicizing Spanish words or hispanicizing English ones:

> The queen was hers and she bet three cents on it knowing that Miguel would raise it to a nickel. "Un neekle," he said . . .
> "Pair of queenas for the Nina."
> "Tenk joo berry mahch," she said in a hammed up Mexican accent. (72, cf. 74)

> "That's my herman," she said to her *hermana*. They had Anglicized the word for sister and used it as a term of endearment with each other. (74)

Whereas here accent and nonstandard language forms make for easygoing diversion and serve as unifying factors for a group of Chicanos, they make for separation and tensions in many other cases.

Together with complexion, an issue not directly related to our subject,[45] language is the most frequently thematized iden-

---

45 "My older sister never spoke to me about her complexion when she was a girl. But I guessed that she found her dark skin a burden. I knew that she suffered for being a 'nigger'" (*Hunger*, cf. chapter "Complexion," pp. 113-139; cf. also *Alhambra* 33, 35, 38, 60, 86, 123, 129, 152; *Buffalo* 189; *Rain God* 127, 141, 144, 150; *Rites* 10; *Tamazunchale* 68; *Tattoo* 192; *Ultima* 33; *Victuum* 188).

tity marker in the corpus.[46] For one thing, it sets off Hispanos
from English-speaking Americans:

> Why were the güeros so set against them? Because they were
> Mexican? Because their skins were darker? Because they spoke
> Spanish? (*Plum Pickers* 141)

> My shrink says, "And is it the same when you hear a new
> song in Spanish?"
> "Fuck, I haven't heard a song in Spanish since I was a kid."
> "Oh? You don't like Mexican music?" he stabs it to me.
> But I don't have time for that racial crap now.
> (*Buffalo* 19, cf. 78)

> He felt calm now that they were on the ground. It was not so
> much relief from the fear of flight as other things . . . the sight
> of other Americans confused in a foreign country while he under-
> stood what was happening, the fact of Mexico itself. The dark
> faces, the men with longer hair and mustaches gave him comfort.
> It was as if a weight had fallen from his shoulders, the weight of
> countless light-skinned, clean-shaven Anglos who ran things back
> in los Estados Unidos. Here he felt unburdened. Somehow this
> was his place to be what he considered his true self.
> A few exchanges in Spanish, and a porter disappeared into
> the milling crowd. . . .   (*Alhambra* 23; cf. *Cockroach* 60;
> *Leaving Home* 29, 233; *Ultima* 191; *Victuum* 114, 154)

For another, it marks divisions between Spanish-speaking
groups that use different languages, dialects, or sociolects.

The texts do not present Hispanics as a homogeneous and
united group, but show tensions and differences between Mes-
tizos and "pure" Spaniards (see 25 above), between Chicanos
and Mexicans,[47] as well as between Mexican Americans who
live in different parts of the United States (*Alhambra* 13, 17;
Buffalo 77), are of different upbringing,[48] or of different politi-

---

46 Religion and Mexican food come in as well but are less direct and
     less conflict-creating markers.
47 See *Cockroach* 185; *Hunger* 113; *Rain God* 13f, 22, 120; *Tamazun-*
     chale 89; *Victuum* 61, 199, 217.
48 See *Leaving Home* 62; *Rain God* 13, 22, 85, 120; *Tamazunchale*
     89.

cal convictions.[49] And, as in the conflicts between Anglos and Hispanics—and again often compounded by complexion—,[50] language serves as the prominent distinctive feature of ethnic identity:

> California, then, was a land of *Pochos*. These California Mexicans were not much higher than the Okies with whom they lived. They spoke English most of the time, while we looked upon life "out west" simply as a temporary respite from the Depression. . . . So, when we left *El Segundo Barrio* across the street from the international border, we didn't expect the Mexicans in California to act like gringos.
>
> But they did. We were outsiders because of geography and outcasts because we didn't speak English and wore short pants. (*Buffalo* 77)

> I envied those minority students who graduated to work among lower-class Hispanics at barrio clinics or legal aid centers. I envied them their fluent Spanish. (I had taken Spanish in high school with *gringos*.) But it annoyed me to hear students on campus loudly talking in Spanish or thickening their surnames with rich baroque accents because I distrusted the implied assertion that their tongue proved their bond to the past, to the poor. I spoke English. (*Hunger* 159f)

> Look at their brown, greedy faces. Listen to their accented speech. We're not members of the same family. We're not even members of the same race. (*Alhambra* 12)

Tensions between different Hispanic groups and intragroup tensions among Chicanos occur throughout the corpus, albeit with uneven distribution. While they are marginal in *Louise, Mango Street,* and *Ultima,* and take a prominent position in *Cockroach* or *Hunger,* they are most insistently emphasized in

---

49 See *Buffalo* 77; *Clemente* 8, 52-58, 103; *Cockroach* 51, 67; *Hunger* 4, 115, 150, 159f; *Leaving Home* 62, 192; *Rain God* 85; *Rites* 64.

50 "Tia Cuca was lighter-skinned than her sister Chona. Nevertheless, like Mama Chona, she was unmistakably Mexican with enough Indian blood to give her those aristocratic cheekbones the two sisters liked the younger generation to believe were those of highborn Spanish ladies who just happened to find themselves in the provinces of Mexico" (*Rain God* 141).

Alhambra (8, 12, 17, 20, 60, 69, 80, 92f, 96, 104, 106, 163, 182f, 191). José Rafa, the protagonist of the novel, constantly stresses his true Spanish roots and dissociates himself from his darker-complexioned relatives who speak less English but better Spanish (12, 17), while the very same features (dark skin and speaking Spanish) make him feel at home in Mexico City: "The dark faces, the men with longer hair and mustaches gave him comfort" (23). On the other hand, an encounter that sets off Chicanos in New Mexico from those in Los Angeles and that involves José's son Joe, also emphasizes the importance of language in the context of identity and self-definition, and illustrates moreover how the perception of what is standard language and what is deviation is reversible:

> He could hear the voices of his cousins by the ditch. Laughing and talking a mixture of Spanish and English. Joe felt drawn to them. . . .
> 'Es verdad que no puedes hablar espanol?' the oldest boy asked.
> Joe flushed. Here it came. The outsider. The one who was different. When Joe did not answer, the boys elbowed one another in the ribs and smiled knowingly. The anger was hot in Joe's chest. . . .
> 'No puedes. No puedes,' came the singsong taunt.
> 'Some kind of Mexican you are,' his oldest cousin said. 'Can't even speak the language.'
> 'It's Spanish,' Joe said. 'Not Mexican.'
> 'And listen to your English,' another said. 'You speak with an accent. A California Anglo accent.' The way he pronounced it it sounded like Een-gleesh.
> 'Whatever I am, I'm the same as you!' Joe said.
> 'Oh no, you're not,' they taunted. 'You're from California, and you can't speak Spanish. No puedes.' (80f)

Once the protagonists have grown up, they frequently idealize the language of their childhood. The expression of dislike for the Spanish language is rare in the corpus and tends to come from not very favorably painted Anglo Americans:

> And don't tell *me* they don't speak any English, because . . .
> Well, *I* am not going to learn any Spanish just to please them. . . .
> I didn't need it as a girl, and I don't need it now. You won't hear

me struggling with that kitchen Spanish . . . it isn't even Spanish, is it? Not the real Spanish anyway. It's one they made up. (*Rites* 97; cf. p. 52 below, quotation from *Plum Pickers*).

Mexican American characters, in contrast, associate Spanish with family life, a sense of togetherness and belonging, with a nostalgic view of childhood (*Buffalo* 73, 186). Spanish "sings" (*Rain God* 142), is "beautiful" (*Alhambra* 26, *Rain God* 163), "soft" (*Hunger* 15, 17, *Alhambra* 121, *Mango Street* 13, *Buffalo* 186, see also Candelaria *Inheritance* 10), and often spoken or sung "softly" or "very softly" (*Plum Pickers* 38, *Rain God* 19, 66, 177). Galarza describes the Mexican Spanish word *chiquihuite* as "musical" (*Barrio Boy* 25). Spanish talk is characterized as "superb" (*Victuum* 324) and "elegant" (*Rain God* 166). Ramona, the central character of a story inserted in *Victuum*, "was extremely fond of her brother. She enjoyed listening to the mastery of his native language [Spanish]" (24). Rodriguez calls the Spanish terms *papá* and *mamá* "tender accents of sound" (24). Only Rolando Hinojosa never presents Spanish as "soft" in his novels and aims his criticism clearly, and in more than one respect, at Rodríguez, when he affirms one year after the publication of *Hunger*:

> What I worked on, as far as my life was concerned, was toward a personal voice which was to become my public voice. . . . I was not ashamed of my parents after I received my education, for I was not ashamed of them before I acquired one; I never ran out of things to say to them because of my education nor did they to me because of theirs. And neither of them spoke in hushed, soft-Spanish voices as some Chicano writers describe those who speak that often strident and vowel-filled language." (*Voice* 13f)

But Hinojosa's stance remains an exception among the authors of the corpus. According to Zeta Acosta, the protagonist and narrator of *Cockroach*, "nobody can learn Spanish sober. It is just too sensual a language, too rolling and flowing to want your tongue stiff and dry" (36f). In his other novel, Zeta Acosta also celebrates Spanish in English. He thus gives the hierarchy that he has established between the two languages by publishing in English an ironic twist:

> And they all are speaking in that language of my youth; that language which I had stopped speaking at the age of seven when the captain insisted we wouldn't learn English unless we stopped speaking Spanish; a language of soft vowels and resilient consonants, always with the fast rolling r's to threaten or to cajole; a language for moonlit nights under tropical storms, for starry nights in brown deserts and for making declarations of war on top of snow-capped mountains; a language perfect in every detail for people who are serious about life and preoccupied with death only as it refers to that last day of one's sojourn on this particular spot. (*Buffalo* 186)

Tía Cuca's definition of Spanish, "the language of love and romance," can be applied to this passage, too, even though the love affair between a narrator and a language may not be precisely what she had in mind.

The praise of the Spanish language in English texts is as such rather Chicano-specific, but is part of a more widespread phenomenon. Rodriguez rightfully plays down the ethnic typicality of his autobiography and insists upon its exemplary function by calling it a "pastoral" (6), and "a parable for the life of its reader" (7). The reconstruction of the past and the idealization of childhood—the "golden age of my youth" (26)—as an irrevocably lost paradise are common and important factors in the human experience as well as in literature.

Margarita, a character in *Plum Pickers*, extends the praise of the "soft" and "intimate" Spanish language to the Mexican American culture as a whole:

> Among Mexicans, she'd heard her teacher Miss Rodríguez say, are exactly the same proportions of docile to aggressive as in other cultural or national groups. That was another lie. There was more of everything in the Mexican character except money or love of money. More sadness, more joy, more love, more ferocity, more intensity, more softness, more intimacy, more warmth, more family, and more hatred. (141)

Although she does not name it, it is obvious which national character is the counterpart of the Mexican in her comparison.

English, "the language of business" according to Tía Cuca, is evaluated differently than Spanish. The word *English* appears about half as much as *Spanish* in the corpus, and the narrators never praise the euphony of the language they use. The protagonist of *Mango Street* compares its sound twice to *tin* (13, 75), while Richard Rodriguez opposes *hard* English to *soft* Spanish (17) and is, as a child, "often frightened by the sounds of *los gringos,* delighted by the sounds of Spanish at home" (*Hunger* 16). In *Horseman,* the sound of English makes for a laugh:

> "I am most pleased to meet you, Hercules," she said in English, and he laughed and said, "Taddalalulalula, lúlala," and they all laughed, for that was how it sounded. (136)

The adjectives that occur in association with *English* hardly ever connote emotion—if they do, they imply rejection ("strange" *Alhambra* 170, cf. *Hunger* 16)—but tend to specify a type of English, or a degree of proficiency, in an unemotional manner. The word *English* appears in the company of: "unaccented" (*Alhambra* 96, cf. 17), "broken" (*Leaving Home* 179), "perfect," "best" (*Rain God* 119-20), "Oxford" (*Tamazunchale* 85), "limited" (*Louise* 68), "grammatical," "garbled," "classroom," "public" (*Hunger* 13, 24, 50, 188).[51] No narrator, protagonist, or character expresses her or his emotional attachment to it. Richard Rodriguez may come to the conclusion that: *"Intimacy is not created by a particular language; it is created by intimates"* (32). Nevertheless, neither he nor any other author ever grow lyrical about English in the way some of them grow lyrical about Spanish.

English is, above all, a practical language. Not only do Chicano texts in English have a better market potential, but learning English also dramatically increases Mario's hustling income in *Clemente* (72), and his knowledge of English helps Fausto, the old protagonist of *Tamazunchale,* when he is detained by the border patrol:

---

51 Unemotional classifying adjectives are occasionally also applied to the Spanish language: "ungrammatical" (*Tamazunchale* 31), "flawless" (*Horseman* 137).

. . . in his most exaggerated Oxford English, Fausto recited without a pause the Gettysburg Address, the Pledge of Allegiance and Franklin Roosevelt's death announcement. It was an old trick, but when the guard heard Roosevelt's name, he was convinced. Fausto was given his clothes and told to leave. (85)[52]

If it comes in handy to get *into* the United States, English is indispensable for Chicanos to get *on* in North America. Not knowing it shuts them off from the anglophone community around them:

"Padre nuestro que estás en los cielos—" I prayed to myself, sharing my prayers with no one. Everyone else prayed in English. (*Ultima* 191)

. . . I believe she doesn't come out because she is afraid to speak English, and maybe this is so since she only knows eight words. (*Mango Street* 73, cf. 74)

English is perceived as a necessity and, together with education, as a key to upward mobility and to success. In many novels, a parent, a relative, a teacher, a tutor, or a superior admonishes a Chicana or Chicano to learn English:

"Hey, *Jefe*, it was only a joke." The young Mexican pronounced the English "j" like a "y" and Felix said to him angrily, "Hey, *pendejo*, why don't you stop being a stupid wetback and learn English?" (*Rain God* 117, cf. above, quotation from *Rain God* on page 43)

"This is an *American* school . . . we want you boys to learn *English.*"
"Even when we play keep-away? Even here?"
"If you want to stay in this school. Yes, you boys will have to speak only English while on the school grounds." (*Buffalo* 187)

---

52 Since the guard does not react before Roosevelt is mentioned, the passage implies a reversal of the stereotype of the illiterate, "stupid Mexican" (cf. *Louise* 68, 84 and *Rain God* 117).

> She said that in school the teachers let them speak only in English. I wondered how I would be able to speak to the teachers. (*Ultima* 30)

> . . . a viejita with the heart in the right place. Patiently pumping English into us. (*Louise* 66)

> Everyone in class speaks Spanish . . . we all do . . . but no the teacher gets mad . . . she says we must speak American . . . I don't know why . . . everyone understands Spanish! (*Victuum* 11, cf. 66, 154)

> Ay Caray! We *are* home. This *is* home. Here I am and here I stay. Speak English. Speak English. Christ! (*Mango Street* 74)

Mexican Americans who do not speak English, or who do not speak it properly, meet little sympathy from Anglos, and are criticized by them:

> Shee yit fugging iggorant bastards mex why they think they are any iggorant nogoods, why they cain't even talk murrican rite lak usns real januwine murrican citizens, U.S.M. (*Plum Pickers* 125, cf. 47)

Although in this case, the criticism may not strike home because the narrator's affirmations are invalidated by his own ignorance and ethnocentrism, the texts agree that if Chicano characters want to make it in American society, their English had better be accent free. English tainted by a Mexican accent can cause shame, rejection, and ridicule among Chicanos, too, and is regarded as a hindrance for a career in the United States:

> She spoke English with a heavy Mexican accent and used it only when she wanted to make "important" statements, not realizing that her accent created the opposite effect. After his first year in school JoEl learned to be ashamed of the way his mother abused the language. The others, including Felix, loved to tease and imitate her. Their English was perfect and Spanish surfaced only when they addressed their older relatives or when they were with their Mexican school friends at social events. (*Rain God* 119, cf. 120, 141)

> . . . I spoke English poorly. . . . But it was one thing for *me* to speak English with difficulty. It was more troubling for me to hear my parents speak in public: their high-whining vowels and guttural consonants; their sentences that got stuck with 'eh' and 'ah' sounds; the confused syntax. . . . Hearing them, I'd grow nervous, my clutching trust in their protection and power weakened. (*Hunger* 14f)

> Pete was picking up the speech patterns of the local Mexican kids. His English was always intermingled with Spanish. And this would not do. He must learn English well; in fact, it did not matter, or perhaps it was important that he *not* learn Spanish. After all, he was American-born. (*Clemente* 11)

In contrast to the overall tendency to acquire English, the impulse to learn Spanish occurs rarely in the texts and is motivated differently. *Clemente* is a case in point. The protagonist Clemente Chacón rejects his Mexican past as an obstacle to a career in the United States and does not want his son either "to associate with semi-literate or illiterate campesinos" (119, cf. quotation above). In the course of the novel, however, he changes his mind, reaffirms his Mexican past, and revises his opinion as to his son's language education: "he has to know where he comes from; he has to learn some Spanish" (124). Clemente acknowledges his roots in an entirely emotional countermovement to his American career and assimilation. The same goes for Zeta Acosta, the protagonist of *Cockroach* who, after having lost his knowledge of Spanish almost entirely in the course of his assimilation, decides one night to join Chicano militants:

> That night I get no sleep. My brain goes off like explosives and by dawn I have made innumerable resolutions. I will change my name. I will learn Spanish. I will write the greatest books ever written. I will become the best criminal lawyer in the history of the world. I will save the world. I will show the world what is what and who the fuck is who. Me in particular. (31)

Summing up and generalizing, we may say that English appears in the corpus as a demanding language, as "hard" and "practical," Spanish as "soft" and "beautiful." English is described as "the language of business," as an active language (it "takes you somewhere"). It is imposed as a necessity and is treated unemotionally and matter-of-factly. Spanish, "the language of love," is dealt with more emotionally and often idealized, but seldom learned or used. It is treated from the outside and has a more passive role. This kind of functional division is very close to what Gary Keller calls "the traditional bilingual dichotomy," with "one language for commerce, education, and public duties in general; the second language for falling in love, being angry, having a good time, family life, and so on" (*Literary Stratagems* 291). In addition, the language dichotomy overlaps with the diglossia that some bilingual education programs create by using Spanish "for teaching Mexican history and literature, for example, but English for mathematics and the sciences, thus fostering the misleading impression that English is the language of a modern, scientific, technological society, but Spanish suitable only for literary, folkloristic, and traditional, 'impractical' purposes" (Peñalosa 10, cf. p. 7n8 above). Furthermore, as I have already mentioned, Spanish appears in this dichotomy as one of the essential elements of a paradise lost:

> I sing Ariel's song to celebrate the intimate speech my family once freely exchanged. In singing the praise of my lower-class past, I remind myself of my separation from that past, bring memory to silence. (*Hunger* 6)

Finally, the way in which the two languages are characterized in the texts coincides with yet two other culturally conditioned binary systems. First, it corresponds to traditional gender stereotypes: English appears as a "male" language, a "father tongue," Spanish as a "mother tongue," a "female" language (cf. Le Guin). Johannes Fabian's *Time and the Other: How Anthropology Makes Its Objects* can be used to elucidate the second binary system: Anthropology tends, or tended, to align reason with the anthropologist, the colonizer; emotion and exotic characteristics with the anthropological object, the colonized. Moreover, it can idealize its objects (11, 121, 135). Extending that assumption to our subject we may say that in the Chicano texts of the corpus English appropriates Spanish in an anthropological way, that it presents itself as the colonizer, while Spanish comes through as the anthropological object, as the colonized. This type of dichotomy between two languages does not break any new ground, does not rewrite any existing textual codes—nor is English the only possible colonizing language. Spanish appears as the colonizer when the 17th century poet Sor Juana Inés de la Cruz included a native Mexican song in one of the poems of her collection *Inundación Castálida*. The song itself is semantically and prosodically clearly marked by colonization. It is a christian prayer and fits the meter of the Spanish *romance* verse to a T. Moreover, and more importantly in our context, the Spanish quatrain which precedes it qualifies the language of the song in exactly the same way as the texts of the corpus qualify Spanish:

> And with the *tender* clauses
> Of the Mexican language
> In a *sonorous* Tocotín
> They speak in *soft* voices:
> Tla ya timohuica
> to tlazo ziuapilli
> maca ammo tonantzin,
> titechmoilcahuiliz.

(357f, my translation from Spanish, emphasis added)

The texts of the corpus and Sor Juana's poem may include the same message as one of their possible subtexts. Anthropological discourses tend to be applied to species in danger of extinction. Native American languages during the conquest and Spanish in the Mexican American context were, or are, such species. Spanish as a theme in the Chicano novel in English could in this case be interpreted as following a pattern that Bruce-Novoa has at one stage defined as characteristic for Chicano literature and exemplified by means of Chicano poetry:

> If Chicano literature is more than an arbitrary conglomeration, one might expect the deep structure of its major works to share elements and their distribution; that is the case. The great variety of Chicano literature derives from one deep structure . . . [that] passes through the following process: threat of disappearance to an *axis mundi* object → rescue of the threatened object's images from disappearance → response to the threat in the form of the work of art as a new object. (*Chicano Poetry* 5)

The thematic treatment of the Spanish language in the corpus makes anthropological and autobiographical discursive registers converge. Reducing it to only one model would be simplistic; both are operative, interact with, and partly devalue one another. Fabian's plea for coevality between anthropology and its object (154), justified as it may be in the context of anthropology, can never be applied to autobiographical discourses. The separation of the adult from the child she or he once was cannot be overcome. At the same time, stressing the personal and autobiographical aspects does not do away with the hierarchy that exists between English and Spanish in the United States. While the autobiographical mode may have been paramount in the process of writing, the anthropological mode may come to the fore in the process of reading. The celebration of Spanish as the "soft," "beautiful," and "sensual" language of their childhood may reflect an authentic personal experience for the protagonists, the narrators, the authors, and maybe for Chicano readers. But the same aspects that signify their personal involvement may confirm stereotypes for "monocultural" readers.

The dichotomy between Spanish and English, as it appears in the corpus, implies and is part of a series of other oppositions. It conditions and is the result of various spatial, temporal, social, and conceptual borderlines that partly coincide, partly diverge. Spanish vs. English marks in the texts love vs. business, the private vs. the public sphere, emotion vs. reason, but stands at the same time as an analogy of Mexico vs. the United States, Chicano vs. Anglo, the Southwest before and after 1848, rural vs. urban, Chicano worker vs. Chicano intellectual, childhood vs. adulthood. All of these oppositions are significant thematic components in the corpus. The last one mentioned, however, the personal experience of cultural and linguistic assimilation, is the one that forms the most recurrent pattern.

The substitution of Spanish by English is the decisive step in the process of acculturation, in the acquisition of a new identity, of a new name at times,[53] and the quintessential condition for a career in North American Anglo-Saxon society. Most texts show protagonists who integrate into Anglo-Saxon society language-wise and, to a greater or lesser extent, also career- and culture-wise. Although the English language and the public American society may make them feel uneasy initially, and the language change is perceived as an imposition, the characters undergo that change without rebelling against it. This attitude contrasts with that of some protagonists in Spanish and bilingual Chicano novels, who refuse assimilation to the extreme of self-annihilation (see chapter 3).

Esperanza, the central character of *Mango Street*, is also caught between the two languages, but is not content with either language. She opts for a third possibility, dreams of breaking out of the dichotomy between English and Spanish. Both languages have negative and positive connotations for her, neither can be reduced to a facile stereotype, though the stereotypes are present for her as well. Both languages are part of her identity, and as in Rodriguez's book, Spanish is dominant in the family, the private sphere, while English is the public language used in school. Esperanza is not content with that functional separation and wishes for a more adequate language to identify with. She wants to break free from the net of culturally conditioned borderlines and stereotypes and exemplifies this dream by means of her name:

> In English my name means hope. In Spanish it means too many letters. It means sadness, it means waiting. It is like the

---

53 *Ricardo* becomes *Rich-heard* (*Hunger* 2, 4, 27), *Pedro* Pete (*Leaving Home* 230), and *Antonio* Anthony (*Ultima* 54).

number nine. A muddy color. It is the Mexican records my father plays on Sunday mornings when he is shaving, songs like sobbing. . . .
  At school they say my name funny as if the syllables were made out of tin and hurt the roof of your mouth. But in Spanish my name is made out of a softer something like silver . . .
  I would like to baptize myself under a new name, a name more like the real me, the one nobody sees. Esperanza as Lisandra or Maritza or Zeze the X. Yes. Something like Zeze the X will do. (12f)[54]

Zeze is, in contrast to *Esperanza*, a name devoid of meaning. *X* designates an unknown quantity. "Zeze the X" gives Esperanza a "room of her own," an undefined and not prescribed space outside gender stereotypes, outside colonial discourses and languages, and outside simplifying binary systems.

---

54 In Villarreal's first novel *Pocho* (1959), which is not included in the corpus, another Chicano protagonist also refuses to decide between his Mexican cultural background and North American values: "Among the various options of absolute value posed for Richard Rubio by Anglo-American culture, by the Roman Catholic Church, by his father's demands, and by his mother's wishes, Richard consistently chooses not to choose. Herein lies Richard's special and generic difference" (Saldívar R. *Dialectic of Difference* 15).

5. The Chicano Novelist as a Translator of Cultural Differences

Friedrich Schleiermacher

Friedrich Schleiermacher begins his lecture on the different methods of translation—*"Ueber die verschiedenen Methoden des Uebersetzens"*—by pointing out that a translator not only has to bridge the gap between two languages but also the gap between the two corresponding cultures (143f). After discussing the dichotomies of translator vs. interpreter, scientific vs. literary translation, and paraphrase vs. reproduction, he goes on to the objectives of the "true" translator:

> Aber nun der eigentliche Uebersetzer, der diese beiden ganz getrennten Personen, seinen Schriftsteller und seinen Leser, wirklich einander zuführen, und dem letzten, ohne ihn jedoch aus dem Kreise seiner Muttersprache heraus zu nöthigen, zu einem möglichst richtigen und vollständigen Verständniß und Genuß des ersten verhelfen will, was für Wege kann er hiezu einschlagen? Meines Erachtens giebt es deren nur zwei. Entweder der Uebersetzer läßt den Schriftsteller möglichst in Ruhe, und bewegt den Leser ihm entgegen, oder er läßt den Leser möglichst in Ruhe, und bewegt den Schriftsteller ihm entgegen. Beide sind so gänzlich von einander verschieden, daß durchaus einer von beiden so streng als möglich muss verfolgt werden, aus jeder Vermischung aber ein höchst unzuverlässiges Resultat nothwendig hervorgeht, und zu besorgen ist, daß Schriftsteller und Leser sich gänzlich verfehlen. (152)

According to Schleiermacher then, the task of the translator consists in bringing together the author and the reader and helping the latter, without forcing him to leave "the circle of his mother tongue," to "as correct and complete an understanding and enjoyment of the former as possible" (my translation). A translator has one of two entirely different and mutually exclusive options open to him in order to accomplish this. He can either leave the author in peace and bring the reader to the author or leave the reader in peace and bring the author to the reader. This idea, as well as the notion of the translator as a mediator between cultures, are useful concepts for the discussion of Chicano literature.

Chicano authors, as well as the authors of other "New Literatures in English" and of "minority" literatures in general, are comparable to translators. Most Chicano novelists who write in English know both the Anglo American and the Mexican American cultural contexts and both languages. The implied authors and the narrators that come to the fore in their texts often mediate between the two by translating linguistic and cultural differences for their intended readership. In doing so, they can adopt one of the two stances described by the German philosopher. They can either leave without clarification tokens, themes, or concepts that the monolingual reader cannot take for granted or that are unknown in the readers' culture,[55] or they can do everything possible to bridge cultural differences by explaining foreign subject matters and using registers and discourses that are familiar to the reader. The "minority" culture can either be presented in a way that endorses the reader's image of that culture and confirms prevailing stereotypes, or its depiction can aim at subverting these stereotypes.

---

55   The *monolingual reader*, or *monolingual English reader*, is a phantom in a way, a stereotype label that moreover does not cover the entire readership of Chicano texts in English. On the other hand, that phantom has a very real existence and is a factor of power in the United States. Furthermore, it is the target of quite a few textual strategies in the corpus; it exists, i.e., as the *implied reader* in Iser's sense. The term will be used in the follow   esignate the stereotype of a white Anglo-Saxon Protestant r   Sollors 12) who does not know Spanish and who is not nec   amiliar with the Spanish loanwords used in the English of tl   est. Dasenbrock uses the same term (15), while Sánchez   a whole set of terms for the same stereotype: "monoling   ence" (852, 857), "nonbilingual audience," "non-Hispanop   57), "Anglophonic readers" (868, 870), and "English-sp   onocultural readers" (858).

Analysis of intercultural mediation, as it appears in the Chicano novel in English, does not necessarily have to rely on Schleiermacher as a starting point. For one thing, the different approaches that Wycliffites and Tyndale took in translating the Bible, and the ensuing disputes made it clear long before him that the character of a translation is shaped by a translator's perspective and procedure as well as by culture- and language-specific factors. For another, his lecture has been superseded by more modern and more thorough studies on translation (Ortega y Gasset, Mounin, Steiner, García Yebra). Schleiermacher's two types of translation are often reflected in newer studies, but he is seldom mentioned. Thus Goethe, who knew Schleiermacher (*Register* 490), seems to base his essay "Übersetzungen" in the addenda to the *West-östlicher Divan* on what Schleiermacher had published some years earlier. And Walter Benjamin, in his—philosophical rather than methodological—essay "Die Aufgabe des Übersetzers" (The Task of the Translator), quotes Rudolf Pannwitz, where he could perfectly quote Schleiermacher, because the former says essentially the same as the latter said a hundred years before him (61). Another often adduced text on translation, finally, Paul de Man's "'Conclusions': Walter Benjamin's 'The Task of the Translator,'" is an excellent piece of showmanship and contains some valid comments on Benjamin's article, but it is not very useful for our purposes. De Man deconstructs Benjamin's article to the point of absurdity and proves that he himself does not know German all that well when he criticizes the translators of "Die Aufgabe des Übersetzers." Moreover, unlike Benjamin or de Man, I am not interested in the question of whether translation is ultimately possible or not. Translation, however imperfect it may be, is a necessary everyday practice all over the world.

The distance between the implied author and the reader has also been dealt with by literary critics. Wayne C. Booth, for example, says in *The Rhetoric of Fiction*:

> The *implied author* may be more or less distant from the *reader*.
> The distance may be intellectual (the implied author of *Tristram*

Shandy, not of course to be identified with Tristram, more interested in and knowing more about recondite classical lore than any of his readers), moral (the works of Sade), or aesthetic. (157)

Booth neglects culturally conditioned distance, and no other theorist on translation presents us with as tangible an image of translation between cultures as Schleiermacher. This has led me to choose his concept that a translator can "either leave the author in peace and bring the reader to the author or leave the reader in peace and bring the author to the reader" as a starting point, although it has to be adjusted and complemented for the discussion of Chicano literature:

- Since Chicano novels do not usually exist in an "original" Spanish and a "translated" English version, the stance of an author cannot be deduced directly from a comparison of these two versions, because it is hidden in the textual strategies employed. Chicano authors translate cultural, not literary, texts.
- Some Chicano authors *do* force their readers to "leave the circle of their mother tongue."
- Schleiermacher does not comment on the hierarchy that may exist between the two languages and cultures involved; the question of "mainstream" versus "minority" language—the "highly asymmetrical relations of power" to repeat Pratt's phrasing (34)—is not brought up in his text.
- His notion that a translator has to choose one of two mutually exclusive positions is too absolute and, even if it were true for translators, not applicable to novelists.

It would be as impossible as it is useless to classify literary texts as corresponding strictly to one of the two options, even if some Chicano novels would rather make Mexican American culture converge on the mainstream North American reader —if there is such a being—, while others can be read as making the mainstream reader converge on Chicano culture. Whereas a translator may prefer to adopt and maintain a stable stance for the translation of a given text, a creative writer in no way has to confine her- or himself to only one discursive register; the perspective presented in a novel need not be consistent or exclusive and less so in a century in which the novel has been defined as "a diversity of social speech types (sometimes even diversity of languages) and a diversity of individual voices, artistically organized" (Bakhtin 262; cf. Todorov *Mikhaïl Bakhtine* 91 and 126-40).

Collage, the fullest and most obvious exploitation of Bakhtin's definition, is rare in the Chicano novel in English. Raymond Barrio's *Plum Pickers* and the novels of Rolando Hinojosa are the only texts of the corpus which use it to some extent. The abrupt juxtaposition of different discourses, a trademark of many twentieth-century prose writers, is more usual in the Chicano novels in Spanish and, for obvious reasons, in the bilingual ones. However, this does not convert Chicano novels in English into monolithic units that either bring the white Anglo-Saxon Protestant American reader to Chicano culture or vice versa. Instead of viewing the dichotomy proposed by Schleiermacher as an either-or requirement that an entire text has to fulfill, it seems preferable to apply it to smaller entities, to evaluate the rhetoric contained in small discursive unities, in words, phrases, and paragraphs. By the same token, the two stances will not be seen as absolute and exclusive categories to which a text can be unequivocally ascribed, but as two poles between which rhetorical gestures place themselves in intermediate and often ambivalent positions. This view seems more in line with such complex subject matters as "culture," "culture conflict," and "acculturation," and with two cultures that are not clear-cut entities but overlapping conglomerates, one mainly influenced by Anglo-Saxon values, the other by Hispanic values. The relationship between two cultures and the mediation between them are intricate issues that escape facile classification. The borderline between the view from within and the view from without, between the cliché and the authentic is thin, and depends a good deal on interpretation.

Schleiermacher presents two attitudes that a translator may assume, but offers no information on what a translation that corresponds to either one of them looks like. He does not provide any methodology for analysis and does not ask, let alone answer, some necessary questions: which concrete features of a textual passage determine a translator's standpoint; how can the position that a given discourse takes between the two cultures be assessed; and how do the textual strategies that work in one direction or the other look.

The position that a textual strategy may take between expressing a "minority" or a "mainstream" stance, cannot be assessed by a simple and generally valid procedure. It cannot be pinpointed empirically, but has to be approached hermeneutically. And though the critic, a translator in her or his turn, can rely on logic, statistical evidence, and secondary literature in such a process of interpretation, the results of that process will in any case also be influenced by her or his personal, social, and academic background and by her or his predilections, preconceptions, and prejudices.

Translation

One of the most blatant and obvious examples of "cultural translation" in the Chicano novel—of leaving the reader in peace and bringing the author to the reader—can be found in Lionel Garcia's *Leaving Home*. Benito Orozco, "a notary who in those days wrote letters for clients, prepared quasi-legal documents and served in a general way as the learned class among the illiterate," says to Adolfo, who has ordered a love poem from him and complains that it "doesn't rhyme": "This is not Shakespeare, this is Orozco." When they talk about his fee, Benito insists: "You want a Browning and you only have money for an Orozco" (240). Shakespeare's fame may be universal. Nevertheless, by having a Mexican scribe refer in Tijuana to two Anglophone poets and not to Hispanic ones, Garcia "translates" the Mexican context into an Anglo-Saxon one in much the same way as van Eyck or Zurbarán "translate" a Palestinian context into a European one in their biblical paintings. Such blunt "translations," in which tokens of the culture depicted are replaced by tokens of the artist's or the receiver's culture, are extremely rare in the Chicano novel of the period analyzed here. Yet this does not mean that "cultural translation" is not present in that genre.

The fact that Chicano novels in English tend to depict a culture different from that of their implied readership surfaces abundantly and on different textual levels. On the thematic level, a text may include cultural manifestations that do not exist, or that exist in a different form, in the culture of the readers, for instance themes like Catholicism, healer wisdom, or mariachi music. On a smaller scale, words that designate material tokens of the Mexican American culture like *tortilla*, *sarape*, or *adobe* may appear in a text without being developed into themes. The interesting point of analysis in the context of intercultural mediation is not so much the inclusion of themes and words from a different culture in a text, but rather the way in which these "foreign" elements are presented. It is significant that *adobe*, for example, is more frequent in the texts of the corpus than probably in any other contemporary literature in English.[56] More significant and interesting than its mere occurrence, however, are the discursive registers that surround the word and that point out its functions.

Nash Candelaria's first novel *Memories of the Alhambra* and Ernesto Galarza's autobiography *Barrio Boy* are two Chicano texts that use *adobe* extensively—both about once every ten pages. In *Barrio Boy*, the word is already used as a marker of difference in the opening sentence: "Unlike people who are born in hospitals, in an ambulance, or in a taxicab I showed up in an adobe cottage" (3). Galarza establishes the contrast be-

---

56 In the literatures in Spanish of our century the use of *adobe* is, for obvious reasons, almost entirely restricted to the Hispanic American *costumbrismo* tradition. Outside that realm, Luis Martín Santos's *Tiempo de silencio* is the only novel in Spanish in which I have encountered the word in my (entirely arbitrary) readings over the last few years: "con adobes en que la frágil paja hace al barro lo que las barras de hierro al cemento hidráulico" (50).

tween his readers' frame of reference—modern North American culture—and the rural Mexico of his childhood right at the beginning of his text. The narrator's singular "I" is opposed to the plural form "people." Being born in an adobe cottage, the norm in rural Mexico at the beginning of our century, is presented as an exception to the norm of being "born in hospitals." To put it in Schleiermacher's terms: the author-narrator Ernesto Galarza brings the world of his childhood to the reader. The other occurrences of *adobe* in *Barrio Boy* work in the same direction. They do not break any new artistic ground, but are employed rather monotonously. With three exceptions (8, 13, 108), the word always appears, as in the example just quoted, as a modifier; almost always in attributive position and accompanying the same stereotype nouns. The reader, who in all probability has never lived in an adobe house, is constantly—up to three or four times per page (8, 12)—reminded that adobe is the prime building material in the protagonist's world. "Little Ernie" not only is born and grows up in an "adobe cottage" (3, 4, 12, 14), but is also surrounded by "adobe walls" (7, 12, 27, 75, 82, 84, 106) and "adobe bricks" (12, 14, 15, 43, 107), goes to an "adobe chapel" (8), and lives or sleeps overnight in "adobe rooms" (83, 183), an "adobe house" (105), an "adobe building" (106), or an "adobe brick building" (104). It seems to be the main function of the word to insistently point out something that is not the norm in the United States though it can be taken for granted in the context of rural Mexico—a gesture that can be interpreted as making the culture depicted converge on the readership. The author's intention to illustrate the Mexican culture to a North American reader also finds expression in the descriptive style and the minutely-detailed realism throughout the text.

Anaya's *Ultima* (4, 85f, 89, 92, 100, 220, 241), Rios's *Victuum* (19, 21, 256, 288), and Villarreal's *Fifth Horseman* (24, 25, 38, 141, 266, 340) use *adobe* similarly, though not as frequently as *Barrio Boy*. They, too, apply it mainly as a modifier in merely descriptive terms, as a marker of difference with no emotional values attached and largely free from any moral or symbolic connotations. This is not the case with the other Chicano novel that makes extensive use of *adobe*. In *Memories of the Alhambra* by Nash Candelaria, the word also modifies nouns like *house* (10, 56, 58, 77, 114, 175, 184, 189), *walls* (62), *church* (63, 75), etc. (see 25, 45, 50, 78, 98, 105, 189) and is used as insistently as in *Barrio Boy*. But since *Alhambra* employs much less detailed description than *Barrio Boy*, this insistence is more striking. During a family reunion at "grandmother's little adobe house," to cite one instance, the narrator informs the reader that "Joe walked off, turning the adobe corner of the house" (77f). Moreover, while the other texts mentioned tend to apply *adobe* matter-of-factly, the word often implies a value judgment in Candelaria's novel. It appears frequently together with the adjective *little* (56, 63, 77, 98, 175, 184), sometimes with clearly pejorative connotations, and can, as in *Barrio Boy*, be part of an explicit or implicit comparison between the Hispanic and the Anglo American cultures in which the former comes out as inferior or more "primitive" than the latter. This is so when Jose, the protagonist, travels to Mexico:

> In the United States the next town would have been an intersection with a gasoline station warily facing a general store. Here there were anonymous adobe hovels, dirt roads, and scrawny chickens. (45)

Or when his son Joe rebels against him:

> This isn't the little ranchito in Adobe Flats. He even wants me to quit school and go to work to make money. Probably to turn my paycheck over to him the way my cousins do to their parents. But, no! I won't! I'm going to finish college no matter what. I want more. I want to be better than him! (98f)

The novel ends with the death of Jose. In New Mexico, after his father's funeral, Joe, a "Californian," experiences a "homecoming" and an apotheosis of sorts, in which adobe serves as a catalyst, loses its pejorative connotations, and acquires mythical ones. A relative talks about the house they are in:

> 'Fifty years old. I built it myself. Adobe. Thick, thick walls.
> Cool in summer and warm in winter. They don't make houses
> like this anymore.'
> The walls, Joe could see, were worn smooth by years of coat-
> ing and recoating. Even from inside he knew that it belonged to
> the earth. He felt from it a solid, heavy inertia that said: This is
> where I belong. No stone castles as in Spain on this new frontier,
> but the earth itself. Leaving no monuments after man has gone.
> For then the elements will erode what was manmade, giving it
> back to the earth from which it came. It is proper that it should
> be so. (189f)

The passage may still be written with a North American reader in mind; moreover, the entire ending of *Alhambra* is pom-
pous and seems motivated rather by the author's wish for a
grand finale than by any interior logic of the text. The ethnocentric attitudes and tensions between Chicanos of different
backgrounds that dominate the novel throughout evaporate too
abruptly. What is crucial in the context of "translation" between cultures, however, is the fact that *adobe* does not serve
primarily as a gloss, as a marker of difference in Candelaria's
first novel, but acquires a symbolic function and is linked to
the personal history of a protagonist. Whereas in the other
instances mentioned so far, the word seems to function in the
first place as an element in intercultural "translation," different functions come to the fore here. This is even more so in
two Chicano novels that are not at the center of the genre. Rudolfo Anaya's *Tortuga*, which, in contrast to Anaya's other
novels, is not set in a Chicano environment, and Floyd Salas's
Tattoo the Wicked Cross, which has been considered as belonging only marginally or not at all to Chicano literature,[57]
both have *adobe* connote a color:

---

57 Bruce-Novoa does not mention Salas in *Authors*, but includes him in
the addendum "Chronological Chart of Publications" as well as in
the bibliography. For Tonn, Salas is, together with Rechy, on the
edge of Chicano literature ("am Rande der Definition," Tonn 39f),
while Lattin and Martínez do not include him at all (cf. Jiménez 3,
255).

. . . a hospital with its adobe colored, cracked walls shimmering in the desert heat. (*Tortuga* 96)

His father's bald head was the dull color of adobe. (*Tattoo* 265)

Tortuga uses it with the stereotype noun *wall*, but not in the stereotype formula "adobe walls"; *Tattoo* removes it entirely from its conventional context. Neither of the two texts emphasize the word through repetition. While *Tattoo* has it appear a second time (274), the example quoted is the only occurrence in *Tortuga*. In both texts the word shows a low profile, is mentioned by the way, integrated implicitly into the discourse, and—though it indicates the author's cultural background—does not function as an explicit marker of cultural difference.

Another expression of intercultural mediation can be found in generalizing statements about Mexican culture which concentrate on the "Mexican mentality," and less on material tokens, and which often explain or justify the behavior of a Mexican American literary character:

. . . for the greatest sentimental moment in Mexican culture is the coming together of a man and woman in holy matrimony. (*Rain God* 55)

. . . it is the Mexican custom, to use a wreath of flowers when a virgin girl dies! (*Victuum* 199, cf. 217)

. . . he sensed another strange feeling, a very Mexican thing, responsibility for his mother's children although he had never seen one until this moment. (*Clemente* 81)

He had, in the Professor's eyes, gone beyond what the normal lower middle-class Mexican-American man was supposed to do—stoop labor. (*Leaving Home* 199)

I must foot the bill for the reception. Chicano protocol dictates that the parents of the bride do this. (*Louise* 97, cf. 67)

The comparison with the North American culture may be made explicit:

> In Mexico we used a liniment from the cactus that had been
> fermented and allowed to spoil. We skimmed the top off, then we
> added chewing tobacco to it and then applied it to the body. Now
> *there* was a smell. Thank God we don't use that in this country.
> (*Leaving Home* 131)

Such phrases, which mediate between cultures and give the
discourse an "anthropological" quality, may still place themselves at different viewpoints. *Barrio Boy* presents a culturally
conditioned gesture from a Mexican view:

> He smiled, and held up a forefinger, crooking and straightening it
> while he looked at us. I had no idea what he meant, for in
> Mexico you signaled people to follow you by holding up your
> hand and closing all the fingers over the palm with a snap a few
> times. (191)

The narrator implies that the Anglo American version of the
gesture has at best a relative value, is but another code. If, on
the other hand, a character makes "the Mexican beckoning
sign, the arm moving downward instead of up" (*Clemente* 14),
the North American culture provides an unquestioned and
absolute frame of reference. Bringing the author to the reader
can in places go as far as projecting the reader's perspective
onto that of a Chicano protagonist. The already mentioned
example of the Mexican scribe who uses Browning as a reference is not the only one in the corpus. In *Letters to Louise*,
Delgado's epistolary novel—a genre which intrinsically
includes mediation more than other types of novels—, the narrator-protagonist relates his life and opinions to an unknown,
but presumably non-Chicano addressee. When writing about
his childhood he remarks that: "One of the things you notice
growing up in Mexico is a lack of toilets of any sort" (39), an
observation which is possible in retrospect, or in comparison
with the North American culture, but which is hardly one of
the things noticed by someone growing up in pre-TV rural
Mexico. "You" refers to Louise, to the reader, to the protagonist as an adult maybe, but certainly not to the protagonist as a
child.

The expression of a narrator's or a character's distance to the world depicted does not necessarily have to name that world "Mexico." The distance can also be made apparent through generalizing formulas which indicate a geographical or temporal distance between the narrator and the setting like "in that country," "it was the custom . . . ," "at that time," "in those days," "in this society," or "in that culture" :

> . . . they will have a black and white photo taken in front of the tomb with flowers shaped like spears in a white vase because this is how they send the dead away in that country. (*Mango Street* 53)

> It was the custom to greet the old. (*Ultima* 10)

Lionel Garcia's *Leaving Home* is the Chicano novel that uses such formulas most abundantly. The expression "in those days" alone appears more than a dozen times.

> In those days, 1941, life expectancy was late fifties, early sixties. (121)

> In those days you didn't need licenses to embalm anybody. (125)

> In those days "virile" meant sexual prowess. (137)

> It was not the custom in those days for the general population to attend prostitute's funerals. (157, cf. 28, 84, 143, 150, 183, 211, 213, 43, 237, 239)

The reader can be addressed directly:

> . . . three dollars was a lot in those days, especially when you consider that his pension amounted to almost thirty dollars a month. (237)

and again, the comparison with the reader's culture, which is already implicit in the formula, can become explicit:

> The sweeping of yards was a common practice in those days. No one had the grass lawns one sees today. (143)

If the comparison contains a value judgment, the North American culture always comes out as more advanced and refined, while the Mexican American culture is characterized as "funny in a way" (43), uncivilized and underdeveloped:

> Both had gotten pregnant under similar circumstances. And at that time, in that culture, where ignorance and cruelty within the family were a way of life, one knew that they had suffered and suffered dearly. (173)

> She had gone from a culture steeped in ignorance into another world. It was unbelievable to her that she had grown up with so many misconceptions. (227)

Since it is in most cases the third person narrator, and not one of the characters, who employs "in those days" and similar formulas,[58] and since that narrator is quite imposing and in no way presented as unreliable, they take on a decidedly authoritative quality. And even though the two longest digressions on Chicano mentality are given by the village priest, a Spaniard, the narrator tops one of them with a short but imperative final assessment:

> No other class of people . . . lived for the present as these people did. . . . The women, he had found, were the mainstay of the family. And although . . . it seemed as if the familes [sic] were male dominated, they weren't. The reason for this maternal dominance, he had found out, was that the male did not want the responsibilities of the home. He wanted to be free to go and come as he pleased. . . . It was an Indian-warrior type of philosophy. Once he was inside the house, though, he exaggerated his importance in front of the children by threatening the wife. The wife's

---

58 "She was one of the few females at that time that had required hospitalization" (145). "Wasn't a popular Mexican song of those days entitled *God Made Woman for the Pleasure of Man*? And if this philosophy extended throughout their cultures it was even more so for Umberta's family of farmworkers" (149). "Both her sons worked in the fields by day and drank by night, as was the custom in this society" (150). "Ever since the days of the Civilian Conservation Corps, Maria had respected Roosevelt. It would be more accurate to say that she loved him, as did most of the Mexican-American people at that time" (174).

mentality, he had found out, was that life was a burdensome jour-
ney that must be endured. . . . Being married was a master-slave
relationship. . . . "You must suffer in order to deserve," was the
saying in those days. . . . He secretly admired the women for
accepting such a devastating fate. . . . They were ignorant and
couldn't work and, if they did work, they couldn't support themselves and their children. So it was an economic problem, he had
surmised. "One day," he said to himself, "when the Mexican
woman becomes educated, there will be no Mexican marriages."
He was wrong, of course. (213, emphasis added; cf. 43f)

Otherness

Like no other text of the corpus, *Leaving Home* makes
Chicano culture converge on the Anglo American reader
form- and content-wise. The "otherness" of the Mexican
American culture will hardly disorient the reader, since the
rhetoric employed in order to present it corresponds to a well-
established and well-known pattern, which can be found in
colonial fiction as well as in travel reports and anthropological
writings. According to Johannes Fabian, modern anthropology
"construct[s] its Other in terms of topoi implying distance,
difference and opposition" (111; see above p. 54-55). Garcia's
novel presents traditional Chicano culture not only as different
from the reader's world but also as strange and exotic, as inferior, more primitive, and more savage than the Anglo American culture, which has the political power and the power of
reasoning. What Fabian says of the anthropologist, can also be
applied to the narrator of *Leaving Home*: "Truth and con-
scious awareness are . . . aligned with the knower, the anthropologist; dissimulation and submission to unconscious powers
are on the side of the Other" (51). Fabian contends that anthropology, through such discourses of colonial appropriation,
"contributed above all to the intellectual justification of the
colonial enterprise" (17):

> American anthropology and French structuralism, each having
> developed ways to circumvent or preempt coevalness, are poten-
> tial and actual contributors to ideologies apt to sustain the new,

vast, anonymous, but terribly effective regimen of absentee colonialism. (68)

Anthropology thus helped to ensure the continuity of the mainstream tradition: it "reflects the organization of a segment of bourgeois society for the purpose of serving that society's inner continuity" (122). When such discourses are used in literature, in spite of the exotic contents that they present, they confirm the expectations of the mainstream readership, rather than undermining them. Of all the texts of the corpus, *Leaving Home* makes the most blatant and most thorough use of "discourses of *otherness*." Galarza's *Barrio Boy*, Villarreal's *Fifth Horseman*, and Barrio's *Plum Pickers* employ them abundantly too, but to a lesser degree. In other Chicano novels they appear, if at all, less frequently, and correspond more often to one of the characters than to the authoritative voice of the narrator:

> From behind came the sibilant murmuring of what must have been prayer, though the language may have been ancient Aztec for all Jose could understand. He rose, made another sign of the cross, and walked past the Indian family still inching their way on their knees to the altar. Jose disapproved of their childlike lack of self-awareness. (Candelaria *Alhambra* 43f)

> . . . talk about the childlike nature of the primitive has never been just a neutral classificatory act, but a powerful rhetorical figure and motive, informing colonial practice in every aspect from religious indoctrination to labor laws and the granting of basic political rights. (Fabian 63)

Antonio Márquez may be right in charging literary works about Chicanos written by *non-Chicanos*—what Lomelí and Urioste have called *literatura chicanesca*—with "ethnocentrism" and with having "largely failed to represent Chicano life and culture honestly and judiciously" (Márquez *Chicanesca* 1). Honest representation and ethnocentrism, however, are not mutually exclusive, and literary works about Chicanos written by Chicanos are not always exempt from conveying ethnocentric attitudes. The fact, for example, that Ernesto Galarza shows instances of Anglo American ethnocentrism in his autobiography does not imply that he does not represent the world of his childhood "honestly." Besides, while blatant ethnocentrism—be it a WASP perspective or a Hispanic one— may be detected quite easily, it is difficult (and for a Swiss critic writing about Chicanos utterly impossible) to create clear criteria for evaluating "honesty" and "judiciousness."

6. Rolando Hinojosa as a Translator: From *Estampas del Valle* to *The Valley*

The rhetoric that the texts of the corpus use in presenting Chicano culture is not the only way to show how Chicano authors translate cultural differences. One Chicano author has literally translated a Spanish-language work of his own into English which thus offers a more straightforward application of Schleiermacher's concept.

Rolando Hinojosa's first novel *Estampas del valle y otras obras* appeared in 1973, accompanied by a quite straightforward English translation by G. Valadez and J. Reyna. It recreates Klail City, a Mexican American and American town in the fictional county of Belken in the Texas Rio Grande Valley. It is made up of short sketches that are arranged in four segments: "Estampas del Valle," "Por esas cosas que pasan," "Vidas y milagros," and "Una vida de Rafael Buenrostro."

• "Estampas del Valle" is Jehú Malacara's first person account of his childhood and youth in episodes that fill about a page each. It includes the diary that his stepfather and circus owner Víctor Peláez wrote in 1920 as a young officer in the post-revolutionary Mexican army. The second half of the segment contains sketches of Klail characters.

• "Por esas cosas que pasan," which may owe its title to a 19th century Spanish novel,[59] recounts the killing of

---

59 According to José David Saldívar, Hinojosa wrote his dissertation on the Spanish realist writer Benito Pérez Galdós (Saldívar J.D. "Klail" 46). "Por esas cosas que pasan" intertextually reflects the following passage of *Fortunata y Jacinta*: "Fue de esas cosas que pasan, sin que se pueda determinar cómo pasaron, hechos fatales en la historia de una familia como lo son sus similares en la historia de los pueblos; hechos que los sabios presienten, que los expertos vaticinan sin poder decir en qué se fundan, y que llegan a ser efectivos sin que se sepa cómo, pues aunque se les sienta venir, no se ve el disimulado mecanismo que los trae" (Pérez Galdós, II, 162). Hinojosa's familiarity with Spanish literature also comes to the fore in other titles. As Héctor Calderón has pointed out, "Generaciones y

Ernesto Tamez by means of newspaper clippings in English, two depositions in Spanish given to Attorney Romeo Hinojosa by Baldemar Cordero (who stabbed Ernesto) and his sister Marta, and one deposition in English by Gilberto Castañeda, who is Marta's husband, Baldomero's friend, and a witness to the crime. The contrasts between the newspaper clippings and the depositions make it clear that the media have entirely misinterpreted the incident.

- The sketches contained in "Vidas y milagros" continue thematically and structurally in the vein of the "Estampas del Valle" sketches.

- The vignettes in the segment entitled "Una vida de Rafa Buenrostro" are even shorter than their counterparts in "Estampas del Valle" and "Vidas y milagros," and spotlight the upbringing and the Korean war experience of the protagonist in first person narration.

In spite of the many characters, the segmentation, and the variety of discourses, *Estampas* comes through as a coherent work. "The segments have most of the characters in common. Each is stylistically similar in use of narrative voice, popular language, and compression of narrative line" (Meléndez, 232). Bruce-Novoa describes the language of Hinojosa's early works as follows:

> His style—precise, clean, with not a word of excess; his ironic and subtle humor, so well within the Hispanic tradition; his undeniably popular and regional themes, incarnating universal verities while portraying faithfully his South Texas neighbors; and a persistent, welcome understatement. (*Authors*, 49)

---

semblanzas," the first section of *Klail City y sus alrededores*, echoes a book with the same title by the fifteenth-century historian Fernán Pérez de Guzmán (Calderón "On the Uses" 133f.). Octavio Paz used the same title for one of his books in 1988. Moreover, Héctor Calderón traces back Hinojosa's novel *Claros varones de Belken* to *Claros varones de Castilla* by Hernando del Pulgar (141n3). That intertextual reference can in its turn be extended to the book that inspired Pulgar's: *Loores de los claros varones de España*, also by Fernán Pérez de Guzmán.

Luis Leal also links the discourse of *Estampas* to the region it depicts and stresses moreover the exemplary function of the novel:

> The verbal structure of *Estampas del Valle* reflects the regional nature of the culture that still prevails in the Valley. This verbal structure describes life, customs, mores, and traditions in Belken County, a county representative of those along the Rio Grande in the State of Texas. The images, metaphors and similes around which the novel is structured give the work its validity, for it is a satisfactory set of verbal symbols for the world it describes. By means of these verbal symbols Hinojosa *ha rescatado* the regional culture of the Chicano of Klail City, Condado de Belken, Valle del Río Grande, y sus alrededores. ("History" 108)

After *Estampas* Hinojosa expanded his saga of Belken County, which he later was to denominate "Klail City Death Trip Series", with several novels in both Spanish and English (see bibliography), the epistolary bilingual novel *Querido Rafa*, and the volume of poems *Korean Love Songs*. The cousins Jehú Malacara and Rafa Buenrostro are the two central characters of this South Texas Yoknapatawpha—mutual alter egos as their family names indicate.

Since 1983, Hinojosa has belonged, together with Samuel Beckett and Vladimir Nabokov, to the small group of writers who themselves have translated part of their work into a second language. Ten years after his first work, he published *The Valley*, his own English version of *Estampas*. The titles of the two books define the former as a collection of texts headed by the title piece, the latter as a single coherent work. The subtitle added to *The Valley: A re-creation in narrative prose of a portfolio of etchings, engravings, sketches, and silhouettes by various artists in various styles, plus a set of photographs from a family album*, shows that postmodernism established itself as the prominent direction of the arts in the decade between the two publications. At the same time, it is a first indication that the work in English is not a close literal translation of its Spanish predecessor.

Since the two texts are written by the same author but address different readerships, and since literal translation from *Estampas* makes up a considerable part of *Valley*, an analysis of those elements that have *changed* in the course of the translation/recreation may reveal Hinojosa's stance as a translator. At first sight, *Valley* shows two major differences in comparison with *Estampas* apart from the different language: one of structure and one of size: The four segments are maintained, but ordered differently. The Rafa Buenrostro sketches come immediately after the Jehú Malacara sketches. The second half of the opening segment "Estampas del Valle"—those sketches that depict characters less directly linked to Jehú Malacara—have been added to "Lives and Miracles" ("Vidas y Milagros" in *Estampas*). The English segment titles extend the postmodernist gesture of mingling different art forms, in this case photography and literature:

- "An Olio: One Daguerrotype Plus Photographs" ["Estampas del Valle"]
- "Rafe Buenrostro: Delineations for a first portrait with sketches and photographs (individually and severally)" ["Una vida de Rafa Buenrostro"]
- "Sometimes It Just Happens That Way" ["Por esas cosas que pasan"]
- "Lives and Miracles: Final Entry in the Photographic Variorum" ["Vidas y Milagros"]

The new order and the subtitles added to three segments may, together with the changed title, serve to stress the unity of the work and to remove any doubts as to whether it should, or should not, be regarded as a novel. The second difference—that of size—and its causes are of more importance to what concerns us here: *Valley* is considerably—more than one third—longer than *Estampas*, even though its text largely follows that of *Estampas* and there are only minor changes in the plot, setting, or characters.[60]

---

60 Mión, for example, *prefers* to be called Mión in *Estampas* (8f), while in *The Valley* there is a plebiscite on his nickname (19).

A list of characters that precedes the segment "Sometimes
It Just Happens That Way," a second epigraph, and the added
subtitles account for a small part of the greater length of the
English version. The rest of the additional material is distributed evenly all through *The Valley*, consisting of words and
phrases added to almost every paragraph.

The greater length of *Valley* is partly due to the author's
making the English version more extensive without changing
the semantic essence with the exception of an increase or shift
in emphasis. In some instances, a word appears in Spanish
accompanied by its English translation:

. . . they went off to live, *a vivir*. (16)

. . . why don't we stop at some roadside place and buy us some
Mexican sausage, *chorizo*. (22)

. . . the Texas Mexicans—or mexicanos—and the Mexico Mexicans—the *nacionales*. (78, cf. 48, 105, 112)

Two English words or expressions may replace a single
Spanish one: "Straight on and from the shoulder, now" (103)
translates "*Sin rodeos*" (29), "naturally and with no affecta-
tion" (103) "*con naturalidad*" (29), "claimed and swore" (37)
"*juraba*"(22) "you *are* a little, ah, heavy, ah, a little fat, you
know" (39) "*estás algo gordo*" (23), and the Spanish version
of:

> Epigmenio sees many things and reads a lot more into them;
> to add to this, those matters which he actually does not see, or
> witness, are then left to his ample imagination. In this way, he
> says, he doesn't have to go on inactive service—he keeps his
> hand in, so to speak; (102)

is considerably shorter, too: "*Epigmenio ve muchas cosas y lo
que no ve lo suple con su imaginación. Así, como dice, nunca
está en servicio inactivo*" (28).

The characters of *Valley* are more talkative throughout. A
short question like "*¿Cómo que no lo sepulta?*"(21) can grow
into two full fledged sentences: "Hold your horses right there,

Father. What do you mean you're not about to bury him?"(35)
And without necessarily providing any additional information,
the narrators have become more wordy in the process of translation, as well: "Tere told each and every one of the Salazars,
again individually and severally, as it were, what it was they
could do with their job" (104) replaces *"Tere mandó a los
Salazar con viento nuevo"* (30), and: "he was worse off than
penniless: he was constantly, endlessly, irreversibly poor"
(37) stands for *"era pobre"* (22). One of the characters tops
the narrators with an impressive list of offensive adjectives in
exchange for the Mexican standard *¡Chingue la suya!*: "Why,
you pug-nosed, pop-eyed, overripe, overbearing, overeating,
wine-swilling, son-of-a-bitch!" (39) Extensive translations of
this kind often add a tone of sheer play to the *Valley*, convert
it into a more baroque text, and make it lose some of the con-
ciseness *Estampas* has been praised for.

Not all the additions consist of *playful* double or multiple
translations. In many cases, the English version is more elaborate. *"Los tennis, llenos de lodo, producían un cuaf-cuaf"* (11)
is lengthened to "the water-soaked high-top tennis shoes were
mud-laden as well, and the mud worked its way in and out of
the canvas" (22); *las botellas vacías se lavaban* (14) to "The
empty bottles would be rinsed, soaped, washed again" (26).
General statements can become more specific: *"Le gustaba la
pezca"* (sic, 5) is transformed to "He loved to fish the sly Río
Grande gray-cat" (14). Characters tend to be more specifically
defined, too. Pepe Figueroa, an *abogadillo* in *Estampas*, is
converted into "a newly assigned civilian attorney on the
General Staff" (28), and *"doctor Nicola Machiavelli"* (109) to
"Dr. Niccolo di Bernardo Machiavelli (1469-1527)" (84). The
author goes at times to great length in order to pin down all
the details of an event or action. *"El otro pedo que tire me lo
van a oír en Ohio"* (8), is extended to "Well, folks, it's been
good here, but the next time Old Hoarsey farts, it'll only be
heard by people living in Ohio, 'cause that's where I'm headed . . . See you" (18). And *"Hoy mandé al Indio Vela a que
recogiera mis cosas y así estaré listo para cuando tenga que*

salir para la capital" (16), reads in the annotated English version: "Indian Vela took my civilian clothes out of mothballs; I'm to wear them during off-duty in Mexico City; M.A.C.'s orders will be posted in short order, and I am to be ready to go to M. City when the time comes" (28). Many additions explain and elaborate on historical or cultural facts that are left unexplained in *Estampas*. Historical or geographical names that appear alone in the Spanish version may be accompanied by explanatory attributes in the English text. *"Carranza"* (16) becomes "President Carranza" (28); *"la capital"* (13) becomes "Mexico's Federal District, that great nation's capital city" (25). Historical events that are mentioned as an aside in the original are equipped with further data in the translation. Thus, *"Algo parecido a lo que había hecho la viruela unos años antes"* (15) is changed to: "Something along the lines of the virulent smallpox epidemics that spread among the armies and general populace from 1916 to '17" (27).

Annotation, a method of bringing the world depicted to that of the reader, not only occurs in the contexts of history and language, but also in that of culture in general and literature in particular. A reference which is taken for granted in *Estampas* may be explained in *Valley*. *"Don Quixote contaba"*(29) appears as "Cervantes, through don Quixote, once said" (103). In the last chapter (see above 64), I have mentioned the Mexican scribe who refers to Browning and Shakespeare in Lionel Garcia's *Leaving Home*. Hinojosa does not go as far as replacing Cervantes by an English poet but changes a direct source to an indirect one. Cervantes's protagonist has become part of the popular tradition in most Spanish-speaking countries. The narrator of *Estampas* reflects this by referring to Don Quixote as if he were a historical character. The *Valley* quotation is less familiar and at the same time more abstract, more scholarly. The words of a legendary figure become the words put into the mouth of a fictional character by an author. Oral tradition is reconverted into a book.

Melitón Burnias, protagonist of one of the "Vidas y milagros" sketches *"no corta figura trágica"* (117). The characterization of his namesake in *Valley* corresponds word for word to the Spanish version but is then extended by three names in parentheses. In "Lives and Miracles," Burnias "doesn't cut a tragic figure (Oedipus, Lear, Millard Fillmore)" (94). And also when introducing the prostitute Fira, the author of *Valley* adds a list of names: "In antiquity, Fira would have had other names: Alicaria. Caserita. Copa. Diabola. Foraria. Noctivigilia. Peregrina. Proseda. Quadrantaria. Scrantia. Scrota. Vaga" (103). The two lists, which are missing in *Estampas*, have all the appearance of a postmodern gesture and bring in at the same time a cultural background that is much less explicitly present in the Spanish version of the novel. Whereas *Estampas* acquaints the reader with a more self-contained Mexican American community, the names quoted (with the exception of Fillmore) position *Valley* explicitly in the cultural and literary tradition of Europe. In addition, the so-called Old World signals its increased presence in the novel in English with the help of German, French, and Latin loanwords or phrases: "what the Germans call *diecke*" (sic, 12), "à la Kaiser" (12), "those who knew Cano au fond" (36), "et alii" (10), "in re the last name" (18), "Nihil novum sub et supra sole" (28).

Cervantes's classic is not the only explicit reference to European literature in *Valley*. The ostensibly uneducated Roque Malacara refers around 1940 to a contemporary Spanish poet: "My father-in-law was a good man; a good man in the best sense of the word *good*, as Machado once pointed out" (14). The Spanish version reads laconically *"mi suegro era un hombre cabal"* (5). Antonio Machado may be one of the most popular Spanish poets today and may have used a very popular register of language in his poetry; moreover, his name was known in Mexican literary circles already in the first quarter of our century (cf. Nervo 38). "Retrato," the poem Roque Malacara alludes to, was first published in 1908 and anthologized in 1912.[61] But in contrast to Cervantes's *Quijote*, Ma-

---

61 "... / y, más que un hombre al uso que sabe su doctrina, / soy, en el buen sentido de la palabra, bueno." *Campos de Castilla*, "Retrato," vv. 11-12. The poem first appeared in *El Liberal* (Madrid).

chado's work was certainly not part of the popular Mexican American tradition by 1940. By quoting him, the narrator imposes his own voice on that of one of the characters.

Explicit references to the classics and to European literature take Chicano literature out of the boundaries of a "minority literature," of a folkloric hinterland, and integrate it into a larger, more universal context. At the same time, however, this integration implies the integration into a mainstream discourse, and while *Estampas* stands implicitly in the Western literary academic tradition, *Valley* does so explicitly.

With the exception of the playfulness of some extensive translations, most of the material added in the process of translation and mentioned so far gives the novel a more cultured tone. Double or elaborate translation, annotation of the Mexican American background, as well as references to European literature all contribute to more academic discourses, to discourses that, in addition to the discourses of playfulness, fit well into postmodern times.

The more academic tone of *Valley* is partly due to such annotations and explicit references, partly to a generally more academic vocabulary and style. Many expressions belong to a more elevated level of language than their counterparts in *Estampas*. "Myocardial infarct" (36) stands for *"ataque al corazón"* (22), "acolyte" (40) for *"monaguillo"* (24). When young Jehú and the circus-owner Víctor, his adopted father, stand in the rain and the mud to fix a flat on their truck, Víctor asks *"Y como dijo Cuauhtémoc, ¿eh? ¿crees que yo estoy en un lecho de rosas . . . ?"* He gets the laconic answer *"Fue Moctezuma"* (10). The analogous English passage:

> You just remember what the Emperor Cuauhtémoc said when put to the torch: "You think I'm lying here in a bed of roses, do you?"
> That's the quote, all right, but it was Moctezuma. (21)

results in a more academic tone because of the explanatory attribute *Emperor* and the information added, but also because of the connotations of *quote* and because of the context in which that word generally appears. A more scholarly vocabulary can also be observed in the 1920 diary of Víctor Peláez: "don Venus was betrayed and thus stabbed in the back literally and figuratively" (28),—"*a don Venus lo mataron a traición*" (16). In *Valley*, Hinojosa also makes increased use of devices that serve to structure written texts: parentheses, dashes, numerals, italics, and uppercased words. These markers diminish the illusion of orality inherent in *Estampas* and create an alienated kind of orality that further contributes to the literariness of the English version:

- Idiomatic Spanish expressions are replaced by English constructs. "*El que no trabaja*"(30) is changed to "he-who-does-no-work"(104), "*los novios*"(155) to "the about-to-be-engaged couple" (50).
- Exclamation marks frame every phrase of Jehú's ballyhooing speech for the Peláez Tent Show in *Estampas*. The corresponding passage in *Valley* uses this device more sparingly but introduces italics and upper case as additional typographic means of emphasis.
- Numerical structuring is added: "In Bascom, people walk softly and carry no stick at all; they go about saying things on the order of: 1. Behave yourself; 2. Keep it down; 3. Don't do anything that'll draw the Anglo Texans' attention; 4. Etc." (51, cf. 20, 24, 37)
- The Bruno Cano story is equipped with stage annotations. "(Smiling)," "(Interruption)," "(Knowingly)," "(sweetly)" are inserted into the dialogue (35, 39), a gesture that blurs the boundaries between genres and points once again towards postmodernism.

Valley replaces the concise and idiomatic vernacular of *Estampas* with an often playful, informal small talk academese and a phony postmodern orality.

Another change are the devices added in order to facilitate the reading of the novel. Not just Mexican expressions and historical facts are explained:

- "he was called Hoarsey, there being some growth or impediment in his larynx" (18) ("*le llamaban Ronco*" 8).

- The decisive words in the central pun of the Faulknerian tall tale "Bruno Cano: Lock, Stock, and Bbl." (*"Al pozo con Bruno Cano"*) are italicized.
- A list of characters heads the segment "Sometimes It Just Happens That Way; That's All" (*"Por esas cosas que pasan"*).
- In order to make family relations clearer, Tere Noriega becomes Tere Malacara née Vilches Noriega.

The changes mentioned so far result in a more imposing role for the narrators. The narrators of *Estampas* keep themselves as much as possible in the background, and the language used is to a large extent that of the characters described. In *Valley*, much more prominent and explicit narrators appear and impose their discourse on the characters. Academese may be expected in those passages that correspond to the third person narrator or to one of the college dropouts, Jehú or Rafa. However, it is also used by characters without any academic background. *Nihil novum sub et supra sole*, for example, appears in the diary of young Víctor Peláez (28). The question of whether a horse trader and Mexican revolutionary was likely to use a biblical quotation (Eccles. 1:9) or not, and even to modify it in Latin, is of secondary importance. What is significant is the change that takes place from the Spanish to the English text: the characters of *Valley* give up their regional vernacular for more literary, more cultivated, and more universal discourses; the narrators impose their language on all the characters.

It is one of the functions of the imposing narrative voice in *Valley* to do away with the illusion of historicity. This, again postmodern, gesture has already been exemplified by means of the Machado quotation, and further examples abound. The title of the sketch *Mesa redonda* is changed to "The Squires at the Round Table," and the diary of Jehú's stepfather, written in 1920, uses in its English version idioms that are highly unlikely for its time, like *upcoming election* or *briefing*.

The narrators also make their role more explicit—*"no podré decirles"* (31) is changed to "is not known to this writer"

(105)—and become more involved: "these are matters which too infrequently are found in one and the same person"(104) expresses a moral stance which is missing in *"cosas todas que, a veces, acuerdan en una persona"* (30).

Characters that appear with an autonomous voice in *Estampas* become puppets on a string manipulated by the narrator. In the Spanish version, Jehú Malacara's grandfather Jehú Vilches receives his future son-in-law with the interior monologue: *"Chaparro, fornido y pisando fuerte a pesar de venir con el sombrero en la mano, Roque Malacara me pone cara de vaqueta y dice que no es por falta de respeto pero ¡qué le vamos a hacer! no tiene padrinos y por eso viene a pedirme a Tere él solo"* (3). In the English recreation of this piece of first person narration, the voices of the character Jehú Vilches and of the third person narrator become blurred:

> Squat, what the Germans call *diecke* [sic] and thus heavy of chest and shoulders, Roque Malacara carries his hat in his hand; this last shouldn't fool the reader, however, since R.M.'s step is firm and resolute.
>
> I'm standing on the doorway on the east porch of a hot Thursday afternoon, and he says: My coming here alone isn't a matter of disrespect, sir, it's just that I've no money for sponsors. (12)

The vocabulary of *Estampas* does not rely exclusively on vernacular. It can be academic, and regional expressions may be explained: "Esta relación, el nombre dado a los tesoros" (22). But the Spanish novel does not mingle the voices of supposedly illiterate characters with those of the high school educated characters that assume narrative functions (Jehú, Rafa, Galindo). Academic discourse is scarce and limited to the narrators and so are the explicit references to Machiavelli (109), Raskolnikov (100), and Américo Paredes (29).

In one passage of *Valley*, the third person narrator uses such a concentrated dose of annotations, of scholarly orthographic markers, and of language as sheer play that it can be read as Hinojosa's own parody of his style of translation:

The *relación*, a local usage for treasure, had been there, according to some, since 1) the time of don José Escandón, first explorer and later first colonizer of the Valley, who died with the title given him by the Spanish Crown: el Conde de Cerro Gordo, and whose honored name, etc. etc.; 2) since the time of General Santa Anna (Antonio López de, 1795?-1876); Mex. Revolutionist and general; president (1833-1835; 1841-1844; 1846-47; 1853-55). Involved in the War for Texas Indep., the Mexican-American War; and under whose leadership Mexico lost the so-called Gadsen (sic) Purchase, not to mention the etc. and etc. and the etc.; 3) since yesterday, a conventional term when speaking of the Mexican Revolution (that grand and glorious Crusade for Justice, whose many advantages present day Mexico now enjoys, etc. etc.) when some greedy-blood-sucking-merchant types who brought gold with them escaping the armies of etc. and etc. And etc., too. (37)

Esta relación, el nombre dado a los tesoros, estaba escondida desde los tiempos de Escandón, según unos; desde los tiempos del general Santa Ana, según otros; y todavía otros, más cercanos, desde el tiempo de la Revolución . . . tesoro que fue ocultado por unos ansiosos comerciantes recién emigrados, etc. (22)

The change from Spanish to English in a novel with a largely Spanish-speaking setting, the added annotations, the increased playfulness, and the more imposing and explicit narrators, give *Valley* a different tone. While the narrative voices of *Estampas* describe their culture in their own language, the still Mexican American narrators of *Valley*, through the language change to English as well as through academese, explanations, and annotations, present Mexican Americans more distantly. If *"Flojo y huevón" (155)* reappears as: "The words 'shiftless' and 'lazy' used to describe him merely reveal the poverty of the English language in his case" (50), the narrator is not commenting mainly on the shortcomings of the English language, but rather on the ineffable laziness of the Mexican American described. A second example illustrating the change of tone and standpoint employs irony and regional vernacular in *Estampas*: *"doña Panchita Zuárez, sobandera, partera al pasito, y remendona fina de jovencitas no muy usadas y todavía en servible estado de merecer"* (22). *Valley* again uses a less regional and more academic linguistic register, and a more playful tone. This contributes to a more pronounced ironic stance and to a greater distance between the culture described and its describer: "doña Panchita Zuárez, bone healer, midwife, and general gynecological factotum (G.G.F.), and a fare-the-well mender of preowned virgos belonging to some of the neighborhood girls of all ages" (36). The words *sobandera* and *bone healer* may stand for the same profession, but they belong to different registers. The description from within is replaced by one from without.

The discursive coherence between characters and narrators contributes to the construction of an ethnic identity in *Estampas*, of an identity which the narrators share. The discourses that the narrators of *Valley* choose work in the opposite direction: they create distance between the narrative voices and the language of the community portrayed. The quest for and the affirmation of Chicano identity that *Estampas* shares with many other Chicano novels (see above 35), is mitigated by this alienation in the English text.

One element of *Valley* that has not been mentioned thus far, seems at first sight to represent a remnant of the more direct and more regional registers employed in *Estampas*. Some Spanish expressions are neither translated nor explained: "The word *amor* was misspelled *roma*" (19). "With wheat flour tortillas?" (22). "An early veteran of the *Revolución*" (27); or "mexicano neighborhoods" (105). However, since most of them are easily recognizable for a monolingual English reader, because they are either formally close to their English counterparts (*mexicano/Mexican, Revolución/revolution*) or because they are part of the small Spanish vocabulary known to the non-Spanish-speaking Western world as characteristic of Hispanics and their way of life (*amor, tortilla*), rather than representing a Mexican element, these Hispanicisms, too, are part of conventional discourses of *otherness* which treat the setting and the characters from the outside (see below chapter 9; cf. Ayala 36f).

In spite of all the evidence presented so far, *Valley* cannot be simply dismissed as Hinojosa's adoption of mainstream

North American discourse and values. The greater distance
between the Chicano narrators and Hispanic culture, the frequent relegation of the characters into *otherness*, are also used
to subvert mainstream discourses. The citizens of the fictional
town of Flora, for example, who are characterized as socially
active, festive, and frolicsome in *Estampas*:

> *Esta gente de Flora es muy alborotadora: tienen concursos*
> *de belleza, una cámara de comercio mexicana, organizan bailes*
> *al aire libre, juegan al bingo en la iglesia y andan siempre con*
> *esto y aquello. No vaya mas allá; es gente mitotera.* (20)

become careless and untrustworthy in *Valley*:

> Make no mistake, the Flora mexicanos do love foofaraws:
> the larger and the noisier, the better. They celebrate beauty
> contests for just about every Saint's Day in the calendar; they've
> got themselves a Mexican Chamber of Commerce, and they're
> forever holding open-air public dances and then they forget to
> pay the band; also, they organize those seventy-two hour bingo
> marathons in the local mission, and if something doesn't need
> fixing, they'll fix it, and then stand in line to charge you for it.
> You know the kind, so why go on? (34)

The final phrase makes it plain that the denigration is parodic,
that the passage is not local color, but a parody of local color.
It caricatures mainstream America's cliché concepts of the
Mexican and ethnocentric prejudices against minorities in the
same way as the earlier quotation on Mexican history parodies
academic writing (see above 88). Nevertheless, such subversions of established discourses appear too erratically to be
interpreted as a central strategy of *Valley*. They help to constitute one of various inconclusive discourses in a postmodern
"everything goes" pastiche—though not an avant-garde collage, the content is still very much the same as in the Spanish
version. *Valley* is not concerned with reproducing mimetically
the language of the group it portrays. It does away with *Estampas'* coherence between the language of the characters and
the language of the novel. The narrators no longer realistically
mime the vernacular used in the community they portray, but

make their own baroque elocution all-pervasive and thus undermine the appearance of verisimilitude and historicity.

Every translation signifies a change of perspective, which a translator can influence but never avoid entirely. Different cultural backgrounds make for different semantic values, and semantic fields may be organized differently in different languages. Moreover, there are no congruent English words for *novio, chorizo, monaguillo* or *chaparro*, and expressions like *un servidor, hombre andariego,* or *con cara de pocos amigos* can only be translated roughly. But the change of perspective from *Estampas* to *Valley* is not primarily due to such problems of translation. *Valley,* as already pointed out earlier, is not a true translation. Since its deviations from *Estampas* tend to follow a limited set of rules, however, it can be read as a translation in the broader sense of the word, as a transformation of one text into another according to certain laws. Most changes introduced in that process can be ascribed to one or more of the following principles: while annotation and academic vocabulary merely tinge *Estampas,* they are the norm in *Valley.* Implicit references are made explicit; what had been left unexplained becomes annotated. The perspective from within gives way to one from without; the *involved* ironic tone is replaced by a *detached* ironic tone, the vernacular by a more universal and more literary discourse. And *otherness* becomes more of an issue—not as a theme, but as an element implied in the discourse.

The more academic vocabulary of *Valley* and the explanation of Hispanic elements make the novel more accessible to non-Hispanics and less accessible to non-academics. The reader of *Estampas,* apart from knowing Spanish (including South Texas idioms), is expected to have some historical and cultural background knowledge of the region. The same, with the exception of a knowledge of Spanish, goes for the reader of the quite literal translation that accompanies *Estampas. Valley,* on the other hand, uses a greater variety of discursive registers but expects its Anglophone readers to have less background information on Mexican American history and culture. These characteristics, together with the several devices that facilitate access to the English work, point towards college students as the target group and the ideal readers of *Valley*.

The changes from *Estampas* to *Valley* follow two main directions: they facilitate reading for non-Hispanics by explaining and annotating Hispanic elements, and they move the contents of *Estampas* from *costumbrismo* to postmodernism. If we accept Schleiermacher's thesis that a translator can either leave the author in peace and bring the reader to him or vice versa, the textual evidence suggests that *Valley* is a translation of *Estampas* in which the translator (who in this case coincides with the author of the original) adheres to the second of these two possibilities, both in the way he translates and in the way he recreates. If, as another possible approach, we take recent cultural history as our starting point, we may say that *Valley* is *Estampas* gone postmodern.

The author of *Estampas* takes language more seriously than the author of *Valley*. The language of the Spanish version appears as a trustworthy means of communication, that of the English version becomes blurred by wordplay and often appears as an end in itself. *Valley* builds up a more scholarly discourse than *Estampas* by means of annotation and explanation and at the same time devalues academic discourses through parody and language as sheer play. It converts the "oral history discourse" of *Estampas* into a more academic historiographical discourse and at the same time devalues historicity. Unlike the Spanish original, the English recreation resembles, not content-wise but discourse-wise, other postmodern novels set in a university context (e.g. John Barth's or Malcolm Bradbury's). Not only the passages where language appears as an end in itself, but also the greater variety of repertoires, contribute to the impression that Hinojosa has worked part of the literary discussion of the seventies into *Valley*.

References to the classics, to the literatures of Spain and England, as well as a more academic discourse, open the English version up, make it step out of ethnic boundaries, make it international. Added explanations make it more easily accessible to readers unfamiliar with Hispanic values and vocabulary. But annotations, references, and academic discourses also close the novel down, make it less open, overdefine it. *Estampas* is not simply a Chicano version of the Latin American *costumbrista* novel, is no Chicano *Martín Fierro* (Hernández) or *Don Segundo Sombra* (Güiraldes), but, as Gonzales-Berry has pointed out in her article "*Estampas del Valle:* From *Costumbrismo* to Self-Reflecting Literature," it is an original contribution to that tradition. Its concise style, its irony and subtle humor make it one of the best Chicano texts of the early seventies. And though it relies on a less modern literary tradition, it is a more forceful, more innovative, and more subversive work than its postmodern rehash.

In a recent article, John C. Akers also compares the two novels, "with the goal to show that Hinojosa's writing is to be understood and classified as a postmodernist experiment that represents more than a simple English language version provided by the author" (92). Whereas Akers and I coincide in pointing out the postmodern countenance of *Valley*—and indisputable characteristics like its greater length and rearranged structure—our focus is different. Akers does less of a close reading—especially of *Estampas*—and largely passes over the question of change in readership that the change of language implies. On the other hand, he embeds *Valley* into Hinojosa's *Klail City Death Trip Series*, comments more amply on the translation of Valadez and Reyna in the first (bilingual) edition of *Estampas*, and brings in the illustrations that accompany that edition:

> *Estampas* has artwork attributed to Oscar Bernal that projects, if even at times abstractly, the milieu of the South Texas Rio Grande Valley. Interspersed in the text of the novel itself are Bernal's renderings of palms, cacti, adobe buildings, animals and human figures. Often the drawings are used as decorative filler between written segments, with the same two drawings (a palm tree and a branch) repeated numerous times. (97)

What Akers does not mention is the double function of these drawings. For one thing they are *estampas* and thus take up

—in a "pre-postmodern" gesture of sorts—the title of the novel, for another, they have a structural function in the section "Estampas," where they indicate whether the character depicted is male or female, or whether the sketch belongs to the autobiography of Jehú Malacara.

Furthermore, I don't entirely agree with Akers in that

> . . . Hinojosa attempts to "tame" the language of the Spanish original in the English version, avoiding the correct but frankly abrasive, literal translations of Valadez and Reyna. There are clearly fewer obscenities in the English of Hinojosa than there are in both the Spanish original and the translation. (99)

It is true that the language of the Valadez translation is rather rude. Akers uses a section from "Una vida de Rafa Buenrostro" to illustrate this, and the dialogue between don Víctor Peláez and Jehú Malacara while they are fixing a flat could be cited as another example, because what in *Estampas* is an inoffensive pun based on the Spanish homonyms *sal* 'salt' and *sal* 'come out' is rendered by Valadez as a pun between *luck* and a four-letter word. But while I cannot discount the possibility that the unrefined language of the English translation that accompanied *Estampas* may have led school boards to reject the book as improper for college kids (cf. below 167n93), and that this in its turn may have influenced Hinojosa's English version, I would nonetheless argue that the difference of tone is between the Valadez translation on the one hand and the two Hinojosa versions on the other, rather than between the two English versions and the Spanish one, as Akers argues. Hinojosa's language is not free of coarseness, but he tends to opt for allusive language rather than blunt vulgarisms, which more often than not constitute Valadez's option, as the passage quoted by Akers convincingly illustrates (Akers 99-100).

The most significant difference between Akers's analysis and mine is the fact that our conclusions are diametrically opposed. I consider—for reasons specified above—*Estampas* a better novel than *Valley*; he does not:

The overall effect of *The Valley* with its projection of cohesion, the emphasis on *novel* over short story, the more polished presentation, added characterization, longer text, and "refined" wording is a considerable improvement over *Estampas*. Rolando Hinojosa has enjoyed the liberties of rewriting—rewriting in a language aptly suited to someone like him who is attuned to the peculiarities of speech and personality that emanate from the Rio Grande Valley. He has not, loosely speaking, changed *Estampas*—the contents are basically the same—but he has reshaped it, expanded it and allowed it to breath more deeply the sense of place that he faithfully seeks to revive in all his novels of life in South Texas. (100)

Hinojosa himself declares in an address to the Texas Library Association convention:

I was born in the Valley; I was nurtured there and educated there both in Mexican and in American Schools. One language supplanted the other for a while, but eventually they balanced each other out. What developed from this, among other matters, was an idiosyncratic vision of the world; an awareness of differences and similarities. What I worked on, as far as my life was concerned, was toward a personal voice which was to become my public voice.

What you see here, this professor, and what ideas I may present, is what you will see in my writings: *the voice doesn't vary.* (*Voice* 13f, my emphasis)

A comparison of the differences between *Estampas* and *Valley* shows that Hinojosa's voice *does* vary in his writings. The differences between the two texts may be interpreted exclusively on the grounds of the author's development and idiosyncrasy,[62] as his change from one language to another, from one literary mold to another, from *costumbrismo* to postmodernism. They may also be seen as indicators of the interplay between English and Spanish in the Chicano novel and of the development that the Chicano novel in particular (and maybe American cultural production in general) has undergone from the late 60s to the early 80s.

---

62 According to Hinojosa, Spanish was the language of his childhood, while English, his second language, became important for him after the age of seventeen (Bruce-Novoa *Authors* 53).

7. The Indirect Presence of Spanish

Hinojosa's recreational English recreation of one of his Spanish novels permits an insight into the interplay of the two main languages of the Chicano novel. But it is not the rule for a Chicano novelist to translate her or his own novels. Most Chicano novels in English have no Spanish counterpart and ·therefore do not offer the possibility of a direct comparison. Nevertheless, they have one feature in common that, to a lesser extent, also permits an insight into the interplay and the roles of the two languages. Since the protagonists of all the texts of the corpus are Chicanas or Chicanos and since the setting tends to be a Chicano community in the North American Southwest between the 1940s and the 1970s, a group is portrayed that is exclusively or at least partially Spanish-speaking. The texts may express this fact by including Spanish words and phrases. Before analyzing such bilingual techniques, however, I would like to deal with more oblique ways of articulating the Spanish-speaking setting: English phrases may adopt a Spanish sentence structure, reproduce Spanish idioms, or pretend to reproduce them; or the narrator may tell the reader that the characters speak Spanish, even though their utterances are rendered in English.

Hispanicized English

One method used to make the reader of a Chicano novel written in English aware that its characters speak Spanish operates on the syntactic level, consisting of Hispanicized syntax in direct speech. English phrases may take on a Spanish sentence structure: "Just what means that, paisano?" (*Plum Pickers* 70), or imitate Hispanic idiomatic expressions: "It pains me greatly" (*Rain God* 146), "our house is your house"

(*Ultima* 46). The last example appears earlier in the same novel also in Spanish: "pase, Grande, pase. Nuestra casa es su casa" (11).

While few authors make use of Hispanicized English at all, José Antonio Villarreal, in his novel of the Mexican Revolution *The Fifth Horseman*, is the only one who does so frequently. The device he employs most repeatedly in this respect is related to the common Spanish use of adjectives as nouns when applied to persons (*Vete, loca*). *Horseman* uses English analogously in a couple of instances: "Away with you, crazy!" (16), or "I shall be back soon, crazy" (301). More often, the same Spanish usage is rendered by an adjective plus *one*. On pages 16 and 17 alone we find: "She was considered a strange one," "He will be a violent one," and "She is certainly a crazy one." The rest of the novel contains about two dozen more examples, though not all of them show the same degree of deviance from a native speaker's usage of English.[63]

The Spanish formula *eso de* is treated similarly:

> She is a little off, you know, and that of prophecies and witches is not true anyway. (17)

> But what of that of Ineses and horses? (18)

> And that of the shot of grace, David. (224, cf. 90, 94, 107, etc.)

Spanish idiomatic expressions or grammatical norms also seem to have led to nonidiomatic English phrases like:

> I have not yet sixteen years. (36) [No tengo todavía dieciséis años.]

---

63 "I am a sensitive one" (5). "Watch your step, little one" (40). "Yes, adored one" (92). "He is an educated one" (98), "here indeed was a rare one . . . he was a queer one" (107). "You are surely a crazy one" (124). "No, old one" (169). "And he, the ancient one . . . a kindhearted one" (184), "old one . . . he is a good one" (186). "The old one had to expire" (206), "is the old man such a great one that he must send messengers?" (207), "there you would be with your old one" (260, cf. 31, 222, 237, 361, 370, 383f.).

. . . a foreigner who knew not a word of the Spanish. (123) [del español]

It matters not. (199) [No importa.]

Sit yourself (164, 255-56) [Siéntate]

Is it that you think me blind? (269) [Es que . . .]

Give me an embrace. (30) [Dame un abrazo.]

I am part of something for the first time in my life, and it makes me well. (173) [. . . y me hace bien]

She gave her hand to the stranger and said, "Xóchitl Salamanca, to serve you." (300, cf. 64) [. . . para servirle]

With your permission, señores. (385) [Con su permiso . . .]

Some of the loan translations result in archaic, dialectal, or literary English. Villarreal also uses such registers without an underlying Spanish sentence structure or idiom: "I beg of you, desist" (130), "you must be of good cheer" (19). The most frequently repeated example is the archaic form "to break one's fast" that he employs consistently instead of "to have breakfast." It is hardly closer to the Spanish verb *desayunar* than the usual English form.

Will you accompany me as I break my fast, don Ysabel? (182, cf. 73)

This expression in particular and Hispanicized and nonstandard English in general manifest themselves mainly in direct speech, but most of the forms mentioned so far also come up in the narrator's discourse:

Heraclio . . . broke his fast there on broiled kidneys and a bottle of mezcal. (192)

On the morning of the clash, the Federal army broke its fast leisurely. (296, cf. 338, 360, 385)

She was considered a strange one (16)

. . . and that of being an Inés (149)

And this of the killing of men. (194)

This was the first he had known about her command of the Christian tongue. (137) [. . . la lengua cristiana]

Nonstandard English phrases in *Horseman*, aside from evoking Spanish, give the text an archaic and epic quality that is in tune with the picture of "México, crude and uncultured" (304) that the novel often presents. But they occur too erratically to lead to any stylistic coherence. By the same token, the narrator alternates between epic or biblical formulas and elevated, fashionable, or foreign language vocabulary;[64] and the same characters that use Hispanicized or archaic English also use sophisticated and modern registers.[65]

---

64 Epic or biblical formulas: "And it was so" (59). "It happened that Crispín had some experience with horses" (69). "And thus it was that Heraclio and Carmen went . . ." (69). "And thus it came to be that . . ." (182). "And it happened that the marauders knew . . ." (341). Elevated, fashionable, or foreign language vocabulary: "discomfiture" (36), "in lieu" (37) "wanderlust" (62), "prerogative" (80), "risqué" (86), "the naïveté of the unenlightened" (112), "double-entendre" (144). The narrator also destroys etymological chronologies by talking half a century before Nabokov of a character's "unsatisfactory hour of fornicating with an ugly, filthy, shapeless glob of flesh called incongruously Lolita" (113).

65 Carmen, the hacendado's daughter, and the peón and protagonist Heraclio, her lover, sound at times in their conversations like two American college kids of the 1970s (88-93). Besides, Heraclio can use Hispanicisms, Hispanicized syntax, and modern academese within one phrase: "The idea of a moral lapse for that of the rurales has left me" (200). Heraclio's brother Teodoro, head of the Inés clan and pictured throughout the novel as dumb and "uncommunicative except, of course, when giving an order or a reprimand" (75), uses phrases like "you committed matricide by the grotesqueness of your delivery!" (79) and is an accomplished user of synonyms: "it is not the fault of the gonads that they hang on the wrong man. There is a respect in me for balls. It is not the testes where the fault is but in the head and in the heart" (337).

Raymond Barrio's novel *The Plum Pickers*, set in more recent times than *Horseman*, also uses nonstandard English in order to render Spanish, although to a much lesser extent. Hispanicized English not only appears on the syntactic level —"Then permit me to ask this of you, cuñado" (72), or: "You have a sharp tongue on today" (214)—but also on the lexical one:

> ¡Mande, mi corazón!
> In the Mexican lexicon—"What is thy wish, my heart?" (45)

> . . . desgraciado hijo de tu maldita chingada? How darest thou speak to me? (113)

The use of the archaic or dialectal pronouns *thou* and *thy*, together with the corresponding nonstandard verb form (*darest*), is no invention of Barrio's. Another twentieth-century American author before him has used the same device in a much heavier dose in order to characterize the speech of a Hispanic character.

> The old man . . . spoke . . . in a dialect that Robert Jordan could just follow. It was like reading Quevedo. Anselmo was speaking old Castilian and it went something like this, 'Art thou a brute? yes. Art thou a beast? yes, many times. Hast thou a brain? Nay. None. Now we come for something of consummate importance and thee, with thy dwelling place to be undisturbed, puts thy foxhole before the interests of humanity. Before the interests of thy people.' (Hemingway 18)

Hemingway and Barrio may have chosen the nonstandard pronouns as a means of mirroring the Spanish distinction between the familiar *tú* and the formal *usted*. However, the possibility that an actual linguistic feature of the Spanish language may lie at the core of their device, does not take away from the "literariness" of that device. *Thou*, *thy*, and *thee* do not bring the English language any closer to the linguistic characteristics of Spanish. Their function does not consist in creating a *replica* of Spanish, but in *evoking* Spanish and in producing an archaic, biblical, epic ring. In *Plum Pickers* they appear rarely and are but another expression of the author's linguistic playfulness, another ingredient in a stylistic pastiche. In *For Whom the Bell Tolls*, the archaic pronouns, as well as other nonstandard English forms (cf. Keller *Literary Stratagems* 277-80), are used more consistently. Apart from their epic quality (ibid. 290f), they also contribute to the primitivist image of Spain and Spaniards that pervades the text.[66] In this respect, *For Whom the Bell Tolls* is closer to Villarreal's *Horseman* (which does not employ archaic pronouns) than to *Plum Pickers*. Hemingway may take a more differentiated approach and be a better stylist than Villarreal; his Spaniards may talk, in contrast to Villarreal's Mexicans, with considerable stylistic homogeneity, and the characteristics of the "Hispanic" discourses created in the two novels may differ from one another; nevertheless, Hispanicized sentence structure and archaic English evoke a similar kind of *otherness* within a similar context in the two novels. In both *For Whom the Bell Tolls* and *Horseman*, nonstandard English forms show Spanish as a more primitive language than English. Furthermore, both novels thematize a civil war; in both of them, a monolithic male hero excels in military cunning and war deeds and proves his superiority over the society that surrounds him and that tends to be depicted as crude in its culture and in its language.

Fictitious Spanish

With the exception of *Tattoo*, all the texts analyzed here—among them some that use Spanish rather sparingly—assert at one or various points that communications between characters take place in Spanish:

---

66 The reference to Quevedo in the quotation above, the portrayal of the characters Pablo and Rafael, and other textual evidence confirm an interpretation in this direction (see, e.g., 22, 29, 136, 187).

The letter was from Carmen . . . Thank God it was in Spanish. She was getting married, she wrote. (*Leaving Home* 246)

He spoke softly to her in Spanish, telling her who was in the room. (*Rain God* 177)

"Be a good soldier," he would say, then in Spanish would assure him that soon they would go away to the far north. (*Clemente* 51)

Once the priest had preached in Spanish against the women who lived in Rosie's house and so I knew that her place was bad (*Ultima* 31, cf. 2; *Tamazunchale* 31, 51, 91)

In more than two thirds of the texts, a particular tension is created by at times applying this assertion to direct speech in English, a device that can already be found, with the language roles inverted, in Cervantes's novel *Los trabajos de Persiles y Segismunda*. There, the reader learns that a certain character speaks Polish (62), Tuscan (86), or English (107), etc., but the direct speech that follows that information is as invariably Spanish as it is English in the case of the Chicano novel.

The soft Spanish words in the semi-dark startled her. "Let me have a cigarette." (*Alhambra* 114-15)

. . . the roller coaster, which we called in elegant Spanish "the Russian Mountain." (*Barrio Boy* 249)

Jesus H. Christ, I was being courtmartialed by a woman! In Spanish, at that!
"The papers say you insulted the hotel clerk." (*Buffalo* 192)

. . . he changed his speech into Spanish, "I wish to present you to my wife." (*Horseman* 136, cf 137)

In Spanish she called through the crowd: "Put a towel on over your shoulders." (*Hunger* 124)

They would say in Spanish,—When the time is ripe. (*Louise* 18)

. . . and saying in her uneducated Spanish, "Do you want to eat my raisin eyes?" (*Rain God* 13)

He makes use of superb, exacting Spanish vocabulary.

"Look into my eyes; you are not to be frightened!"
(*Victuum* 324, cf. *Valley* 83)

With one exception, the narrators do not comment on the incongruity between the language announced and the one used. Only in Delgado's *Louise*, the narrator intervenes once and makes the incongruity explicit:

> I feel hot too, ese, maybe I'm sick—I answered, all in Spanish, of course. I retell all this in English for form's sake but we, my friends and I, actually wouldn't be caught dead talking English to each other. (*Louise* 80)

While some novels, like *Cockroach* or *Tamazunchale*, use the device without any recognizable strategy, others give it a specific function. The author of *Leaving Home*, a novel that relies to a considerable extent on dialogue, applies it to the first appearance of direct speech, thus making it clear from the start that the conversations to follow may be carried out in Spanish, even though they are rendered in English:

> "Good morning," he said in Spanish.
> "Good morning," she answered. (1)

Alhambra and *Rain God* are the texts which most frequently state that their characters speak Spanish and have them then speak English,[67] frequently enough that the repetition may be interpreted as a strategy. Neither of the two novels presents difficulties in understanding for monolingual English readers and neither of them uses hermetic Spanish dialogue, and yet the reader is constantly reminded that the language in which the novel is written is not the "original" language of its characters. Moreover, both novels show the conflict between an older generation obsessed with ethnic identity, with being of pure Castilian, not of Mexican origin, and a younger generation that calls such distinctions into question:

---

67 *Alhambra* 26, 38, 48, 80, 114, 170, 179; *Rain God* 12, 13, 19, 22 (not direct speech but a letter in this case), 66, 76, 123, 124, 128, 130, 141, 166, 169.

> I said: "Hablas espanol?" When she nodded, I told her we were
> Spanish. Real Spanish. Descendants of conquistadors. Not that
> so-called Spanish from south of the border. Indians with Spanish
> names. (*Alhambra* 106)

> Later, in his adolescence and while she still retained her wits,
> Miguel Chico hated her for this very trait, seeing it as part of the
> Spanish conquistador snobbery that refused to associate itself with
> anything Mexican or Indian because it was somehow impure.
> (*Rain God* 27)

Although both texts coincide in postulating repeatedly the
Hispanophone nature of passages rendered in English, the different way in which each treats the Mexican language and culture and the different overall context that they offer make for a
different effect. On one hand, the protagonist of *Alhambra*
belongs to the older one of the two generations just mentioned,
the protagonist(s) of *Rain God* to the younger one. On the
other hand, *Rain God* keeps the theme of ethnic identity rather
in the background, treats it in a more implicit way. The ethnocentrism of the all-consuming protagonist permeates *Alhambra*: José Rafa is fixated on searching for his true roots and on
judging other people mostly on the grounds of ethnic and
national stereotypes. The paradoxical thing about his attitude
is the discrepancy between his insistence on his "true Spanish"
roots (see quotation above) and his all-American tourist reaction to the Hispanics he meets when the quest for his identity
leads him to Mexico and Spain. He identifies skin-deep with
the inhabitants of Mexico when he first arrives there: "The
dark faces, the men with longer hair and mustaches gave him
comfort" (23). However, this first impression is not long-
lived: "But eventually Gomez did [phone], late, like almost
everything in Mexico . . . But then you never know how these
Mexicans work. Some with their office in their hat. Ready to
run quickly comes the next revolution" (31). All José can
"conjure of Spain" are "Captains from Castile in leather and
shining metal breastplates, castanets, snapping fingers, and
thundering big-horned bulls with shouts of 'Ole!' " (142, see

also 143f.). His views impose themselves on the text and on its discourse; the glimpses of a different perspective that other characters or the narrator offer in places are far outweighed.[68] The two texts also treat explicit Spanish language entries in different manners. *Alhambra* uses Spanish as abundantly as sloppily (see below 109n70) and includes some often repeated clichés. The most often repeated Spanish words are *senor*, *adobe*, and *tortilla*. The use of Spanish in Candelaria's first novel "leaves the reader in peace," to use Schleiermacher's phrasing. Islas's first novel *Rain God* disturbs that "peace" somewhat more, applies Spanish entries more scarcely and in a more differentiated way, and even insinuates at times that the rendering in English is less meaningful and less expressive than the Spanish "original" would be (cf. below 133).

The gap between the language announced and the language rendered indicates in both novels the importance of Spanish in the Chicano culture. In *Alhambra*, however, the context and the way in which explicit Spanish entries are introduced, give the Spanish language the quality of a folkloric ingredient; Spanish does not come through as a language on par with English. *Rain God*, though it also marks the two languages as different from one another, makes a less abundantly present Spanish language appear as a peer of English. Islas makes it clear that whatever reason he may have had to prefer English over Spanish in telling his story, it was certainly not because Spanish has less of an expressive potential.

---

68 Trujillo evaluates *Alhambra* more positively than I do (131).

Spanish-Language Entries

8. General Aspects

Spanish language entries appear in all the texts of the corpus, although their size, frequency, type, function, and manner in which they are presented differ from novel to novel. They may appear without being marked typographically, set off from the English text by quotation marks or italics,[69] spelt correctly or not,[70] and with or without inverted exclamation marks, question marks, and accents.[71] In addition, a novel may or may not be consistent in the treatment of Spanish.[72]

The Spanish entries in the corpus include a great deal of vernacular words and expressions from the Southwest and Mexico. By the same token, the *spelling* can be vernacularly marked. *Seseo* (the pronunciation of Castilian /θ/ as /s/) and the dropping of the intervocalic -d- in the participle ending -ado- are the two most frequent dialectal characteristics which

---

69 *Barrio Boy, Hunger, Leaving Home,* and Hinojosa's novels in English use italics throughout for Spanish entries, except for well-known loanwords like *barrio, corral,* or *tortilla. Buffalo, Cockroach,* and *Mango Street* use italics mostly but not always. *Louise* either does not mark Spanish entries or puts them between quotation marks. In *Alhambra, Clemente, Horseman, Plum Pickers, Tamazunchale, Tortuga, Ultima,* and *Victuum* Spanish is not marked.

70 *Alhambra* shows the most inaccurate Spanish, including double consonants: "abrazzo" (94, 95), "baille" (51), "raza suffrida" (32, 77, 89); Anglicized Spanish spelling ("sanctuario," 72); and faulty adjective endings: "La turista es muy malo" (40). *Victuum* has quite a few orthographic mistakes in both English and Spanish. In the rest of the corpus orthographic flaws in Spanish are rare.

71 *Alhambra* and *Victuum* use neither inverted marks nor accents; *Leaving Home* puts the accents in and includes no questions or exclamations in Spanish; *Louise, Hunger, Plum Pickers, Rites,* and *Ultima* use inverted marks and accents.

72 *Cockroach* and *Buffalo* apply accents and inverted marks inconsistently. The latter uses the inverted marks repeatedly on page 191 but not in analogous phrases on 189, and it does not put in any accents, except for an isolated one in *"pásamela cabron"* (sic, 186).

are reflected orthographically. For example, *Alhambra* (47), *Ultima* (32f, 102f), and *Victuum* (12, 106f) use the standard spelling of the past participle in the case of *chingada* and *chingado*, while *Clemente* (70), *Rites* (108), and *Tortuga* (51) employ *chingao*, and *Louise* uses *chingao* (104) or *chinga'o* (112). The augmentative noun to the same stem appears as *chingazos* in *Louise* (56) and, reflecting *seseo*, as *chingasos* in *Tortuga* (155).[73]

The frequency of Spanish entries ranges from a few words per text (*Tattoo, Leaving Home, Mango Street*) to several words and phrases per page (*Clemente, Louise*, see 16.1-3). In some novels, bilingual strategies function as distinctive stylistic features (*Louise, Plum Pickers, Rain God*). The corpus contains thousands of Spanish entries, which I have divided, according to their length, into the four groups *single words*, *short entries*, *long entries*, and *songs*.

• Spanish *single word* entries in the Chicano novel in English are comparable to the Native American vocabulary that became part of the Spanish language in the process of the Conquest (cf. Lope Blanch, Zamora Munné, and Mejías). Most of them consist of no more than one word, and more than 95 percent of these close to a thousand different *single words* are nouns, from *abonos* (*Louise* 111), *abrazo* (*Alhambra* 94f, *Barrio Boy* 74, 215, *Clemente* 91, *Cock-*

---

73 Further examples include dropping of intervocalic -d- in the participle ending: "cansao" (*Clemente* 153), "desgraciaos" (*Clemente* 118), "fregao" (*Louise* 122). More examples of *seseo* are "descalsa" (*Victuum* 58, 172), "dies centavos" (*Buffalo* 194), "morsilla," "fregasos" (*Louise* 53, 67), "surumato" (*Alhambra* 124), "tristesa" (*Ultima* 55). There is an instance of hypercorrection due to *yeísmo*: "tlacollo" (*Clemente* 37), and another due to *seseo* (or English language influence?): "'Clean the *graza* off of your face!' (*Greaser!*)" (*Hunger* 119). Other vernacular spellings reflect confusion of *v* and *b*: "vívora" (*Ultima* 223); relaxation: "gracias a dios que venites" (ibid. 220), "enbrujado," "basudero," "escusado" (*Louise* 13, 43, 49); assimilation: "probrecito" (*Victuum* 111, 159); or assimilation and vowel change: "parpariar" for *parpadear* (ibid. 137, cf. Santamaría).

roach 178, *Louise* 54, *Ultima* 58, 129, 214), and *abuela* (*Louise* 14f, 22, 28), to *zócalo* (*Alhambra* 24, *Barrio Boy* 8) and *zopilote* (*Barrio Boy* 6f). The dominance of nouns can be exemplified with a representative sample. Only nineteen of about four hundred different single Spanish words starting with a-, c-, or m- are not nouns: there are seven adverbs (*ahora, aquí, así, atrás, cuándo, cómo, mañana*), five adjectives (*mucho, magnífico, maldito, condenado, correspondido*), four interjections (*adiós, ay, caramba, chingado*), two imperatives (*cálmate, mira*), and one infinitive (*cochar*). If the same calculation is done on the absolute number of single Spanish words, i.e., if each repetition of a given word is counted individually, the percentage of nouns goes way beyond 99 percent.

As a rule, Spanish nouns are accompanied by English articles. Spanish articles are only used for institutionalized entities like *la familia, la misa, la muerte,* and for names that have the article included by convention, be they toponyms,[74] nicknames,[75] public places,[76] songs,[77] institutions,[78] or religious or legendary figures.[79] Apart from

---

74 "Las Pasturas" (*Ultima*), "Los Angeles," "El Segundo Barrio" (*Buffalo* 77, *Louise* 75), "La Boquiilla" (sic, *Louise* 15).

75 "El Perro," "El Longo" (*Louise* 102); "El Tigre" (*Leaving Home* 26); "El Borrachín" (*Rites* 12).

76 "El Calcetín (the sock) or 'El Calce' in Caló" (*Louise* 110); "the old neighborhood theatre, *El Calsetin . . . La Pinata*, the grocery store" (*Buffalo* 185). "La Despedida, a night club" (*Louise* 55).

77 "La Barca de Oro" (*Leaving Home* 101); "a polka, *La Playita*" (102; "the first five notes of La Cucaracha" (*Alhambra* 19).

78 "I read a little paper called *La Raza*," "the meanest Mexicans in all Mexico, *los tarascans*" (sic, *Buffalo* 196, 188). "The paper is called *La Voz de Huitzilopochtli*, after the principle [sic] ancient diety [sic] of the Chicanos" (*Cockroach* 33); "a club of Mexican girls called 'Las Rucas'" (*Rain God* 85).

79 "La Llorona" (*Barrio Boy* 43, *Buffalo* 87, *Ultima* 23, 26, *Tortuga* 66f, 103, etc.; exception: *Clemente* 91, "the llorona"), "la Malpagadora" (*Plum Pickers* 62), "la Virgen de Guadalupe" (*Cockroach* 19, 44, *Plum Pickers* 41, *Ultima* 12, 42, *Victuum* 132).

institutions and names, the use of the article is rare. Examples like "Sundays, *el domingo" (Buffalo* 185), or "She has him by the balls, *los huevos*" (*Leaving Home* 122) are statistically negligible; *Louise* is the only text to use Spanish articles with some consistency,[80] and in one case even for an English expression: "los slow ones" (67).

• The more than six hundred and fifty different *short entries* contain between two and four words; are mostly short expressions or compound nouns and sometimes full sentences. They range from *a chingao* (*Clemente* 70), *buenos días* (*Barrio Boy* 21, 119; *Clemente* 49; *Horseman* 66, 338), and "Contéstame, tonto. ¿Estás herido?" (*Clemente* 76) to "voy a tirar tripas" (*Ultima* 198), *yerba de la vívora* (sic, ibid. 223), and *zona rosa* (*Cockroach* 189, *Louise* 49).

• *Long entries* of five or more words occur less than two hundred times and consist, apart from a few combinations of nouns and adjectives—"hijo de la chingada bruja" (*Ultima* 241); "Virgin Maria Pursima, Sagrado Corazon de Jesus" (sic, *Victuum* 152)—, mainly of phrases and entire sentences: "¿A quién le va a quedar todo ese terreno y todos esos animales, eh?" (*Clemente* 25). "Buenos días te de Dios, a ti y a tu familia" (*Ultima* 10). "Vamos a dar la vuelta" (*Clemente* 92). "Yo soy Guadalupe Jiménez Rodríguez, un arriero. No esté chingando" (*Louise* 37). Spanish prose entries very rarely are longer than one sentence or one line of text. Two exceptionally long Spanish entries in *Barrio Boy* and *Plum Pickers* are dealt with below (149-50), and only in *Louise* do we find a few complex sentences like:

> La palabra quiche, queche o quechelah significa bosque en varias de las lenguas de guatemala, y proviene de 'qui', 'quiy' (muchos) y che (árbol) [muchos + árboles = quiche] palabra maya original. (17; cf. 18)

---

80 "la botella" (107), "la cabalgada" (67), "la cobija" (105), "una cruda" (107), "los locos" (123), "la peda" (61), "una pulmonía" (107).

. . . asked me to go out y darnos en la madre. Yo le contesté,
Pos'aquí está suave, pa' que vamos pa' fuera y le puse dos cabro-
nazos y lo senté. (112)

Y nos dicen los gringos,
—Ustedes los mejicanos no hacen planes.
—Pos con que ojos, divina tuerta. (120)

The reluctance to use long Spanish entries contrasts with
the entire paragraphs and sections in English that can be
found in some of the Chicano novels of the same period
written in Spanish (e.g., Brito 45-48; Elizondo 13f, 102;
Hinojosa *Klail* 31, 89-91; Rivera 20).

• Various novels include a stanza or some verses of a *song*
or poem in Spanish: a *corrido*, a *romance*, a Mexican or
Hispanic folk rhyme, or a popular song. *Songs* form a
category apart. In contrast to the *long entries*, they do not
necessarily appear in those texts that use Spanish most frequently. They are present in *Rites* and *Tortuga*, but not in
Louise and *Clemente*, the two novels which include the
greatest number of *long entries*. *Songs* in a secondary language have a long tradition in literature, the inclusion of a
Portuguese song in Fernán Caballero's novel *La gaviota*
(1846) could be mentioned as an early example (243).

The majority of the texts use *single words* and *short entries* exclusively (*Mango Street, Rain God, Tattoo*) or almost
exclusively. *Tortuga, Tamazunchale, Leaving Home,* and
Hunger include less than three *long entries*, and most of the
remaining English texts less than ten. At the other end of the
scale are *Ultima* (eighteen), and in particular *Clemente* and
Louise, which both contain about fifty *long entries*. Tables
16.1-3 in the *Statistics* section below show how frequently
each of these four categories occurs in the texts of the corpus.

There are different ways of arranging Spanish entries
within a text. For obvious reasons, Spanish language entries
appear mostly in the context of Hispanophone settings and in
direct speech. Their function is often to indicate representa-
tively the Hispanophone nature of a dialogue that is otherwise

rendered in English. Moreover, *Louise, Rain God, Rites,* and *Victuum,* for example, have them dispersed quite evenly, while *Horseman* uses them above all in the "First Book," set on a Mexican hacienda, and less in the "Second Book," which deals with the Mexican Revolution. *Buffalo* uses Spanish throughout, but shows an increase in frequency when the setting changes from the United States to Ciudad Juárez towards the end of the novel (187-194). *Leaving Home* scarcely uses Spanish for the first eighty pages (*caliche* 4, *tequila* 57, *serape* 67, *arrimado* 73), comes up with concentrated portions of Spanish on pages 82 (*barrio, carne guizada* (sic), *picadillo, fideo, caldo de res, jalapeños*) and 84 (*toronjil, flor de canela, yerbabuena, barreteada*), only to fall back into its previous rhythm afterwards. Some clusters of Spanish vocabulary occur in specific semantic contexts and will be treated in chapter 11; others have a structural function.

Like the author of *Leaving Home* (see above 103), Rudolfo Anaya makes it clear to his readers at the very beginning of *Ultima* that his characters speak Spanish. But in contrast to Lionel Garcia, he then renders their direct speech in Spanish:

> "Está sola," my father said, "ya no queda gente en el pueblito de Las Pasturas—"
> He spoke in Spanish, . . . (2)

> "Jasón no está aquí," she said. All of the older people spoke only in Spanish, and I myself understood only Spanish. It was only after one went to school that one learned English.
> "¿Dónde está?" I asked. (9)

After both quotations, the direct speech switches to English interspersed occasionally with Spanish words or expressions. But before this switch, Anaya inserts an extended narrative passage that helps to make the language change less perceptible. The same procedure can be observed in *Clemente* (14f).

Spanish language entries interspersed in direct speech passages in English tend to represent the Hispanophone nature of a dialogue. They primarily function as stylistic devices with little claim for mimetic accuracy. And only in very few cases do they reflect code switching or depict a speaker who uses both languages:

> "Hey Nacha," said Pete. "No me des any of that Messican stuff. Dame cornflakes y peaches y luego un egg y mucho toast." (*Clemente* 11)

> "No mijita. I thought I was dead." Fausto sat up. "It happens, you know. From one day to the next, poof! Al otro mundo."
> "Well, you come down and eat in this mundo." (*Tamazunchale* 38)

As I have pointed out in the second chapter, the length of secondary language entries and the way in which they are arranged within a text are not the only significant factors of literary bilingualism. Secondary language entries can be classified not only according to their *form*, but also according to their *type* and to the *method* by which they are introduced into primary language discourses. *Type* does not refer in this context to any semantic classification of foreign entries, but to the degree in which and the reason why these may already be familiar to monolingual readers. In this sense, four types of entries may be distinguished which in the following will be analyzed under the headings of *Loanwords, Clichés, Etymological Pairs*, and *Hermetic Spanish*.

While *type* denotes the degree of accessibility of Spanish entries to the English monolingual reader, *method* signifies their degree of translation. Here, too, four subgroups can be distinguished, depending on whether Spanish entries are translated *literally*, by *paraphrase*, or by *context*, or whether they are left *untranslated*. The arrangement according to *type* and to *method* of translation makes the approach to the uses and functions of Spanish entries in English texts easier, but represents by no means a rigid system. Neither of the two classifications implies clear-cut boundaries between its subgroups, and many Spanish entries can be ascribed to more than one *type* and one *method*.

9. Types

Loanwords

From Spanish, once the Mississippi was crossed, and particularly during and after the Mexican War, there came a swarm of novelties, many of which have remained firmly imbedded in the language. Among them were numerous names of strange personages and objects: *rancho, alfalfa, mustang, sombrero, canyon, desperado, poncho, chaparral, corral, bronco, plaza, peon, alcalde, burro, mesa, tornado, presidio, patio, sierra* and *adobe.* . . . Some of the borrowings . . . underwent phonetic change. . . . *Vamos*, the first person plural of the Spanish "let's go," became *vamose* or *vamoose* in American, and presently begat an American verb, *to mosey.* . . . *Estampida* was converted into *stampede, frijol* into *frijole* (pro. *freeholay*), *tamal* into *tamale, tortilla* into *tortillia*, and *vaquero* into *buckaroo*. *Chile*, a pepper, came in with *frijole* and *tamale*, and at the same time the pioneers became acquainted with the Mexican beverages, *mescal, pulque,* and *tequila*. Such words as *señor, señorita, padre, siesta, sabe, poncho, pinto, yerba, hombre, casa* and *arroyo* began to bespatter their speech. (152)

Most of the Spanish words mentioned in H.L. Mencken's classic *The American Language* also appear in the Chicano texts we are discussing. Here, however, the term *loanword* will designate only those Spanish or Mexican-Spanish expressions that are listed in *Webster's Third New International Dictionary* and that have preserved their spelling. This excludes words that had the spelling naturalized, like *hackamore, lasso, lariat, ranch, cockroach,* or *barbecue,* but includes their synonyms with conserved Spanish spelling—*jáquima, lazo, reata, rancho, cucaracha,*—as well as regional forms like *laso* or *riata*).[81]

---

81 *Barbacoa* is not counted as a *loanword,* though it appears in the corpus as well as in *Webster's.* While the texts use it with the denotation "barbecue," the dictionary lists it as "a Chibchan people."

Mexican *loanwords* in Chicano novels, like Mexican-Spanish words in general, go back to different roots that range from Iberian (*cama*), Arabian (*alacrán, alcaide*), and Latin (*álamo*) to native Mexican languages (*huarache, sarape, tamale*). Furthermore, the *loanwords* used may be more or less widespread in the English-speaking world. *Huarache, metate,* and *riata,* for example, are used mainly within the Southwest; *plaza* and *guacamole* are common in American English, while *guerrilla, mosquito, patio, tequila,* and *marijuana* are Hispanicisms used in English generally.

Loanwords can also be subdivided according to their position in the U.S. American cultural context. Some words, *peyote, tequila, papaya,* or *llama,* for example, stand for Mexican or South American tokens and are thus still clearly linked to their Hispanic origin; others, like *patio* or *plaza* have been fully integrated into American English and do not necessarily stand for Latin American objects. A third group has even become part of the myth of the North American West, part of the North American identity. This is not only true for *alamo,* the Spanish equivalent for poplar, in combination with the English definite article and the verbal form *remember,* but also for a whole range of Spanish expressions that have been taken over—together with a set of cultural practices—by settlers of Anglo-Saxon and other origins from the Hispanic population of the Southwest (see chapter 11: "Ethnographic Terms"). *Corral, burro, bronco,* and *rodeo* belong to this group, as well as Hispanicisms with adopted spelling (*barbecue, hackamore,* etc.), which will not be further analyzed here.

While some Spanish terms have made their way into the vocabulary of the myth of the North American West, others are also used as loanwords in American English, but with a different value, especially in the Southwest. *Adobe* and *frijoles,* together with native Mexican expressions like *huarache* or *tamale,* have become part of the English vocabulary of the Southwest, but not of the mainstream American heritage. They are *loanwords* that denote *otherness* rather than identity in the Anglo American context, and they will be treated more extensively in the sections on *ethnographic* and *culinary* terms in chapter 11.

Clichés: Formulas and Stereotypes

A relatively small group of Spanish words (and *loanwords*) appear very frequently in the corpus and make for an easily accessible Hispanic element. They correspond by and large to the command of Spanish displayed by Mr. Frederick C. Turner, the greedy landowner caricature in *Plum Pickers*: "I speak their language even though I don't talk a word a Mexican. Oh, I know sombrero and mañana and saludos amigos and crap like that, just enough to get by" (79). They differ from words that either stand for material tokens in a realm that has Spanish as its first colonial language (*tequila, peyote*) or that have been fully appropriated by the culture and language of the American North like *corral* or *sierra*. *Clichés* are stereotypical representatives of the Spanish language and of the Hispanic character in the non-Hispanic Western world. They consist on the one hand of *formulas* that could easily be replaced by the corresponding English expressions, if it were not for the advantage that they bring an instant Hispanic flavor: greetings like *buenos días, hasta la vista*, or *adiós*, forms of address like *señor, muchacho, señorita*, and swearwords or interjections like *caray, caramba, Dios mío*, or *Ave María Purísima*. Expressions belonging to this group often function as synecdoches in the Chicano novel. Interspersed in English dialogue or, more often, introducing it, they suggest that it is carried out "originally" in Spanish. They function on a smaller scale, but in much the same way as the direct speech passages in Spanish at the beginning of *Ultima* and *Clemente* (see above 114):

Well senor. I don't like to tire you. (*Alhambra* 40)

Welcome to México, señorita. (*Clemente* 15)

"Muchacho," his hoarse voice whispered, "I need confession."
(*Ultima* 162)

". . . thank you, Mam!"
"Yes, muchísimas gracias, Senora!" (*Victuum* 183)

Formulas are among to the most frequently used Spanish
entries in many Chicano novels (see chapter 15), and they
appear with much the same function as in many non-Chicano
novels or in Hollywood movies that include Hispanic characters (see Robinson and Pettit): they give a Hispanic hue to the
English discourse without complicating its understanding.
Examples of ironic use are scarce.

In a few cases, Chicano novelists employ faulty Spanish
formulas in order to satirize ethnocentric attitudes. Raymond
Barrio seconds Mr. Turner's already mentioned *saludos amigos* with "Now you keep away from me, spic. You comprain-
da?" (101) A further example can be found in Villarreal's
Horseman: "To lay with a gringa was somehow a great desire
to the dark sons of Cuauhtémoc, such as it was to the fair-
haired Saxons of the north to mount a hot tamale señoreeter"
(280). Villarreal rephrases the very same idea in *Clemente*:
"The Mexican likes a güerita now and then, especially a
young one, just as the gringo likes our young beauties" (110).

A second group of *clichés* appears less frequently and
repeatedly than the *formulas* and could be denominated *stereotypes*. They represent the Hispanic way of life rather than the
Spanish language. They often lack a directly corresponding
English term and are used to signify the stereotypical *otherness* of the Mexican or of the Hispanic in general to the rest of
the world. Words like *don* and *hombre* (which are at the same
time *formulas*), *macho, mañana, siesta,* and *olé* do not present
the monolingual reader with any unexpected concepts, but
confirm cliché views of the Hispanic mentality in the same
manner as does the (Mexican) Spanish vocabulary pointed out
by Keller in the context of a poem by El Huitlacoche (Keller's
pen name):

...*"campesinos," "sombreros,"* and *"frito bandito"* (instead of *bandido*) are all examples of Spanish lexicon that are well-known to English speakers and have actually been partially assimilated into English. What the poet does is to show how these words have been used in the Anglo world to stereotype the Hispano. Thus they become "alien" to the Hispanic world to the degree that they are used by the Anglo to characterize (and caricaturize) the Hispano. (*Literary Stratagems* 297)

As with *formulas*, authors may comment on *stereotypes* by parodying the way in which non-Hispanics use them: "you lousy dirty rotten nogood lazy mexicans all you think of is pot and mañana and mañana" (*Plum Pickers* 156), or "I know you, hombre. And you can take anything, right? Mr. Macho" (*Buffalo* 56). Barrio and Acosta point out and subvert *stereotypes* with some consistency by treating them in an ironical and detached manner, while the protagonist and the narrator of *Alhambra* use them abundantly and with little ironic distance (cf. above 104-5). In all the other texts, *stereotypes* play an insignificant role, if they are used at all.

Stereotypes that typify Hispanics are systematically employed only in a few texts. One *stereotype*, however, appears in the majority of the texts and is one of the most frequently repeated Spanish terms: *gringo* counterpoints and reverses the perspective inherent in *macho, siesta,* or *mañana,* typecasts the North American from a Hispanic point of view, and shows that clichés on ethnicity and *otherness* are not only imposed by a dominant on a dominated group but also vice versa.[82]

---

82   "So, when we left *El Segundo Barrio* across the street from the international border, we didn't expect the Mexicans in California to act like gringos. But they did" (*Buffalo* 77); "give these lame gringos hell" (*Cockroach* 178); "Washingtón, who was the Miguel Hidalgo of the gringos (*Horseman* 86); "My father continued to use the word *gringo*. But it was no longer charged with the old bitterness or distrust" (*Hunger* 23); "what I had heard in Juárez was true, —Those gringos throw good things away" (*Louise* 86); "what do gringos know about misery? Or compassion? Or sympathy—?" (*Plum Pickers* 74); "gringos . . . they have that superiority complex, and that is something the Mexican must face . . . gringos are a funny breed . . . they may be curious . . . uncultured and sometimes crude . . . but they are the most sympathetic of all nationalities . . . why, if they know you're down and out . . . there isn't anything,

Etymological Pairs

As a consequence of the Norman conquest, a large Romance vocabulary became part of the English language. It is therefore not astonishing that a considerable number of those Spanish entries in English Chicano texts that go back to classical roots can be recognized by an English monolingual reader with little or no effort. The following is a representative but far from complete list of such Spanish terms that appear in the novels analyzed:

> *aeroplano, compañero, comunista, conquista, correspondido, desgraciado, domicilio, enamorado, esmeraldas, espíritus, falsete, fiesta, idiota, imbéciles, inocente, lámparas de carburo, memoria, pasatiempo, perdón, políticos, sal, saludos, vecindades, vino, veterano.*

Etymological pairs do not require translation, because they simply replace an English equivalent with similar or identical meaning, similar spelling, and identical syntactical function. Although the vast majority is of Latin origin, there are also a few that go back to other common roots (*chal, ricos, tripas*), or that have become part of the English language via Spanish (*café*).

Some Spanish words, be they *etymological pairs* or *loanwords*, differ from their English counterparts merely by an accent. *Horseman* is the only text that opts constantly for the Spanish form in such instances (*patrón, peón, México*; see chapter 11. "Terms of Address" for *mamá, papá*). If a word has exactly the same spelling in Spanish and English, it will be read as English in an English-language context: "Bonnie Ess,

---

they won't do for you!" (*Victuum* 154f; cf. *Alhambra* 39, 43; *Buffalo* 112, 139, 167, 188; *Clemente* 15, 78f, 110, 120, 122, 125; *Cockroach* 67, 211; *Horseman* 126, 219, 221, 273, 280, 339; *Hunger* 12ff, 21f, 27, 31, 53, 81f, 86, 113, 115f, 118, 135, 147, 176ff; *Leaving Home* 161, 179, 191, 221, 232; *Louise* 15, 16, 33, 35, 45, 66, 68, 120; *Plum Pickers* 32, 40, 112, 157, 219; *Rain God* 38, 59, 126; *Victuum* 81, 104, 114, 256, 260).

you miserable prick!" (*Rites* 47), or "these miserable migrant workers" (*Plum Pickers* 57). An exception to this rule can be found in *Plum Pickers*, where the same adjective may be read as either English or Spanish, depending on whether one has it concord with the preceding Spanish article or with the English noun that follows: "Whatsa matter, el miserable pal?" (31)

Clemente also uses a Spanish word that exists with exactly the same spelling in English. In this case the two corresponding terms are neither *etymological pairs* nor *loanwords*, but homonyms across the language barrier. Their identical form, in spite of the entirely different contents, makes for confusion rather than for easy recognition: "the woman . . . reached into her purse or what those things are called, as big as a red it was" (90). English *red* does not fit the context at all and might be interpreted as a typographical mistake if it were not for the facts that Spanish entries can be expected in *Clemente* and that 'net,' the denotation of Spanish *red*, fits the context perfectly.

Hermetic Spanish

Loanwords, etymological pairs, and *clichés* can be understood by English monolingual readers without much need for translation or explanation. All texts rely on these *types*, *Alhambra, Buffalo, Hunger, Mango Street,* and *Rain God* to a greater extent, and *Leaving Home, Louise,* and *Rites* to a lesser one. Nevertheless, the corpus also includes a considerable amount of standard or regional Spanish vocabulary that is less comprehensible. *Hermetic Spanish* words and expressions like *antojitos, nagua, pañales, güera como el,* or *navajas de razurar,* and especially *long entries,* will create a tension in the text and make a dictionary necessary, if they are left untranslated (cf. table 16.4).

Spanglish and Pachuco, hybrids of the North American Southwest, hold a special place among this type of entries. Since many Spanglish words have been taken over and Hispanicized from English, it could be argued that they are comparable to *etymological pairs* as far as their accessibility for English monolingual readers is concerned. However, the changed spelling of the stem-vowel, a feature seldom found in *etymological pairs—coffee* and *café* would be an exception—, obstructs a first sight recognition of words like *daime* (dime), *lonche* (lunch), or *rinche* (ranger). Their inclusion among the hermetic entries is therefore appropriate, even though they go back to English roots. Hermetic Pachuco slang in its turn occurs in the bilingual and Spanish novels, but is scarcely used in the English texts. *Tattoo*, the English text which uses Spanish least, treats Pachucos or zoot-suiters most extensively as a theme and includes the most hermetic Pachuco term in the corpus: "'Chudini! Chudini!' Rattler shouted in Pachuco slang, meaning pussy" (176).[83] The quotation shows that the inclusion of hermetic foreign language entries in a text does not necessarily make the text itself hermetic. The difficulty of a given text for a monolingual reader depends not solely on the *types* of Spanish terms that are used, but also on the *methods* employed to integrate these terms into the text.

---

83 *Chudini* does not appear in any of the Pachuco slang and Mexican vocabularies or dictionaries consulted (Barker, Blanco, Galván, Polkinhorn, Santamaría). With the exception of *jaina* (*Louise* 75), which is not listed in Santamaría, and *feria* (*Cockroach* 125), which is not listed in Blanco, the other Pachuco entries in the texts tend to appear in the reference works, and their etymology can in many cases be retraced with the help of Santamaría: *ruka* (*Cockroach* 51, 64, 91, 129, 164; *Rain God* 85), *ruquito* (*Clemente* 16), *yesca* (*Clemente* 109, see below, chapter 14).

10. Methods

Literal Translation

Translation of Spanish occurs, with more or less frequency, in all the novels analyzed. While it is for obvious reasons a sporadic and marginal phenomenon in the novels that use Spanish least (*Tattoo, Mango Street*), it becomes in different ways a distinctive feature of the discourse in *Alhambra, Plum Pickers, Louise, Rain God*, and *Ultima*.

Several methods of translation are used. The most frequent one lets the literal English counterpart of a Spanish word, expression, or phrase directly accompany, in most cases follow, the latter as an attributive, separated by a comma, a full stop, or a dash: "the curse was put on a bulto, a ghost" (*Ultima* 216); "you puta. You prostitute, puta" (*Plum Pickers* 217). "She has him by the balls, *los huevos*" (*Leaving Home* 122). "The *viejitos*—the old men, thank him, as always" (*Valley* 112).

Abelardo Delgado also uses direct attribution: "una lámpara de petróleo, a kerosene lamp" (*Louise* 40), "mental calculations. Calculaciones mentales" (69), but opts sometimes for a more academic rendering by putting the English terms into parentheses "La Boquiilla [sic] (the small mouth)" (15), "patillas (sideburns)," (107) " 'El Rorro' (the doll)" (99), and "El Calcetín (the sock)" (110). Parentheses as translation markers occur in Hinojosa's novels, too: "*eso es cuento de nunca acabar* (that's a story without end)" (*Rites* 111).

Direct translation is also used for groups of words or entire phrases: "*Dicho y hecho*. Said and done" (*Leaving Home* 129). "Numero cinco. Calle de Los Libreros. Number five. Street of the bookshops" (*Alhambra* 144). "*Hace mucho frio*, it is very cold" (*Buffalo* 191). " 'El monte,' the old men said, 'no es de nadie y es de todos'—the forest doesn't belong to anyone and it belongs to everyone" (*Barrio Boy* 5). A song is translated literally in *Plum Pickers*, with very little additional text interspersed:

> Ando borracho
> ando tomando
> el destino cambió mi suerte . . .
> —for when I'm drunk, moaned the girl on the radio singing soft-ly, I go around drinking, and fate has changed my luck. . . . The coffee pot bubbled merrily, joining contrapunta to the singer's romantic warbling.
> Yo—yo, que tanto
> lloré por tus besos . . .
> I—I, who cried so much for you [sic] kisses
> —Yo—yo, que siempre
> te hablé sin mentiras . . .
> I—I, who always spoke to you without lying . . . (38)

Hinojosa, too, includes the *literal translation* of a song in *Rites*, but opts for a more distanced form of attribution. In one of the "Witnesses" sketches—a genre Hinojosa already used before in *Estampas* and other novels of his "Klail City Death Trip Series"—Abel Manzano, a Spanish-speaking character, talks about the killing of Mexicans by the Texas Rangers. His account is rendered in English but includes a song in Spanish:

> En el camino a esa ciudad mentada
> En un domingo por la noche con nubarrón
> Estos rinches texanos de la chingada
> Mataron a más mexicanos del Galveston.* (*Rites* 110)

The narrator translates the stanza in a footnote, with some additional explanation:

> * A literal translation of the *canción: Otra matanza, Señores* (Trans. note: in this instance, *señores* is translated as friends; the context of the song clearly shows this.) *Another Bloothbath, Friends.* "On the road to the aforementioned city (Ruffing); on a rainy Sunday night; the sonsofbitching Texas Rangers; murdered more Mexicans who worked at the Galveston Ranch."

Attributive connection is the most common, but not the on-ly method of *literal translation*. The coordinating conjunction *or* offers another possibility of linking a Spanish term and its English counterpart: "fans or *aficionados*" (*Barrio Boy* 52, cf. 109), "stories or *cuentos*" (*Rain God* 161), "the five estancias, or stations" (*Horseman* 24). Delgado uses this technique most frequently: "a witch or curandera who could rid him of the spell" (*Louise* 13); "my insanity or my tontera which increases as my age does" (33); "la lotería mexicana, or the equivalent of bingo" (52). Though the English and the Spanish terms in the last two examples are not totally congruent, the syntactical structure makes the reader believe that they are. Delgado often prefers rough translation over rendering a Spanish term as exactly as possible.

The closeness of the English and the Spanish terms in the methods of translation mentioned up to now create an impression of tautology, of needless double naming. Some authors, Barrio and Delgado in particular, make this redundancy complete at times by connecting a Spanish expression and its English synonym as if they were not synonyms, and their contents were different. One way of doing this consists in connecting the two synonyms with the conjunction *and*:

. . . the corn patches and the *milpas* on the mountain. (*Barrio Boy* 17)

He throws his arms around my neck and gives me an *abrazo*. (*Cockroach* 178)

It acually gives me gas and yields many pedos instead of sexual desire. (*Louise* 52)

Were they not their brothers and *cousins and primos* and uncles and compadres across the border? (*Plum Pickers* 125, emphasis added)

Another possible reason for tautology is that synonymous qualifiers follow each other as if they had different meanings. Thus, the adjective *güero* in "blond güero kids" (*Plum Pickers* 65) already includes the connotation 'blond.' By the same token, *ronca* would be read as an attributive translation in a phrase like "his voice was husky, ronca." However, in "he had a very husky, ronca voz" (*Louise* 107) the word order does not suggest synonymity between *husky* and *ronca*. *Voz* does not need translation, given the reduced field of application of *husky* and the similarity between *voz* and *voice*. To quote another example of redundancy, the Mexican Spanish noun of Nahuatl origin *petate*, "palm leaf mat, sleeping mat" becomes part of a compound noun and a mere qualifier in: "She pulled the baby along, on her petate mat on the ground" (*Plum Pickers* 184). And Lionel García employs the preposition *with* to overdefine a Mexican dish: "*caldo de res* with beef and potatoes" (*Leaving Home* 82).

Double or even multiple naming may also be applied to achieve a comic effect: "short-eared son of a jackass of a depraved burro" (*Plum Pickers* 72); "my insanity, madness, locura, abnormality" (*Louise* 17); or: "Face it, goddammit: the girl's *preñada*; fat; *panzona*; knocked up; that fucking way; in trouble; *está pa' parir*; the works" (*Rites* 18; for *Valley* see above 80-81).

A Spanish expression and its translation do not necessarily have to follow each other directly: "Your abuelito is dead, Papa says early one morning in my room. *Está muerto*," (*Mango Street* 53) or " '¿Si o no?' she stopped me cold. Just yes or no" (*Buffalo* 193). Parallel syntactic construction may be used in order to make clear which English term is the translation of a Spanish expression:

> . . . for even a clerk is less than a horseman.
>   How can a five-peso-a-day clerk be less than a fifty-centavo-a-day jinete? (*Horseman* 18)

> . . . she doesn't have the bun! . . . she doesn't have the molote! (*Victuum* 12)

The disjunction of a Spanish entry from its English counterpart not only allows parallel syntax, but makes more elegant translations possible, as well. Since it permits the two corresponding terms to appear independently and sometimes with different syntactic functions, the impression of redundancy can be avoided. The recurrence of "synonyms" loses its tautological aspect, the translation becomes less apparent, and the style less clumsy and repetitive: "no cowboy either, but he knows our vaqueros" (*Rites* 63). Another example of this method is:

> Leopoldo had returned a few months later. "Call me *Licenciado*," he said. "Any gringas you know want a divorce?" He hopped gaily. "Let my young friend off for the day," he said to the store owner. "Today I received the results of my examinations. I am a licensed lawyer." (*Clemente* 79)

The text that separates the two corresponding entries may extend over one or several phrases. In a passage that mingles the voice of the third person narrator with the informal register of the character Silvestre, Barrio sets a Spanish word and its English counterpart off from the text by giving them the status of full phrases: "Hombre. He could really lie down and really go to sleep on that carpet. Man. What a son of a bitchin carpet" (*Plum Pickers* 52). In the following example, Villarreal carefully defines a Spanish term before introducing it. He first uses the English term *donkey*, sets it off against *horse* after that, and only then introduces the Spanish equivalent for *donkey*, the Southwest *loanword burro*.

> "You had better take the donkey with you," said Vásquez.
> "You take it," called Concepción. "You are the one who insisted the new boy should not ride the spare horse."
> "Sheepherders always ride burros, you know that. You should not have brought the horse for your brother." (*Horseman* 32-33)

If the distance between a Spanish term and its translation grows, it may produce yet another effect. An author may create *translational suspense* by introducing a Mexican word and not translating it until some phrases, paragraphs, or pages later. In García's *Leaving Home*, for example, *picadillo* and *fideo* are first mentioned without being translated, even though the context makes it clear that they refer to edible items: "workers in the area came and ate . . . their *picadillo* and and [sic] *fideo* with rice and beans." Half a page later, the Spanish terms are defined more clearly: "She ordered the *picadillo* with *fideo*, or the ground beef with spices and vermicelli" (82). *Rites* suspends the translation of a Spanglish term for even longer. The word *rinche* pops up first in a conversation: "he's a *rinche*, and he doesn't take shit from anyone" (63). A dozen pages later a character pins down the word somewhat more: "First thing they see is this circled star of mine, and right away: Pinche rinche! Well, I'll pinchy-rinchy them, goddammit" (76). After a further gap of ten pages, another character talks extensively about the Texas Rangers. Over three whole pages he uses the English term *Rangers* to denominate them, and but once its Spanglish equivalent:

> The Mexicans on *this* side didn't mind the Army too much . . . but it was the Texas Rangers they looked to, and the Rangers walked around like the big muckety-mucks. . . . Not saying they liked the Army, no, but the Rinches rankled, y'understand? (87)

Although the English monolingual reader might still have to look up *pinche* in a dictionary, she or he knows now at least the etymological source for *rinche*.

The concatenation of two or more Spanish terms and their English counterparts in a rhetorical pattern constitutes yet another form of elaborate translation, as in the following quotation from *Ultima*, where *vaqueros* and *cowboys* frame *horsemen* and *caballeros* in a chiasmus:

> Then they imported herds of cattle from Mexico and became vaqueros. They became horsemen, caballeros, men whose daily life was wrapped up in the ritual of horsemanship. They were the first cowboys in a wild and desolate land which they took from the Indians (*Ultima* 119)[84]

Plum Pickers has a chiasmus directly followed by an attributive translation: "Yes. A fool. Tonta. Sí. A crazy dream. Un sueño loco" (44).

---

84 Another bilingual chiasmus in *Ultima*, though this time without translation: "when anybody, bruja or curandera, priest or sinner, tampers with the fate of a man . . ." (80).

Translation fits well into the often quite academic narrative voice of many Chicano novels, but less into direct speech passages. It is not surprising that a character is called *David* in the narrator's discourse and *Daví* in direct speech (*Horseman* 25f), or that a narrator translates direct speech: " '¿Qué—ah, qué pasó, corazón?' He wanted to know what the matter was, my heart . . . 'Nada.' No, nothing, my heart" (*Plum Pickers* 39). " 'Eres Mejicano?' Are you a Mexican?" (*Alhambra* 92). But the translation frequently lacks motivation when it occurs in the direct speech of one of the many Spanish monolingual characters who express themselves among Hispanics in Chicano novels. There is no evident reason for the enunciator to use both the English and the Spanish form. Direct speech among Spanish-speaking characters is generally rendered in English. The inclusion of Spanish elements in it may serve to express the importance of Spanish in the Chicano context, and may be interpreted as an endorsement of the Spanish language in a country where English dominates. The translation of these Spanish elements, however, tends to slow down the discourse unnecessarily and seldom contributes anything to the novel on the aesthetic level. If the inclusion of Spanish vocabulary—especially of hermetic Spanish—creates tension and heightens the intensity of a text, these characteristics are frequently flattened out again by the inappropriate discursive register that the translation brings about. The translation seems motivated more by the author's wish not to leave the reader without clarification than by any inherent logic of the character's:

Woman, mujer, I said enough, basta. (*Plum Pickers* 121)

"Why why why? God, God, God." Sobbing over and over.
"¿Por qué por qué por qué? Dios, Dios, Dios." (ibid. 122)

I was only kidding, mijito, no te enojes, es un chiste nomás. (*Louise* 37-38)

. . . it's a bug . . . why, it's a piojo. (*Victuum* 134; cf. *Alhambra* 55)

On the other hand, translation can become an integral part of the discourse if the enunciator is not a Spanish monolingual speaker, but uses mimetic code switching, and if repetitiveness is that character's trademark anyway:

> six hundred and ninety-five dollars, spot cash, mind you, for a brand new Plymouth? 'Cause that's what he did: dollar for dollar. Went up to Heck Barth's and from one to six ninety five, al contado, too. No credit, no sir. (*Rites* 77)

The same goes for the translation of *cliché* Spanish in the imaginary dialogue of a landowner with his Mexican workers in *Plum Pickers*: "Until we meet again. Hasta la vista, you all. Love you pickers." (82) In both instances, the verbosity of the characters goes hand in hand with the playful and repetitive discourse used by the narrator. The translation is perfectly motivated, too, in the following dialogue between two bilingual characters on an, as it seems, flawed phone line:

> "When you leaving?"
> "¿Qué?"
> "Que ¿cuándo te vas?"
> "Oh; next week sometime . . ." (*Rites* 107)

The examples listed so far make the English equivalent of a Spanish term explicit, but they do not make the act of translation explicit. Most novels rely mainly or even exclusively on this *en passant* manner of translation. Nevertheless, some of them also include translations that are dealt with in a more explicit way. Translation can be made more apparent by stating that a Spanish entry "means," "is," or "is the equivalent of" an English expression:

> Extremadura, Jose mused. 'Hard extremes' was what it meant in English. (*Alhambra* 174)[85]

> "I'm standing in water, and it comes up to here." In Spanish it went like this: "Hasta aquí me llega el agua." (*Barrio Boy* 86, cf. 8)

---

85 Jose's translation is etymologically inaccurate, but fits the argument.

"*Mondado*," she said, which was the equivalent of calling someone a dumb ass. (*Leaving Home* 127 cf. 118, 154)

La lotería mexicana, or the equivalent of bingo. (*Louise* 52)

"*Basta!*" cried Lupe, meaning Enough! (*Plum Pickers* 115)

. . . *abuelita*, the Spanish equivalent to granny. (*Rain God* 4)

Chudini! Chudini! Rattler shouted in pachuco slang, meaning pussy. (*Tattoo* 176)

My mother called Ultima la Grande out of respect. It meant the woman was old and wise. (*Ultima* 3)

Explicit translation in *Plum Pickers*, *Louise*, and *Rain God* deserves a special mention. Barrio's playfulness with language comes through also on this level, for example in the form of internal rhymes: "'¡Mande mi corazón!' In the Mexican lexicon 'What is thy wish, my heart?'" or as a merry-go-round translation:

. . . the Jonsons were from Alamaba [sic] where they were considered something like poor white trash. Trash was basura which was garbage. It was with great difficulty that Lupe wondered how the white güeros could treat their own kind like living garbage too. (65-66)

Abelardo Delgado belongs, together with Raymond Barrio, to the authors of Chicano novels in English who use Spanish most extensively and with many different functions. And whereas Spanish entries seem to function mainly as an exotic seasoning in *Alhambra*, *Leaving Home*, and *Victuum*, they sometimes acquire a privileged position in *Louise*:

I really liked that chavala. Chavala means little girl, little bitty girl. It is an old Chicano word now seldom used. Mi chavala. My girl. I was even then a bit clever with words. For my friends I used the term camarada. This was long before I learned the communist implication in the term. In one of my jobs I was actually nicknamed "El Camarada." It does mean friend and not necessarily a party follower. (*Louise* 127)

The narrator's personal attachment to the two Spanish expressions is as plain as is his struggle to come to terms with them in English—as if English did not offer enough words, or not the right words, to render the full meaning of *chavala* and *camarada*.

Islas uses Spanish not very frequently, but efficiently, in *Rain God*, the only novel in which explicit translation prevails over mere attribution. The comments and explanations that accompany and accentuate Spanish entries are in keeping with the voice of the narrator who is, after all, a university professor:

> "That's my herman," she said to her *hermana*. They had Anglicized the word for sister and used it as a term of endearment with each other. (74)

> She brushed the ants from his legs, saying their diminutive Spanish name, "*Hormiguitas*, . . ." (122)

> His certainty was fixed when he heard the tone of voice in which Lola called his father a *sinverguenza* as he relinquished her to his son. The word is untranslatable; literally, it means "without shame" and can be used as a noun. It was one of Miguel Chico's favorite expressions from childhood. Lola said it darkly, the way lovers would in an embrace. (56)

Sinvergüenza in the last example assumes a similarly privileged position as *camarada* and *chavala* in *Louise*. Two other words that are treated with distinction in *Rain God* are *cabrón* (134) and *malcriado*, which moreover is a case of translational suspense (125, 147, 160, 180). All these words require a large amount of English in order to counterpoint their weight, to reflect their quality; and all of them are identity markers of sorts and thus have a function that English words do not tend to have in the Chicano novel. Finally, it is interesting to note that the Spanish words that Delgado treats in this way are terms of endearment, while Islas does the same with offensive expressions that, through their contexts, become terms of endearment, too. As *sinvergüenza* above, they acquire a connotative richness that goes beyond their dictionary definition and a subtleness that defies stereotyping.

Nonliteral Translation

Nonliteral translation comprises the three subgroups *paraphrase, explanation,* and *summary.* The criterion for differentiating them is one of size.

Paraphrase includes those *nonliteral translations* in which a Spanish entry and its English translation are of about the same length. It suggests itself whenever there is no literal English translation of a Spanish expression or idiom available: "la misa de gallo, midnight mass" (*Ultima* 170). "Ni modo, he had no choice" (*Tamazunchale* 83); "that he is in a spell, *enhierbado*" (*Leaving Home* 122). "He used to get drunk. Cuando se le pasaban las copas . . . (*Louise* 49). "Morisco. Converted to Christian" (*Alhambra* 159). "You all want some *pan de dulce?* Esther can go over to La Nacional for some; biscuits okay?" (*Rites* 23). Furthermore, *paraphrase* can function as a means of avoiding rigid parallel constructions and obvious redundancy: "¿Y por qué no? And what the devil is so wrong with that?" (*Plum Pickers* 47).

Translation by paraphrase can be made explicit in the same way as *literal translation*: "I know very well what a novio is. Almost engaged" (*Plum Pickers* 213). "Go on, lose that goddam eye. Who cares? Lose it, you son-of-a-bitch, and then the Mexicans'll call you Tuerto. Serve you right" (*Rites* 47). In contrast to the examples of explicit translation quoted above (131-33), which are all voiced by a third person narrator, these two cases occur in direct speech, and are more convincingly embedded in the discourse than most of the attributive translations in that mode (see above 130).

The term *Explanation* is applied to English translations which are considerably longer than the Spanish entry they refer to:

It was because Ultima was a curandera, a woman who knew the herbs and remedies of the ancients, a miracle-worker who could heal the sick. (*Ultima* 4)

As middleman between them and the promises of North America, he knew he was in the loathsome position of being what the Mexicans called a *coyote*. (*Rain God* 115)

He wears a white T shirt and a blue beanie, the traditional garb of the *vato loco*, the Chicano street freak who lives on a steady diet of pills, dope and wine. (*Cockroach* 89)

Next to the back door, on a wooden peg, hung the *bule*, a large gourd mottled gray and brown. The *bule* was a dry, leak-proof container about eight inches across, with a wide belly and a short neck cut at the tip and plugged with a cork. Drinking water kept cool and sweet in the *bule*. (*Barrio Boy* 28)

In all these quotations, the semantic quality of a Spanish expression is counterbalanced with a distinctly longer English text that elucidates the Spanish concept for the monolingual reader. This kind of annotation is frequent, has already been encountered in *Valley*, Hinojosa's English version of *Estampas*, and occurs above all with Spanish terms for items or concepts that stem from the Mexican side of the Mexican American cultural tradition and that do not belong to the Anglo American heritage. *Explanations* often give the discourse an anthropological or historiographical tone.

Ernesto Galarza's autobiography, *Barrio Boy*, uses the most extensive *explanation* scheme. The text is the only one in the corpus which translates its Mexican Spanish terms in a glossary (267-275). While some entries in that glossary correspond to *literal translation* (*arroyo:* a stream, creek; *cervecería:* brewery; *trabajo:* work; *zopilote:* turkey vulture), the majority of them are translated by *explanation*. The tone used for these *explanations* is not consistent. Some Mexican terms are dealt with by means of scientific discourse, in a detached and matter-of-fact manner:

> *charro:* horseman bedecked in tight pants, bolero jacket, wide-brimmed hat, spurred boots, sarape, cartridge belt and holster, the most of it trimmed with silver ornaments and gold braid.

> *machete:* a heavy steel blade about thirty inches long, with a single edge, a grip, and a rounded tip; an all-purpose work tool and weapon.

> *metate:* a three-legged slab of stone, about nine by fourteen inches, slanted forward, on which *masa* for tortillas is ground by hand.

At times North American items are adduced in order to illustrate a Mexican object. At least since the *cronistas de las Indias* explained the fauna and flora of the New World with the help of tokens from the old one, it is a standard procedure in colonial and anthropological texts to explain the unknown by means of the known:

> *aguardiente:* brandy or rum, literally burning water; the cheapest brands are in the American class of rotgut.

> *candil:* if an ordinary beer can were cut in thirds, the bottom part capped, a wick inserted and the drum filled with kerosene, the result would be a candil.

> *peso:* a unit of money once worth fifty cents of the American dollar, now devaluated to slightly more than eight cents; . . .

> *mesón:* a sort of rough motel for *arrieros* and their *atajos*; a caravansary entered by a *zaguán* consisting of a large open patio where men and beasts rested overnight.

In these comparisons, the Mexican object tends to come out as cheaper or inferior than its North American counterpart. *Mesón,* the last example quoted, further confirms the general tendency in the glossary to present the traditional Mexican culture as less civilized than the culture of the North American reader. Whereas *motel* fits well into a North American frame of reference, *caravansery* points towards an entirely different cultural context. However, both terms help to create a primitivist image of the Mexican culture—an image that the heavy dose of local color humor in the glossary further enhances:

> *atole:* corn gruel, about the consistency of thin mush; best when served too hot to drink.

comadre: a lady's relationship to parents whose baby she has presented for baptism, of whom she is the *madrina; comadres* frequently became intimate to the point of not being on speaking terms.

corrido: a dramatic or heroic story sung to the accompaniment of guitars; a sort of Mexican folk opera on subjects such as The Disobedient Son, The Great Flood of Papasquiaro, Juan Charrasqueado the Valiant One; a form of art of which every Mexican is capable.

curandera: a woman who practices folk medicine with herbs, unguents, brews, compresses, poultices, a little prayer, and much faith on the part of the patient.

filarmónica: a town or village orchestra culturally a peg or two above the *mariachi.*

The narrator makes fun of the culture depicted in a belittling way. He seems to identify rather with the culture for which the glossary is meant than with the culture that the glossary depicts. North American cliché views of Mexican culture are confirmed rather than questioned, a tendency that can also be observed in the autobiography as such, as Tonn has convincingly shown (81-90). I can therefore only partly agree with Carlos B. Gil, when he defines Galarza's autobiography as a

> study of the migrant's vicissitudes seen through a child's eyes. Far more valuable and persuasive than the many anthropological studies of exotic Mexico which clinically discuss *compadrazgo* systems and mating preliminaries in an Indian village, *Barrio Boy* warmheartedly relates everyday images about real country people. (447)

Barrio Boy, although it does not employ 'clinical' discourses, is not that far removed from "anthropological studies of exotic Mexico." Galarza constructs his childhood, as Fabian would say, in "terms of topoi implying distance, difference and opposition" (111). His narrator "leaves the readers in peace," as Schleiermacher would put it, he bridges cultural differences by explaining the foreign subject matters in ways that are familiar to his readership. Maybe, *Barrio Boy is* what it declares itself to be: "a true story of the acculturation of Little Ernie" (2), of the author-narrator-protagonist Ernesto Galarza. One word does not seem to fit into the picture. *Vergüenza* is translated as "a sense of shame, of personal dignity; conscience; doing right; modesty; responsible behavior; trustworthiness not based on the fear of being caught." There is no local color in this definition, but an attempt at coming to terms with the concept of *vergüenza* and a contrast to the pejorative view that dominates the glossary otherwise. Or, to put it in the context of dichotomous stereotyping of ethnic *otherness*, *vergüenza* presents the reader with the "noble," the virtuous side of the "Mexican character," while most other *explanations* in the glossary show its uncivilized, its "savage" traits (cf. Berkhofer 72-80, Sollors 129). Galarza's definition of *vergüenza* resembles the treatment of its antonym *sinvergüenza* in *Rain God* because the Spanish term is heavily charged with positive meaning—it differs from it in that this positive meaning is more institutionalized and less personal.

The use of *sinvergüenza, malcriado,* and *cabrón* in *Rain God* or *chavala* and *camarada* in *Louise* (see above 132-34) falls into the category of *explanation*, too. A large amount of English is applied to translate a single Spanish term and to bring a Spanish token closer to a reader who is not familiar with Hispanic values. What is different is the underlying attitude of the narrator, whose voice signals more personal involvement and identification and less interest in anthropological explanation than Galarza's narrator and other *explanatory* voices quoted earlier in this chapter. This is not to say that the discourses of personal involvement and explanation are mutually exclusive. The semantic field in which this comes out most clearly, is food (see chapter 11. "Culinary Terms").

Long Spanish entries are rare in the Chicano novel in English, and even more so is their English rendering by *summary*. *Summary* stands for those translations that are much shorter than the "original." Galarza uses a generic term in order to translate collectively the names of several tropical plants that also exist in English as loanwords: "Under the shady canopies of the giants there were the fruit bearers—*chirimoyas, guayabas, mangos, mameyes,* and *tunas*" (*Barrio Boy* 6); Acosta subsumes different Mexican dishes under the word *food*: "vendors of tortas, tacos, tamales, helotes on a stick and whatever kind of food one wanted for a buck or a penny" (*Buffalo* 188). In other instances, a translation by *summary* eases the tension created by the insertion of a longer Spanish entry in an English text and offers at the same time a way around tedious *literal translation*:

> Then my mother came to give me her blessings. I knelt and she said, "te doy esta bendición en el nombre del Padre, del Hijo, y el Espíritu Santo," and she wished that I would prosper from the instruction of her brothers. Then she knelt by my side and Ultima blessed us both. She blessed without using the name of the Trinity like my mother, and yet her blessing was as holy. (*Ultima 234*)

The narrator-protagonist summarizes the Spanish entry by employing the word *blessings* before it and following it up with the comment that his mother uses "the name of the Trinity" in blessing him. In a similar manner, the first person narrator of *Louise* tells us of a waiter who

> used to be a real lover. He was short and ugly and very old but at times se le juntaban la esposa y sus queridas y no hallaba el pobre por qué puerta salir. (102)

The comment that the waiter "used to be a real lover" condenses the more detailed information contained in the Spanish sentence. The way in which Delgado excludes the monolingual reader from the full picture makes this passage belong to the category of "insider puns" discussed under "High Impact Terms" (chapter 11).

Villarreal, in turn, uses a combination of *summary* and of historiographical *explanation* to render a Mexican *corrido*:

> Moya se fué por delante
> mirando por las laderas

se llevó cincuenta gallos
pero de los más panteras

This was the ballad of the fearless old man, José Luis Moya,
who with fifty men had taken the Bufa and the city back in 1910.
(*Horseman* 8)

The difference between the Spanish stanza and the text that renders it in English is much the same as the difference between certain Spanish passages of *Estampas* and their English counterparts in *Valley*. Like the names of *Don Quijote* and *Cuauhtémoc* in *Estampas*, *Moya* appears in the *corrido* without further need for comment. And just as *Valley* gives additional information on the two characters (see above 82, 84), the English rendering of the *corrido* resorts to annotation. The contents of the song are summarized in "Moya, who with fifty men had taken . . ." The *corrido* does not spell out that the hero's christian name was "José Luis," that he was a "fearless old man," or that he had taken "the Bufa and the city back in 1910." All of this contributes to bringing the culture that is depicted in the text closer to the culture of its reader. On the other hand, the *corrido* informs us that Moya went ahead keeping an eye on the slopes and stresses the fearlessness of the fifty men he took with him—information that, together with the poetical form in which it is presented, falls prey to *summary*.

Contextual Translation

Translation by context is the most complex *method* and cannot be defined as easily as *literal, paraphrastic, explanatory*, or *summarizing* translation. The *methods* dealt with thus far may present some difficulties as to their mutual differentiation—gray areas exist between, say, *literal translation* and *paraphrase*, or between *paraphrase* and *explanation* or *summary*. Nevertheless, they constitute clearly recognizable textual strategies. Context, on the other hand, is an omnipresent phenomenon that works for all the words in a text, not only for foreign language entries. The functions of contextual elements are therefore less precisely definable and more open to interpretation.

Translations by context can be more or less specific. When a character in *Clemente* says: "Too much dinero, boy. Five dollars for a little trim" (71), *dinero* obviously means 'money.' In other cases, the context provides readers only with a rough or partial idea of the connotations of a Spanish entry. Thus, the context of the word *perico* in the sentence: "Like a good perico I prided myself on being able to rattle off long prayers and give standard theological answers to standard theological questions" (*Louise* 91) suggests that the word might designate someone who talks a lot or who memorizes well, but does not define it unequivocally as 'parrot' or, in the figurative sense, as 'talkative person.' By the same token, the context of the terms *metate* and *molcajete* in:

> Across the kitchen, Rosa . . . was on her knees over a metate, grinding corn to be used during the day. At another table, Manuela . . . made chile in a molcajete. (*Horseman* 34)

tells us that the two words stand for kitchen utensils that can be used for grinding corn and making *chile* respectively, but leaves us uninformed about the shape of these utensils and the material they are made of. If they represented commonly used kitchen items in the United States, the terms *metate* and *molcajete* would have their English counterparts, and their partial definition in the passage quoted would give North American readers enough clues to fully comprehend them. Since these material tokens behind the signifieds are not used in the English-speaking United States, however, the reader who is unfamiliar with them has to consult a dictionary or encyclopedia in order to visualize them more exactly.

Contextual translations employ manifold strategies. One of the most frequently used ones follows an action-reaction scheme in which the content of a Spanish entry in the action element can be deduced by the reaction in English. The action can be a question, the reaction an answer: " 'Cómo te llamas?' she asked. 'Antonio Márez,' I replied" (*Ultima* 54). When the protagonist of *Clemente* is picked up by his wife after work, his first words are: "Vengo más cansao que la chingada," to which she responds: "I'll fix your tub as soon as we get home" (153), thus indicating that he might have mentioned his being tired. The quotation is at the same time an instance of *summary*. The same goes for the following example: "The clerk said to the older man, *'¡Dile que si no le gusta, que se vaya a la chingada!* 'Well, fuck you too, you sonofabitch!' I shouted in my finest English" (*Buffalo* 191). The reverse pattern, in which a Spanish expression is part of the answer, occurs more seldom: " 'Ready to pick apples?' he asked. 'Sí tío,' I replied" (*Ultima* 44).

Spanish terms can also be defined by antonymy or antithesis rather than by analogy:

> "It is for bigger things that your padrino has taken an interest in you."
> "Then I wish I had never been his godson," said Heraclio. (*Horseman* 18)

> Mario was the only boy on the street who wore shoes, always highly polished. Some wore huaraches but Ramón had not had anything on his feet for two years. (*Clemente* 74)

> Fausto . . . waited for his niece.
> "Tío, are you awake?" (*Tamazunchale* 28)

The question-answer scheme may be replaced by a statement and the reaction to it, or an order and its being carried out. Most translations of this sort use direct speech in at least one element: " '¡Vamos! ¡Vamos!' my uncle called and we clamored aboard" (*Ultima* 45); "one of them said, 'Vamos a dar la vuelta.' I didn't even hesitate. I simply walked with them" (*Clemente* 92). The action-reaction scheme, which is used in almost all Chicano novels in English, becomes the preferred mode of translation in *Tamazunchale*. " 'Cálmate,' Fausto said, trying to think of some consolation" (50). " 'I'll give him some anís,' Fausto said. 'That usually helps.' He removed the crystal liqueur bottle from the cupboard shelf" (66). Synecdoche and metonymy offer further ways of contextual translation. The meaning of a Spanish entry can be made clear by mentioning parts of a signified with a Spanish signifier: "where the cottonwoods make a thick bosque" (*Ultima* 81), "a gay fiesta for everyone, for everyone likes to dance and sing a little" (*Barrio Boy* 123), or: "they was having themselves a baile *and* a barbacoa; you know. Beer. Meat. And Music" (*Rites* 72). Also in *Rites*, a prominent member of the Blanchard-Cooke clan gets a thirteen-year-old maid pregnant, and a relative bursts out: "Just what did you think, goddammit? No . . . you listen. No one's coming into this Ranch with some goddam curandera and her rusty coat hangers, you hear?" (19). *Curandera*, which for once in a Chicano novel does not connote a positive and mythical element of the Chicano cultural tradition, is sufficiently defined by the context, and by the token "rusty coat hanger."

Metonymy, the use of attributes or characteristics to define a Spanish entry, can also be encountered: "His head is all white with canas," (*Louise* 120) "the clump of red-branched manzanita" (*Tattoo* 24). "The light cast by the farol revealed the wild, frightened eyes of Chávez" (*Ultima* 14). *Cana* can be pinned down as 'white hair,' the *loanword manzanita* as a plant, and *farol* as a lantern by means of the words *head* and *white*, *red branched*, and *light* respectively. The protagonist of *Victuum*, on the other hand, uses three types of smell to inform readers of the semantic contents of a Spanish term. Her reaction when walking into a *zapatería* is: "Ooh, it smells like shoe polish and smelly feet and old leather" (52).

The coupling of Spanish and English terms belonging to the same semantic field makes for yet another method of translation or rough translation by context:

. . . the chirimoya and avocado trees. (*Tamazunchale* 39)

. . . all the celebrities were present. The president of the city of Fresnillo, the alcalde of Río Grande. (*Horseman* 144)

Most of them have died by now, una cruda, una pulmonía or
simply exposure and malnutrition. (*Louise* 107-8)

José sucked and huffed the repertoire of *corridos* and lullabies
and marches he carried in his head. (*Barrio Boy* 47)

Louise is an abundant source of further types of translation
by context. The context may, for example, illustrate what a
person does: "the 'gambusinos' who used to smuggle silver
out of the mine" (42),[86] or elucidate what a thing is used for:
"the coal of the bracero we used for cooking" (29), "her black
chal wrapped around her dark hair" (28), "She would sell
small pieces of it to men or women who would tie a knot
around it with the corners of their panuelos and carry it with
them" (94). Villarreal uses this kind of contextual translation,
too: "Get my traje de etiqueta—I will take it along and change
at the office" (*Clemente* 115); or "Elías came from the side,
twirling his reata, and lassoed the forelegs so the colt did a
half somersault, landing heavily on its back" (*Horseman* 43).
And in the following example, the context makes it obvious
that *taco* for once does not appear as a culinary *loanword*, that
it does not denote a tortilla sandwich, but a type of trousers:
"He was a figure in bronze, from his low brown boots, the tacos on his calves, to the narrow-brimmed hat" (*Horseman* 2).

The author of *Louise* defines Spanish words using more
than one contextual element or embeds more than one Spanish
word into the same context: "I would fantasize all kinds of
episodes based on conversations I had heard that day or on the
many cuentos my bedridden blind great-grandmother, Andrea
Flores, used to tell me" (27). Two contexts help to constitute
the meaning of *cuentos*, one before and one after the word itself appears. For one thing, *cuentos*, like conversations, can
serve as the basic material for fantastic episodes; for another,

---

86 Cf. "In Saltillo, the compadre Urbina reigned as *cacique*" (*Horseman* 323, emphasis added); "the *Jefe Político*, who represented the
government" (*Barrio Boy* 33).

they can be told by a great-grandmother. In the following two examples, on the other hand, two Spanish words or locutions appear within one context: "He used to have big arguments with my mom and at times se la sonaba. She was never muy dejada, so she used to hit back" (109-10). "There was a tiendita close to the school where a lot of us would hang around buying candies o nieve raspada" (69).

Adolfo, the protagonist of *Leaving Home*, has been invited to stay overnight at the house of a woman he met on the bus. The narrator comments on his feelings the morning after: "He felt that she did not owe him an explanation. That went with being an *arrimado*. No one owes you an explanation about anything" (73). The context defines the Spanish term about as clearly as the glossary of *Barrio Boy*: "*arrimados:* poor relatives or friends who stayed with a family temporarily when they had no place of their own; from *arrimarse*, 'to get close to.' "

Those Spanish entries that appear once or twice during a novel, will have an ephemeral effect on the reader. But if a Spanish entry appears repeatedly and in different contexts, it will become increasingly familiar to the reader, who will end up integrating it into her or his passive vocabulary. This occurs with *carnal* 'close friend' in *Louise*, or with *ese, vato*, and *vato loco* in *Cockroach*. By the same token, a few novels use Spanish keywords and their English counterparts alternately and in parallel constructions, both so frequently that they become entirely interchangeable. This is the case with *bruja* and *witch* in *Ultima*, *tortuga* and *turtle* in *Tortuga*, and *jinete* and *horseman* in *Horseman*. However, most Spanish words that appear more than ten times in the texts of the corpus are *clichés* and thus do not lead to any learning process.

No Translation

All in all, translation is not used economically in the corpus, is not only applied to *hermetic* Spanish. A lot of *loanwords* and *etymological pairs* are translated:

Catolicos? [sic] Si. Somos Catolicos. Of course. We're Catholics. (*Alhambra* 108)

Take the idea of the anti-Christ. El anti cristo [sic] . . . (*Louise* 18)

. . . she knew what it meant to die in agony. *La Agonia* [sic], the Mexicans called it. (*Leaving Home* 164)

Moreover, a given Spanish entry can be translated repeatedly. Thus, *corazón* appears as many times translated (39, 45, 64, 88, 122) as untranslated (46, 116, 120, 190) in *Plum Pickers*, and, in the same novel, the internationally known *loanword machismo* is translated three times: "What was important was to let Danny keep his budding machismo intact, his budding manhood, like the young bull he was" (46); "that viejo pendejo kept his machismo intact, his manhood" (135); "Dan with his overpowering need to constantly assert himself and his manhood, what their mother called machismo" (141). Those Spanish entries that are not translated by either *literal* or *nonliteral translation* and are at best vaguely defined by the context are mainly *loanwords*, *clichés*, or *etymological pairs*. This is why the absence of translation rarely leads to a difficulty in understanding. Terms like *barrio, tortilla, fiesta, sombrero, gringo, señora,* or *gracias*, which belong to the most often used Spanish *single words* in the corpus, and are easily recognizable for monolingual readers, contribute at the same time the biggest share of untranslated Spanish entries.

Hermetic Spanish entries that are not translated can be found above all in *Clemente, Louise, Plum Pickers, Tamazunchale, Ultima,* and *Rites,* in those texts, in other words, that use Spanish most extensively (with the exception of *Barrio Boy*) and where more *long entries* appear:

. . . suddenly one of the young black men leaned forward and began to laugh.
    Mario laughed back with all his soul and said to Ramón, "*¡Pero mira qué bonitos dientes tiene este cabrón!*" (*Clemente* 70, emphasis added in this and in the following four quotations)

I had a little dog with which I played constantly. One time my mama Luz . . . told me not to handle the dog as dogs had many germs and I was sure to catch some of them. *Nunca me hubiera dicho eso.* I threw the dog against the wall and ran away crying. Every day from then on for a period of almost a month, I would not look at my hands and would hide them behind me. (*Louise* 28-29)

Frowning, Manuel lifted the screaming infant in his strong, rough, calloused hands. He pressed the child's face to his shoulder. The baby's shrieks gradually subsided. *"Qué pasó, gordita,"* he murmured, holding her coconut head to his face, smelling her. (*Plum Pickers* 120)

This little man—*chaparrito y con una gorrita*—took him just before you came. (*Tamazunchale* 78)

We pressed through the curious, anxious crowd and they parted to let us pass.
"¡La curandera!" someone exclaimed. Some women bowed their heads, others made the sign of the cross. *"Es una mujer que no ha pecado,"* another whispered. (*Ultima* 96, cf. 30, 123)

A Spanish proverb that remains untranslated in *Leaving Home*, on the other hand, stands out, because the novel is one of the texts which use Spanish least, and only in the form of single words or short entries that tend to be translated literally:

He took special pains to dress as well as he could with what clothes he had brought with him. He bathed daily, shaved daily, and she never, never, saw him without his teeth. *El hambre lo tumba, y la vanidad lo levanta.* (235)

While all the italicized Spanish entries in the last six quotations contain information that complements the argument or comments on it, or that—as in the first quotation—brings in an additional aspect, none of them is crucial for the argument. But since they are all *hermetic*, and since none of them is translated, the monolingual reader is left with a feeling of missing something, and the narrator provides no help to ease that feeling. In order to ease it, monolingual readers have to consult a dictionary or ask a Spanish-speaking person. They are forced to leave their native language and to make a step towards the language of the culture that the texts depict. This may be different in the case of a phone conversation in *Rites* which is marked by code switching and by a considerably higher Spanish ratio than the rest of the novel (107f). One of the Spanish entries is translated literally (see above 131), some by context, others remain untranslated. The whole conversation is pure tall small talk, and the monolingual reader may rightly assume that its Spanish part does not contain more substance than the English one.

In a passage from *Clemente*, to add a further example, all the direct speech is rendered in—mostly *hermetic*—Spanish:

> "Epa, Leopoldo," Mario called. He made the Mexican beckoning sign, the arm moving downward instead of up. The young lad came to the door, mop in hand.
> "Quiero que me laves ese carro," said Mario. He pointed toward the car. "Pero que quede limpiecito porque le pertenece a un amigo." He gave the older boy a five-peso bill. "Pero 'horita —pronto, eh."
> "Al ratito, ya mero acabo aquí."
> "Gracias, eh."
> "Las gracias a ti, Mario."
> They walked on. Ramón, against his will, counted. . . . *another dollar for the car wash, altogether 30 pesos. He gave that guy five pesos to wash the car.* (14-15)

No *literal translation* is given, but the narrative voice and the interior monologue of Mario's friend Ramón inform the reader on the gist of the argument through a translation by *summary* of sorts.

In none of the examples listed so far is understanding the Spanish entry necessary to follow the main line of the argument. However, since monolingual readers cannot be sure of this until they have translated it and since novels are not merely a matter of argument and information, the use of *hermetic* Spanish instead of more easily understandable *types* increases the distance between these texts and their readership, and makes for a difference in reading and evaluating them. The comparison of two structurally very similar and thematically related passages in *Barrio Boy* and *Plum Pickers* may serve to illustrate this difference. Galarza describes in his autobiography how, as children, he and his brothers used to get up in the morning:

> One by one we came down the notched pole, still snug in our sarapes.
> "Buenos días, muchachos."
> "Buenos días, Don Catarino."
> "Buenos días, Tía"
> "Buenos días, Tío"
> "Buenos días, mamá."
> We huddled around the fire in the *pretil* as close as we could without getting in the way of the business of preparing breakfast.
> (*Barrio Boy* 21)

The definition of *sarape* and *pretil* is taken care of by previous mentions, by the context, and by the glossary added to the text. The fivefold repetition of the *formula buenos días* plus a name in parallel construction is not translated and does not need to be. Galarza removes the text from his monolingual readers by using Spanish, but employs at the same time all possible means of minimizing the distance that the foreign language creates.

Plum Pickers also renders a greeting ceremony in Spanish. The first three lines almost coincide with the direct speech passage in *Barrio Boy*, even though it might be argued that *qué tal* is a more *hermetic formula* than *buenos días*. After that, the greeting develops into an *albur*, the playful exchange of verbal wit that appears in several Chicano novels in Spanish, too (Hinojosa *Klail City* 74, 131; Méndez *Peregrinos* 18; Elizondo *Muerte* 54, 86, 98):

> ¡Qué tal, compadre!
> ¡Qué tal, comadre!
> ¡Qué tal, viejo!
> ¡Quiúbale, hermano!
> ¡Qué tal está tu cola, chango!
> ¡Igual a la de tu iguana, tu esposa!
> ¡La tuya!
> ¡Tu Tu Tu!

¡Ja ja ja!
Good friends, buenos amigos, having fun. (68)

The narrator translates *buenos amigos* literally, summarizes the *albur* in the words "having fun," and goes on to describe a cheerful Sunday get-together among friends. Neither of the two passages in Spanish affects the main argument of the novel; their effect on the reader, however, is quite different. The second one imposes more and more difficult Spanish, creating problems of interpretation even for a Hispanophone reader not familiar with Mexican Spanish and the *albur*. The juxtaposition of Spanish and English marks both quotations stylistically but leaves monolingual readers with the feeling of missing something, excludes them from the "fun," so to speak, in the case of *Plum Pickers*, where the Spanish entry *shows*, what the English comment *tells* (cf. Booth 8).

While most untranslated Spanish entries are not *hermetic* and the major part of the *hermetic* Spanish entries that remain untranslated do not carry the gist of the argument, some Spanish entries in Delgado's epistolary novel *Louise* are essential to the argument and thus remove the text even further from the language and the culture of the monolingual reader—they make that reader move more, to use Schleiermacher's rhetoric. In the example that follows, the narrator-protagonist Santiago Flores talks on behalf of the migrant council at a hearing of the Occupational Safety and Health Agency:

> I play more with words, showing that we Chicanos are not pendejos now nor have we ever been pero eso sí de vez en cuando nos hacemos pendejos nosotros mismos. (65-66)

The statement that "we Chicanos are no fools now nor have we ever been but it is true that sometimes we play dumb ourselves," is more than mere wordplay. This is also true for a quotation from the Popol Vuh in the same novel, which constitutes one of the longest prose sentences in the corpus. The author does not translate it, but does not leave the reader entirely without background information either:

How timely that I read the "Popul Vuh, las antiguas historias del Quiche" and in such a way prepare myself to greet July 4, 1976. The "American" roots as explained in this real mythology resemble greatly all other myths dealing with the creation of mankind. . . .
"La palabra quiche, queche o quechelah significa bosque en varias de las lenguas de guatemala [sic], y proviene de 'qui,' 'quiy' (muchos) y che (árbol) [muchos + árboles = quiche] palabra maya original."—Popul Vuh—
Placed in the magnificent development of this continent the bicentennial celebration seems indeed insignificant and a minute minute in the various centuries, epochs maybe. (16-17)

The Spanish entry relativizes not only the predominant language of the text, but also North American cultural values, which the narrator puts into a larger American perspective by adducing Mayan mythology. The official history of Anglo-Saxon America is questioned by a quotation in Spanish. However, since this quotation in turn refers to native American languages and is itself a translation from Mayan, it does not follow the already encountered dichotomous pattern of English versus Spanish in which the latter is idealized (see chapter 4). This narrator's attitude could best be summarized by an already quoted sentence from *Buffalo*: "Spanish is the language of our conquerors. English is the language of our conquerors. . . . No one ever asked me or my brother if we wanted to be American citizens. We are all citizens by default" (198).

11. Semantic Fields

The analysis of the Spanish entries in more than thirty Chicano short stories leads Penfield and Ornstein-Galicia to the conclusion that:

> these terms fall into basically five semantic categories: (1) terms of address—be they endearment or blasphemy; (2) swear terms; (3) interjections—highly affective and emotional idioms; (4) terms for regional food; and (5) terms for groups of people. (88)

Though most of the *single words* and a considerable part of the *short entries* in the corpus fit into one of these categories, I have opted for a slightly different classification on which I have also based the Spanish entry lists in chapters 14 and 15:

1. *Terms of address*, be they formal (*señor, señora, don, buenos días, adiós*) or familiar (*mamá, papá, comadre, tío, hola, vámonos*); and including words like *gracias, por favor, sí*, and a few verbal forms like *dame, cálmate, entiendes, vete, voy*—correspond largely to the first category above, but do not contain blasphemic terms.

2. *High impact terms*—interjections, swearwords, terms of blasphemy, highly affective and emotional idioms, and euphemisms—bring together the second and third categories above and parts of the first.

3. *Ethnographic terms* represent or describe Mexican (American) culture, its material tokens, values, surroundings, flora and fauna.

4. *Culinary terms*, a subgroup of *ethnographic terms*, are prominent enough to be dealt with separately. They appear above as "terms for regional food" (general *ethnographic terms* are not mentioned by Penfield and Ornstein Galicia).

5. *Terms for groups of people*—identical to category five in Penfield and Ornstein-Galicia.

The classification reflects my intention to cover the greatest possible part of the Spanish language entries in a limited number of categories. Although each entry appears only in the category that corresponds to its most frequent use in the corpus, the categories are not mutually exclusive and many entries could belong to more than one category. Thus, *panocha* denominates a sweet in *Barrio Boy*, while *Louise* uses it as a euphemism; *gringo*, which I list in the last category, also appears in the texts in the first and second categories; *hombre* is used in most cases as a *term of address*, but comes up as an interjection, too. *Macho*, which mainly represents traditional Mexican American values in the texts, designates at the same time the members of a group, and can moreover be a *term of address*. Finally, many terms listed under *groups of people*, are at the same time *ethnographic terms (alcaide, arriero, campesino*, etc.). In contrast to such polysemantic entries, homonyms are separated: corresponding to its general application in the corpus, *taco* appears as a *culinary term*, but it is also listed as an *ethnographic term*, since it is used once as 'chaps' (*chaparreras*), the heavy leather trousers worn by cowboys to protect their legs (*Horseman* 2). Chapter 14 lists the five categories.

Not all the Spanish entries in the corpus lend themselves to detailed analysis. The numerical prominence of *clichés*, for instance, is an important factor in the overall assessment of the Spanish language entries, but the application of many of these *cliché* terms is rather monotonous. Therefore, this chapter will focus on those categories which, apart from being widely represented in the corpus, offer at the same time food for thought. The large category *terms for groups of people*, which contains the bluntest brackets of identity and *otherness* (*anglo, bolillo, chicano, gabacho, gachupín, gringo, mexicano, pachuco, raza*), will not be further treated, although the application of these words would in some instances be well worth analyzing—the changing value of *gringo* in *Hunger* and *Clemente*, for example (see above 120). By the same token, only those *ethnographic terms* that belong in the context of rural Mexican (American) life are considered, and the *terms of address* have been narrowed down to kinship terms, thus ex-

cluding very frequent *formulas* like *don, maestro, señor,* or
señora. Two semantic subgroups of the *High impact terms* are
not taken into consideration. Interjections like the *stereotype*
"ay"—which appears in nine texts as a *single word* or in *short
entries,* and is heavily used in *Plum Pickers* and *Ultima*[87]—are
not analyzed, nor are the few but frequently repeated religious
high impact terms; not because they are used almost exclusively by women, but because their application is quite monotonous. Spanish entries from the field of religion are in most
cases invocations of the Virgin Mary or of a saint: " '¡Jesús,
María Purísima!' my mother cried, 'Blessed Virgen de Guadalupe, thank you for your intercession! Blessed St.Anthony,
Holy San Martín, Ay Dios Mío, gracias a San Cristobal!' She
thanked every saint she knew for her sons' safe delivery from
war.["]88

Terms of Address: Kinship Terms

My *mother!* My *father!* After English became my primary language, I no longer knew what words to use in addressing my parents. The old Spanish words (those tender accents of sound) I had
used earlier—*mamá* and *papá*—I couldn't use anymore. They

---

87 *Ultima* contains more than half of the corpus's *short entries* starting
    with *ay*: *ay diablo* (159, 241); *ay Dios* (27, 59, 121, 157); *ay Dios
    mío* (7, 56, 82); *ay Dios, otro día* (48); *ay, gracias a Dios* (215);
    ay, Grande (122); *ay, hijito* (38); *ay maldecido* (153); *ay, María
    Luna* (10); *ay mi Antonito* (94); *ay mi hijito* (174); *ay, mujer* (49,
    215); *ay no* (48); *ay, papá* (46); *ay, pendejo* (157); *ay que diablo*
    (154); *ay que Lupito* (15); *ay sí* (126); and in the anglicized form:
    aye, Gabriel Márez (214).
88 *Ultima* 56, cf. 12, 80ff, 121, 172, etc.; *Barrio Boy* 104f; *Cockroach*
    19, 44; *Louise* 62; *Clemente* 26; *Horseman* 95; *Hunger* 85; *Plum
    Pickers* 109f; *Tortuga* 88; *Victuum* 132, 152, 164. Religion as a
    theme is an important factor in the corpus and is treated in a more
    varied way: *Alhambra* 41ff, 49, 86, 108; *Barrio Boy* 8f, 49f; *Cle-
    mente* 28, 91; *Cockroach* 12-17, 77, 161; *Horseman* 75f, 162, 367;
    Hunger "Credo" 77-110; *Leaving Home* 33, 162f; *Louise* 91; *Plum
    Pickers* 41; *Rain God* 16; *Tattoo* 84; *Tortuga* 88, 90ff, 107, 140;
    Ultima 25, 29ff, 42, 189f; *Victuum* 45, 53, 65, 132f, etc.

would have been too painful reminders of how much had changed in my life. On the other hand, the words I heard neighborhood kids call *their* parents seemed equally unsatisfactory. *Mother* and *Father*; *Ma, Papa, Pa, Dad, Pop* (how I hated the all-American sound of that last word especially)—all these terms I felt were unsuitable, not really terms of address for *my* parents. As a result, I never used them at home. Whenever I'd speak to my parents, I would try to get their attention with eye contact alone. In public conversations, I'd refer to 'my parents' or 'my mother and father.' (*Hunger* 23-24)

Spanish terms designating family members or relatives, together with Mexican swearwords and the culinary Mexican vocabulary, belong to the semantic fields that are most widely represented. This is mainly due to two reasons. For one thing, kinship terms, like terms of address in general, can be integrated very handily into an English text. They can be added to the beginning or the end of an English phrase without obstructing its understanding, as if they were proper names. They appear, in fact, often with the function of names (*Mama Chona* and *Tia Cuca* in *Rain God*, *Tia* in *Victuum*, *Tío* in *Tamazunchale*). The second reason for the abundance of kinship terms is the fact that the Mexican American family is present in all the texts, although in differing degrees and forms. *Family*, in the corpus, can be anything from a couple and their child to a large clan. It is the dominant *setting* in *Barrio Boy, Rain God, Ultima*, and *Victuum*, while *Alhambra*, *Hunger*, and *Leaving Home* treat it extensively as a *theme*. *Alhambra*, *Ultima*, and *Victuum* in turn rewrite and relativize Anglo American history by depicting protagonist Mexican American families that have played an important role in their region for centuries.

Certain traits recur. The Mexican American family, as represented in the texts, is an institution with clearly distributed male-female and generational roles and a strict set of values that requires loyalty, responsibility, and pride towards a name, a clan, and a tradition:

It was the custom for a Hispano young man and his parents to pay a call on the girl's family as a preliminary to engagement. (*Alhambra* 57, cf. 14ff, 59f, 62)

It was just that deflowering the girl was the surest way to get her. Refusing to marry meant severe violence to the suitor, even death. How they reconciled after the wedding was funny in a way. The priest never could understand it. A few moments before the wedding, the family would threaten to kill the young man and immediately after the wedding the whole relationship would change. Now, the new groom was one of them. It was the damndest thing he had ever seen. It reminded him of the Sicilians. (*Leaving Home* 43f, cf. 27, 84, 149, 213)

They were not our kinfolk but the *respeto* I felt for them, after Doña Henriqueta's lectures, was genuinely Mexican. (*Barrio Boy* 187, cf. 17, 45f, 146, 177, 215, 236f, 239)

Our parents always called him the *older* brother. I have had to treat him with the respect that a Chicano gives to the eldest son. (*Cockroach* 189, cf. 106f)

. . . he also knew that if he failed in any way, another one of them would do it. It was impossible that the family should lose to a horse. (*Horseman* 151, cf. 44, 54, 145-155, 367, 374ff)

"The family," as usual—more concerned with its pride than with justice— had begun to lie to itself about the truth. (*Rain God* 85, cf. 4f, 36, 142)

It was the custom to greet the old . . . a family was judged by its manners. (*Ultima* 10)

Surely I've been strict ... especially with the girls ... but a father must with his girls ... he must make sure they become young ladies ... goddesses for a man to worship ... virgin princesses ... (*Victuum* 146, cf. 138, 150f; *Louise* 100; *Mango Street* 53)

Another imperative that appears repeatedly expects a family not to reveal its private concerns to strangers, let alone to Anglos:

Writing is one thing, the family is another. I don't want *tus hermanos* hurt by your writings. And what do you think the cousins will say when they read where you talk about how the aunts were maids? Especially I don't want the *gringos* knowing about our private affairs. (*Hunger* 178 cf. 129f)

Pregunton means nosy and minding other people's business. *Preguntar* means just to ask about things you don't understand. It is not good to be nosy. It is good to ask. Just be careful who you ask and what you ask. You can always ask me or your uncles. (*Barrio Boy* 95)

This "Mexican attitude" of *no rajarse*, of 'not opening oneself up,' which for Octavio Paz is the quintessential attitude of *machismo* (see above 37, cf. also Mirandé 165-181), is also described by the careerist Clemente Chacón after he has been beaten up by a group of militant Chicanos on the day he is going to be promoted. His boss wants to call the police, but Clemente quiets him down:

They will hate me, ignore me or curse me, but they will do nothing to have the 'white' man destroy me. You will notice they did not touch my face. Why? Because they will not spoil my day. They have a strange idea about la familia. The familia concept insists that we keep our things to ourselves. Our enemy, the 'white' man, will never have our support against one of us. (*Clemente* 58-59, cf. 53, 81, 121ff)

The protagonist being caught between Anglo and Mexican values is the main theme of the novel and is obvious in the quotation, too. At its beginning, Clemente looks at Mexican culture from the outside, from the position of his boss, the Anglos, and, we may assume, many readers: "They have a strange idea about la familia." However, immediately after judging Mexican American concepts as "strange," he switches his perspective and identifies with the "other" culture: *they* becomes *we*.

The pressure of the strict codes of behavior that the family imposes, and that is most apparent in Villarreal's novels (*Clemente, Horseman*) and in *Alhambra*, is not the only family characteristic that comes to the fore in the corpus. *Family* also signifies the togetherness, intimacy, and protection within a household, and the happiness of childhood: "when the family was happy, the house sang and the sofa played music" (*Rain*

God 125, cf. *Horseman* 360; *Barrio Boy* 11). The two facets—
codes of behavior and closeness—often condition each other.

> "You and him are pretty tight, are you? I mean, army and
> school, being cousins and all."
> "We're close, if that's what you mean. And, we're family."
> "Took you in as a kid, did they?"
> "Yeah; I was only five or six then . . . but it wasn't charity,
> Noddy. I mean, I was already family when I went there; do you
> know what I mean?" (*Rites* 50)

> . . . the women welcomed him with open arms and in the manner
> of women remembered every connection, every date important to
> the family, and filled him with tales of the history of the Inés
> clan. (*Horseman* 56f)

> "Just remember to have respect for your parents," Mama
> Chona told Miguel Chico and his cousins in her beautiful Span-
> ish, "and everything will be all right." (*Rain God* 163)

> . . . there's nothing more beautiful than the love between a man
> and a woman . . . and that love is freely expressed after marital
> vows. (*Victuum* 146)

The authority of the clan and the closely knit family, while
still functioning during the childhood of various protagonists
(e.g., in *Barrio Boy, Horseman, Hunger, Ultima,* or *Victuum*),
tend to be altered, if not disrupted, by forces which impose
themselves from the outside and which once again can be sub-
sumed under the heading of acculturation. The English-speaking school, the draft for Korea or Vietnam, and the social
pressure of a North American way of life—living in a city,
greater mobility, looser family ties[89]—lead to generational
conflicts and alienate the younger generation from traditional
Chicano family values.

Although the Spanish term *familia* is used in the corpus occasionally (see quotations from *Clemente* above and from *Rain
God* towards the end of this section), the texts generally label

---

89 See, e.g., *Clemente* 11, 125; *Cockroach* 25; *Hunger* 179-185; *Plum
Pickers* 73; *Ultima* 60f.

the social unit described here in English. The English term *family* thus acquires the connotations that the Spanish term *familia* tends to bear in the Mexican American context. In contrast to the nonstandard English forms mentioned in chapter seven, this form of Hispanicized English operates purely on the semantic level without implying any morphological or syntactic changes. It brings a cultural concept to the reader without touching the language surface.

Aside from the semantic Hispanization of the English term *family*, the semantic field of *family/familia* also contains many of the Spanish terms in the corpus. The most frequent ones are: *mamá, compadre, tío, comadre, papá, hijo, tía, familia, hermano, padrino*, and *primo* (see chapter 15). The terms of endearment *mamá* and *papá* appear a dozen times or more in some texts (*Plum Pickers, Ultima, Horseman, Victuum*),[90] and mostly in direct speech. The more formal expressions *madre* and *padre* are used very rarely and never connote a parent,[91] but form either part of interjections and swearwords (*madre mía, chinga tu madre*), or have religious or patriotic connotations (*Padre Hidalgo, Madre Purísima*). *Mamá* is the most often-used kinship term by far, and the only one that outnumbers its male counterpart. It appears much more frequently in the corpus than *papá*. As far as all the other terms belonging to this field are concerned, however, the male forms (*hijo, tío, compadre*) clearly have a stronger showing than their female equivalents (*comadre, tía, hija*, see chapter 15). This may be so because the male form can be used inclusively, but also because almost all authors, narrators, and central protagonists are male. At the same time, the fact that many of the novels

---

90 Since *Victuum* is one of the texts that does throughout without Spanish accents, the spelling of *papa* and *mama* alone does not reveal if the Spanish or the English form is meant. The expression "mi Mama" (87) points toward Spanish.

91 The exception that confirms that rule is: "His father always admonished him, 'With corn, mi hijo, with corn you live.' Yes. Sure. Corn nourishes, keeps whole tribes and nations alive. But where do you plant it? Where, padre?" (*Plum Pickers* 132).

show this male protagonist growing up or include his child-hood reminiscences may account for the primacy of *mamá*.

Kinship terms in Spanish, if they show any discernible function beyond their use as *formulas*, express—as in the opening quotation by Rodriguez—closeness between family members and can serve as intensifiers. This is, apart from *mamá* and *papá*, especially so for *primo* and *compadre*:

> She continued. "My stepfather is a good man."
> Clemente remembered the bloated taxi driver pimp. "Cipria-no?" he asked.
> "Yes," she said. "I call him Papá. I have taken his name since I never had one. My mother loves him very much." (*Clemente* 82f, cf. 77)

> ". . . it does my heart good to see an old compadre, an old vaquero." (*Ultima* 214)

> Serafina beside herself, smiling and pleased at all the pleasure her company, her compadres and compatriotas were giving her. (*Plum Pickers* 68)

Horseman never uses *compadre* as an intensifier, but employs it always detachedly to designate the "compadre Urbina," a relative of Pancho Villa (215, 274, 276, etc.). *Primo*, on the other hand, has a part in the celebration of male friendship that pervades that novel:

> "Primo," said Heraclio, and he was embarrassed to call him cousin, almost as if he was now accepting him as an Inés, and embarrassed also that now, when he needed help, he was being intimate with a man whose table he had shared. . . . (188)

> He placed a hand on the man's arm with kindness, almost tenderly. "Thank you for your courage and for your selflessness, mi primo. Let us have one drink or two. . . ." (190)

The treatment of both *primo* and *compadre* in the corpus is not restricted to relatives. Given their intrinsic connotation of closeness, which Galarza uses for an ironic comment in his glossary—"two adult males may bestow the honorary title of *compadre* on each other in an excess of fondness, especially when drunk"—, the two terms can be applied as intensifiers when asking for a favor or in order to persuade somebody. Tenorio, a character in *Ultima*, employs *compadre* when he tries to talk sense into Lupito, who runs amuck: "It is me, hombre, your compadre. Listen my friend" (19). A landlord in *Alhambra* who attempts to convince a reluctant client to take an apartment brings in *cousin*, the English equivalent to *primo*, for additional endorsement:

> See the bedroom? It hardly needs paint, but for you, compadre—You say you're from Albuquerque? I have a cousin there. He loves it. Wonderful people, he says. I'm from Chihuahua. Almost a blood brother. (14)

The landlord tries to make a bond by insinuating that he and his customers might be, however remotely, *familia*.

Arturo Islas's novel *Rain God*, which includes a chapter entitled "Compadres and Comadres," uses *mama* frequently, but only three times in the accented Spanish form. In one instance, it bridges the gap created by *fictitious Spanish*:

> "But Mamá," Jesus Maria began in the elegant Spanish she had learned from Mama Chona, "how can you . . ." (166)

In another it functions as an intensifier:

> "Come on, Mother, say it again," Magdalena pleaded.
> "*No seas malcriada*," Angie said and waved her hand close to Lena's cheek.
> "No, Ma, not in Spanish. Say it in English." Lena and her summer boyfriend were on the front porch . . . Every night at exactly nine-thirty, Angie went to the screen door behind them and said, "Magdah-leen, kahm een." Lena shrieked with delight; the sad boyfriend smiled apprehensively.
> "Oh, Mamá, just a few more minutes." She said "mamá" in the Spanish way.
> "No, *señorita*, Joo mas kahm een rye now." More howls, as the boy said an embarrassed good night and slipped from the swing and the porch into the dark. Lena barely noticed. She was too taken up by her mother, whom she adored. (*Rain God* 119f)

Magdalena does not share Rodriguez's scruples about using English terms of address for her mother (see quotation above 154-55). But the moment she wants a favor from her, she resorts to the Spanish form of endearment. The authoritarian and yet ironic quality of *señorita* in Angie's answer distinguishes this word, too, from its *cliché* use elsewhere in the corpus (*Barrio Boy* 150; *Horseman* 70, 95; *Victuum* 202).

The subtlety with which Islas treats Spanish entries is also manifest in the most magical and most realist part of *Rain God*, the final pages, which include the third occurrence of *mamá*. They show the last years of Mama Chona, the head of her clan, who still cultivates a "beautiful Spanish" (163) and personifies traditional Spanish-Mexican values but has not been able to prevent the deterioration of these values—nor of the Spanish language—in the generations that follow hers (142). In her old age she acquires mythical dimensions. When she wanders through the apartment at night searching for her lost children, she becomes an implicit reference to the legend of *La Llorona* that is treated explicitly in other texts of the corpus and that also appears in Spanish and bilingual Chicano novels.[92] Mama Chona disintegrates as a woman and as a mother. She loses her uterus, an experience that she perceives as a childbirth (176). At the end of the novel, her entire family, including her dead son Felix, are gathered around her deathbed, and the nit-picking and petty animosities make it clear that it is only because of her that they are still together. With her death, her *familia* will cease to exist, too. Islas, who otherwise uses relatively little Spanish, uses three Spanish words within the last lines of his "Autumn of the Matriarch":

> The old woman looked at them for the last time.
>   Even Felix had finally come to visit her. He was standing between Miguel Chico and JoEl. She reached out to them but was unable to lift her arms.
>   Miguel Chico felt the Rain God come into the room.

---

92 See *Barrio Boy* 43; *Buffalo* 87; *Clemente* 91; *Tortuga* 66, 67, 101, etc.; *Ultima* 23, 26, 72. Cf. Brito 20, Cota-Cárdenas 90ff.

—Let go of my hand, Mama Chona. I don't want to die.
"*La familia,*" she said.
Felix walked toward her out of the shadows. "Mamá," he
called in a child's voice that startled her.
"All right," she said to the living in the room, "if you want
to, you can cry a little bit."
To Felix, she said, "Where have you been, *malcriado*?" He
took her in his arms. He smelled like the desert after a rainstorm.
(179f)

Rain God uses much less Spanish than, say, *Barrio Boy*,
Clemente, or *Louise*, and does not make Spanish entries stand
out through frequent repetition either, as is the case, for
example, with *jinete* and *rurales* in *Horseman*, or *Ave María
Purísima* and *curandera* in *Ultima*. Instead, Islas uses some
Spanish words as keywords which appear a few times in the
novel, in different contexts, and with different values, and
may moreover be commented upon explicitly. *Mamá, malcriado, chile, comadre, compadre,* and *sinvergüenza*, are thus
enriched with meaning during the novel. *Familia*, on the other
hand, has the function of linking the beginning of the text with
its end. The reader learns about Mama Chona's death at the
very start of *Rain God*: "On her deathbed, surrounded by her
family, she recognized Miguel Chico and said, *la familia*, in
an attempt to bring him back into the fold" (5). And since the
novel deals extensively with the different characters and the
different facets of the protagonist family, it also fills *familia*
with meaning and significance between the first and the second
(and last) appearance of the word.

The ending of *Rain God* is not only effective because it
brings together *familia, Mamá,* and *malcriado*, which have
become meaningful in the course of the novel, but also because three English keywords that have gone through the same
process of acquiring meaning along the novel come together in
the last sentence, too: "smelled," "desert," and "rainstorm"
are part of a network of associations in the text: The title of
the novel is *Rain God*, the subtitle *A Desert Tale*, one chapter
is entitled "Rain Dancer," another "The Rain God." The desert is an essential setting and theme (4, 6, 8, 34, 40, 48, 50,

56 113f, 137, etc.). Smells are important (18, 132, 145, 153). The three elements "smell," "desert," and "rainstorm" (and more generally "rain" or "water") already appear combined before in the novel: " 'They're coming. I smell them' . . . 'The angels' . . . From then on, JoEl could tell them when it was going to rain" (114); or "Felix loved those quiet moments at dusk as much as the smell of the desert just before and after a thunderstorm" (ibid.). Moreover, one or several of these elements are also used in the context of death: Felix is murdered in the desert (18, 137) and Tony drowns (47). Smelling, water, and death also are combined in the sentence: "smelling her hair and feeling her voice of truth moist on his ear, love and death came together for Miguel Chico and he was not from then on able to think of one apart from the other" (19). It is this richness of the textual fabric which makes Islas's novel one of the most compelling texts in the corpus.

High Impact Terms: Swearing and Sex

Spanish swearwords appear in all the texts except for *Hunger*. Spanish entries that include the Mexican verb *chingar* and its derivatives, for instance, show up in two-thirds of the texts, in most of them repeatedly. Their list is extensive and includes *single words, short entries, long entries,* and one *song*:

A chingao. (*Clemente* 70)

A chingar la muerte! Let us go fuck death. (*Horseman* 210)

A la chingada. (*Ultima* 198, *Alhambra* 79)

Al ratito me la pagas, perro hijo de la chingada. (*Clemente* 140)

Bien haya, chingao. (*Rites* 108)

chinga (*Horseman* 113; *Alhambra* 42)

Chinga tu madre, cabron! (*Buffalo* 119)

¡Chinga tu madre! · (*Ultima* 124)

Chinga'o (*Louise* 112)

chingada (*Ultima* 32f, 102f, 138f, 144, 147, 150, 185f, 200, 203, 209, 230; *Alhambra* 47; *Victuum* 106; 107, 110)

Chingado (*Victuum* 12, 32, 107)

Chingados! (*Alhambra* 124)

chingando la verga some goddam place. (*Rites* 108)

Chingao (*Tortuga* 51)

Chingao no a venido aquella, andará con el Sancho. (*Louise* 104)

Chingasos (*Tortuga* 155)

chingazos (*Louise* 56)

chingo (*Louise* 79)

chingón (*Tamazunchale* 112; *Cockroach* 104)

. . . what was left out was 'de la chingada' or 'of a bitch.' (*Valley* 88)

Denle sus chingazos. (*Clemente* 56)

. . . desgraciado hijo de tu maldita chingada. (*Plum Pickers* 113)

¡Dile que si no le gusta, que se vaya a la chingada! (*Buffalo* 191)

En el camino a esa ciudad mentada
En un domingo por la noche con nubarrón
Estos rinches texanos de la chingada
Mataron a más mexicanos del Galvestón. (*Rites* 110)

Eso, chingao. (*Rites* 108)

The grandfather-chingada of all headaches. (*Alhambra* 47).

. . . gringo güero heroes hijos de la chingada . . . (*Plum Pickers* 127)

. . . gringo güeros chingados . . . (*Plum Pickers* 43)

. . . gringo hijos de la chingada . . . (*Plum Pickers* 45, 94)

Hijo de la chingada bruja! (*Ultima* 241)

¡Hijo de la chingada cabronada maldita que fue la pendeja que te crió you bastard! (*Plum Pickers* 130)

¡—Hijo de tu chingada! (*Ultima* 153)

hijos de la chingada. (*Alhambra* 42, 48, *Plum Pickers* 152, 155)

Me cantaba por chingazos. (*Louise* 112)

. . . *no estés chingando* . . . (*Valley* 68)

¿No puedes hacer callar esa criatura, Rosalba? ¡Con una chingada! (*Clemente* 25)

. . . para acabar la chingada . . . (*Plum Pickers* 70)

¡Pinches, cabrones, hijos de la chingada! (*Cockroach* 19)

Vengo más cansao que la chingada. (*Clemente* 153)

¡Vieja hija de la chingada! (ibid. 26)

¡Ya chingamos! (ibid. 25)

Yo soy Guadalupe Jiménez Rodríguez, un arriero. No esté chingando. (*Louise* 37)

Octavio Paz treats *chingar* lyrically and lucidly in his essay "Los hijos de la Malinche." Roberto Galván and Richard Teschner, on the other hand, seem to have some difficulties in defining the term and its derivatives in their dictionary of Chicano Spanish. They translate *chingar* as "to copulate (etc.); to cheat, to avenge; to defeat (in a contest)" and render the meaning of *Hijo de la chingada madre* as "interj. (strongest and most vulg. interj. possible) 'XXXXXXX XXXX.' " It is not astonishing, therefore, that the authors of the corpus, while using Spanish words and expressions that include the stem *ching-* abundantly, tend to leave these terms untranslated.

Chingar is not the only Mexican swearword that appears frequently in the corpus. Similar, though shorter, lists could be made with *cabrón, pinche, pendejo*, and their derivatives. The texts with the highest rating of Spanish swearwords are *Clemente, Louise, Plum Pickers, Rites, Ultima, Victuum*, and the two novels of Acosta (*Buffalo, Cockroach*). Since swearwords belong to the least translated semantic fields and include many *hermetic entries*, they function as euphemisms of sorts for monolingual readers and can create a similar impression as the one Delgado's protagonist experiences in the reverse situation:

> I could hear the gringos cussing at me,
> —You stupid sonofabitch, stupid Mexican.— I thought they
> were complimenting me on my speed and dexterity. (*Louise* 68)

The euphemistic function of swearwords is especially effective in *Ultima* and *Victuum*, where the offensive Spanish entries contrast with the rather inoffensive English registers in which they are embedded.[93] In the other novels mentioned, Spanish swearwords are accompanied by English counterparts of about the same caliber. Yet in these novels, too, the monolingual readers, though they may gather from the context that a Spanish entry is offensive, are left at odds about its exact meaning, and Chicano characters are not necessarily helpful either, if an Anglo asks them to translate a swearword:

> "Regular Army, *cabrón.*"
> "What does *that* mean? You and Joey and Sonny are *always* saying that ... and now you got Frank doing it too. ...."
> "Aw, it's just a word ... it doesn't mean anything . . ."

---

93 *Victuum* includes the offensive *single words burro, cabron, cabrona, caca, chichi, chifletera, chingada, chingado, cochina, diablo, fundillo, mierda, pendeja, puta*. In bilingual New Mexico, the fact that *Ultima* employs offensive language mainly in Spanish has not prevented it from being banned from a class in cultural humanities by the Bloomfield school board in 1981. "By some reports, the book was even burned. Anaya said the overt reason for the book's banning was 'parents' objections to language' in the book" ("Banned").

"Yes it does; what's it mean?"
"Well, sometimes it means ass hole; in a nice way. . . . You know . . ." (*Rites* 91)

The most frequently used Mexican swearwords have sexual connotations either originally (*chingar*) or as euphemisms (*cabrón, pendejo*). In many cases, however, their frequent use as offensive terms or interjections has rendered their sexual connotations secondary or entirely negligible. This is true for Mexican (American) society as well as for the novels of the corpus. Nevertheless, the sexual connotations are still dominant in the case of some less abundantly used Spanish entries:

> With us was a woman from Caracas who enlightened us with a few of the Caraguians' terms for sex organs. She claimed "cuchara," a spoon, was the term for the female sex organ. I made a contribution by saying how New Mexicans refer to a sort of cookie as "panocha." We in Texas and Mexico think of a "panocha" as a "cuchara." One afternoon one of the secretaries in the Colorado Migrant Council where I was director brought up quite a chuckle as she offered me "panocha." Since I had been without a woman for many months I didn't think her offer was merely a cookie. (*Louise* 40-41)

Whereas Delgado comments explicitly on Spanish euphemisms, some other Chicano novelists who write in English seem to have come to a tacit agreement to include in their work at least one euphemism, obscene joke, or sexual allusion hidden amongst the nontranslated Spanish entries —a Spanish insider pun, a private joke for the bilingual, that is, for the Chicano readership.

The expression "a la veca" or "ah la veca" is used often by the kids that surround Antonio, the protagonist of *Ultima* (34, 102, 138f, 145, 149, 198, 200). The context suggests that it is a swearword. However, when Miss Violet, the teacher, wants to know its meaning, she gets the answer "It means okay!" (145, cf. Dasenbrock 15f) Since *veca* is not listed in any Spanish or Mexican dictionary, the translation offered by the kids is the only one available, and the only clue to the Spanish term—unless one notices the one instance in which *veca* is spelled differently. On page 139, after it has appeared in its usual form twice, it is used a third time, at a moment where the reader is bound to concentrate on the tension that is built up in the text and to overlook the different spelling:

> "She blinded a man!" Abel nodded vigorously.
> "How?"
> "Witchcraft—"
> "Ah la verga—"
> They were around me now, looking at me. The circle was tight and quiet. Around us the playground was one jarring, humming noise, but inside the circle it was quiet. (139)

Any Spanish dictionary will inform those who do not overlook the one instance of changed spelling, that the kids have lied to Miss Violet, that *veca* does not mean "okay," that *Verga* is no Mexican Spanish word for *mountain* either, as Hinojosa's suggestive pun "the tip of the ice-verga" (*Rites* 28) seems to indicate, but a general Spanish word for penis, and an *etymological pair* to *verge*. Hinojosa uses *verga* a second time in *Rites* without translating it: ". . . chingando la verga some goddam place" (108).

Other hidden euphemisms in *Ultima* are: "my father came whistling up the goat path . . . and we ran to meet him. 'Cabritos!' he called. 'cabroncitos!'" (42) and: "'And what is Purgatory?' / 'Purga,' Abel whispered. The boys giggled." (192) The effect is difficult to reproduce in a translation. This may be the reason why Tonn, in his translation of *Ultima*, leaves *cabritos* and *cabroncitos* in Spanish and renders the second example as: "'Und was ist das Fegefeuer?' / 'Da fegt der Schornsteinfeger', flüsterte Abel" (176).

Carmela, one of the protagonists in *Tamazunchale*, is not too familiar with Spanish, and misquotes a word her uncle uses:

> "I told you, it's chicha. They drink it in Peru . . . something like pulque."
> "Tío, be serious. Why would that . . . chichi be here?"
> "Chicha." (61)

The alteration of the final Spanish vowel, a regular phenomenon in native English speakers, leads here to an involuntary semantic change: *chicha* is a beverage, *chichi* means 'tit.'

What is common to the Spanish puns quoted so far is that they are, for one thing, presented in a way that facilitates overlooking them, and that for another, the sexual allusion is not essential to the argument of the novel. Anyone who fails to notice it misses a joke, an insider pun, but no essential portion of the argument.

Rain God builds a different and more elaborate scheme around a Spanish euphemism. At the center of the section "Chile" stands a dinner of spicy *chile jalapeño* at Nina's and Ernesto's place, an ordeal that only their friend El Compa, their son Antony, and Nina herself can handle:

> "Let me tell you a joke I heard about chile," El Compa said one winter evening as they sat down to eat.
> "Is it dirty?" Juanita asked.
> "No, comadre, would I tell a dirty joke in front of you?"
> "That's what my husband always says before he goes ahead and tells one."
> "Leave him alone, Juanita. Go on, Compa, tell it. I love stories about chiles," Nina said with a little girl's smile on her face. She could be salacious without being obscene and Juanita watched her carefully because she wanted to learn that talent. Juanita's best friend Lola, who was married to El Compa, had the same skill.
> "I'm not talking about that kind of chile," El Compa said. "I'm talking about the kind we're eating."
> "Go on, get it over with," Tony said, resigned to having to listen to another bad joke.
> "Well, there was this gringo who was in Mexico for the first time. At a restaurant he ordered a mole poblano that was real hot. I mean hot, hotter than this." (37-38)

By insinuating that *chile* can be used with sexual connotations, and not clarifying them, Islas points out the insider pun to the reader and pushes her or him to consult a Mexican dictionary. At the same time, the word *chile*, which in a North American context evokes mainly Mexican or Southwestern cuisine, experiences a process of enrichment in the chapter that bears its name. It is used in its *cliché* function as a spicy dish, appears as a euphemism, and is moreover a personal symbol for some of the characters, with differing value for each of them. Since the use of Spanish words as keywords in *Rain God* has already been commented upon more than once, I need not go into further detail here. Suffice it to say that *chile* becomes a polysemous signifier which leaves the reader not with a stereotype of the Mexican culture, or with the simple subversion of that stereotype, but with a complex picture.

Ethnographic Terms: Rural Life

The (mostly Mexican-)Spanish terms that refer to life in the rural areas of Mexico are more unevenly distributed over the Chicano novels in English than the terms of the other three semantic fields treated in this chapter. While they show up in many texts sporadically, and *Tamazunchale, Clemente, Louise,* and *Ultima* include them with a certain frequency, they appear most often by far in *Barrio Boy* and in the almost two hundred pages that make up the "First Book" of *Horseman* called "Hacienda de la Flor." Since *Barrio Boy* has already been treated extensively, Villarreal's text will serve to illustrate their use.

"Hacienda de la Flor" deals with everyday life on a Mexican hacienda in the times of Porfirio Díaz. The hierarchical structure, organization, and administration of the estate are described as are different kinds of farm work, clothes and tools, funerary and festive rituals. The detached descriptive prose and the amount of detailed information in passages like the following have their literary predecessors—Matthew Bramble's letter of Oct. 11 in Tobias Smollet's *The Expedition of Humphry Clinker* (1771) is a curious early example—, but would also fit perfectly into a textbook on Mexican agrarian history:

> Because it was almost entirely self-sufficient, it was necessary that the estate be so large. Although la Flor was not agricultural,

> it was imperative that there be a good-sized acreage of tillable soil. This was located south and west of the main buildings. Directly south, the Tecolote Mountains, the entire range completely within the hacienda proper yielded stone, lime, and other minerals for the small open hearth. From the north, beyond the grazing lands which immediately surrounded the main part of the hacienda, clay for adobe, wild herbs, and salt abounded! Eastward, in the foothills barely visible, were small forests which supplied timber, and beyond that was rocky wasteland, mountain land where the hacienda's seventy-five thousand sheep grazed. (25)

The attempt at rendering an authentic image of rural Mexico before and during the Revolution manifests itself not only on the thematic, but also on the linguistic level. Most Spanish entries, with the exception of a *corrido* stanza (see above 139-40) and a small number of short formulas (*buenos días, buenas noches, qué tal, mucho gusto*), are *single words* which do not render a *description* of the historical object, but *represent* it, are part of it. They do not *refer* to history: they *are* history. However, they can be integrated into a descriptive historical discourse through explanation or translation: " '*Cuaco!*' that word for horse which also means *move!*" (9), or:

> The *encomienda* was a protectorate, as the word implied, and a worthy Spaniard—usually one who had performed a service to the king, or a relative, or a bankrupt member of the court—was given an extensive area to protect. They owned the land and lived as lords, but the life and soul of every Indian within their domain was their responsibility. (80, cf. 20, 31)

This explanatory way of dealing with foreign words, which can be found in fictional and factual texts from Christopher Columbus's diary (Colón: *canoa* 122, 133, *aje* 139, 147) to Cooper's *The Last of the Mohicans* (12), Ernesto Galarza's *Barrio Boy*, and other texts of the corpus, is not the norm in *Horseman*. Although Villarreal uses much explanatory and anthropological discourse *outside* Spanish entries, he prefers to bring in Mexicanisms without explicitly explaining or translating them.[94] He creates a less didactic and more aesthetically

---

94 See, e.g., *tamales* and *alcaide* (120); *tacos, birria,* and *antojitos* (144); *jaripeo* (161); and *vaquero* (179); cf. *Clemente* 23.

oriented literary discourse than Galarza. This discourse cannot be found in historiography,[95] but stands in the *costumbrismo* tradition. The dominant semantic subfields are food (*antojitos, tacos, tamales, menudo, birria, aguardiente, tequila*), clothing (*huarache, sarape*), housing (*adobe, choza, jacal, zaguán*), horsemanship (*reata, jinete, vaquero*) and administration (*alcaide, rurales*). Some of these terms are of Nahuatl origin; most of them are linked to Mexican rural culture, to the life of the vaquero. As words and as the material objects they stand for, they are historical tokens that belong to a certain region, to a certain society, to a certain time. In those cases where the author refuses to translate or to explain them, a tension is created between their exotic form (as words) that attracts the reader and the reader's difficulty in understanding them. Their meaning has to be constructed with the help of the context or of a *diccionario de mejicanismos*. Whereas a scientific and explanatory discourse appeals mainly to the intellect, their primary appeal is a sensual one.[96] However, an intellectual effort is required in order to give meaning to these exotic elements.

---

95 Unless one compares the Mexicanisms in *Horseman* with the Latinisms in scholarly historical texts. The important difference is that Latinisms represent the humanist tradition and stem from a cultural elite, whereas *vaquero* jargon comes from a nonliterary background and has entered literature in local-color fiction and *costumbrismo*. The *otherness* that Latinisms intrinsically convey is that of a model to follow, while that of the vaquero tends to be anthropologically connoted.

96 Mexican vernacular and Spanglish entries may be put to similar use in the Chicano novel in Spanish. They form part, for example, of one of the various discourses of Elizondo's *Muerte en una estrella:* "Al Alafa le gustaba platicar donde fuera: si estaba en las piscas de tomate en Ohio se acordaba de Texas; y si estaba en Texas era porque allá les contaba de Ohio y era cuento de nunca acabar, pero al Alafa no le faltaba de qué platicar. . . . En el Rincón del Diablo había por las calles lagunas de agua verdosa que eran más viejas que muchos de los que vivían por ay. Lagua nomás se movía despacio cuando pasaban las trocas, como que se veían color champurrado nomás meciéndose y luego como que sin ganas se calmaban sin hacer mucha ola, ni los zancudos se criaban en esa agua. Pero pos ni modo, ay vivía la gente y ay tenían sus casitas" (53).

The author can reduce this effort—bring the text to the reader, that is—by using a word repeatedly. *Jinete* and *vaquero*, for instance, are used frequently enough in *Horseman* to become familiar to the reader; *molcajete*, *jaripeo*, and *birria*, on the other hand, can gain their meaning from only one context and require more of an effort from the reader.

From a standpoint outside the American Southwest, the use of Hispanicisms in "Hacienda de la Flor" can be interpreted as a question of jargon and dialect, rather than as a question of Spanish versus English. For one thing, quite a few terms are of Aztec and not of peninsular origin; for another, and more importantly, words like *huarache, reata*, and *sarape* have become part of the English language of the American Southwest as *loanwords*. They are familiar to the population on both sides of the Mexican-U.S. border, but unfamiliar to the New Englander as well as to the Paraguayan. Their literary function is similar to that of the *gaucho* vocabulary in Argentinian *costumbrismo*. Within the context of the Southwest, on the other hand, Villarreal's novel may be read differently. Because Mexicanisms are familiar to the population in the Southwest, they function less as exotic elements. They are not neutral terms either but can, depending on who uses them or who reads them, denote either identification with or contempt for the traditional Hispanic way of life in the region. They belong in the field of tension between English and Spanish, between the United States and Mexico, between the North and the South.

One effect of the Mexican Spanish vocabulary in *Horseman* works in the context of the Southwest as well as for an international audience. "Hacienda de la Flor" rewrites mainstream history. It can be related to two fictional models, one Hispanic, the other Anglo American. First, it is rooted in the tradition of *costumbrismo* literature. Secondly, it depicts a lifestyle that has become famous as an essential part of the Anglo American heritage through Western novels and movies. On the one hand are *Martín Fierro* and *Don Segundo Sombra*, on the other Zane Grey and John Wayne. *Horseman* combines the two traditions. It is a novel written in English and published in the United States that presents Hispanics as cowboys. It rewrites the history of the Southwest and redefines terms like *rancho, corral*, and *rodeo*, which have become an integral part of the American English vocabulary and are marketed as cultural elements of the Anglo American Southwest.[97]

For reasons which I have explained elsewhere ("Fifth Horseman"), *Horseman* does not come off as a novel of the Mexican Revolution and is an utterly misogynist text. I cannot agree with Bruce-Novoa's positing the protagonist as a positive figure of identification for the modern Chicano (*Authors* 38). The rewriting of an all-American myth and the "deterritorialization" of the Anglo American language (cf. Deleuze and Guattari 24-39) in "Hacienda de la Flor" are the novel's most subversive and most convincing gestures—stylistically as well as politically.

---

97 Cf.: " 'Papa, this magazine is written in Spanish and all the pictures are about cowboys . . . Papa, are there Mexican cowboys?' / 'Why, of course . . . the Mexican was the first cowboy here in the West, they were called Vaqueros. The Mexican taught foreigners, the gringos, how to rope and guide the steer. The southwest was full of cattle ranches; the Southwest was Northern Mexico, you might say. Why, everyone spoke Spanish . . . it wasn't until those pioneers, or shall I say pirateers, from back East started trodding upon this land, that we began to speak English. You see, this is why I always speak Spanish; it actually is the Southwest's native tongue! . . . After the Indians, of course!' / 'But, Papa none of the cowboys I see . . . like Tom Corbit, Lone Ranger . . . none of them speak Spanish!' / 'Because . . . the movie industry has made a flimsy fraud of what really occurred during the wild-West days . . . why, it's disgusting how they insult a person's intelligence . . . it's ridiculous . . . the bad guy dressed in black . . . the good guy dressed in white . . . the men of the old West . . . were dirty, dusty smelly, foul-mouthed creatures creeping behind a rock ready to shoot you for small change . . . there was nothing but constant killing. . . . The Hollywood version is an out and out lie' " (*Victuum* 114).

Culinary Terms

Mexican culinary terms are, as a subgroup of the ethnographic category and the rural life context, important enough to be treated separately. They occur in all the texts except for *Hunger* and *Tattoo*. Their list is large and various and ranges from internationally known Mexican dishes like *chile, tacos,* or *tortilla,* to dishes that are less widely known, like *birria, polvorones,* or *morcilla,* and to beverages like *atole, mezcal, pulque,* or *tequila* (see chapter 14.4). The most frequent of these terms are *tortilla, tamales, tequila, menudo, enchilada,* and *tacos* (see chapter 15). In a few instances terms from this semantic field serve as folkloric stereotypes. *Tequila,* for example, is presented by Galarza as the responsible agent in turning a celebration of the Sixteenth of September into a fight (*Barrio Boy* 241f). *Tequila* also emphasizes—when drunk in a gulp or from the bottle—the manliness of Villarreal's heroes (*Clemente* 43f; *Horseman* 111-14). *Menudo* repeatedly shows efficiency as a hangover cure (*Cockroach* 41; *Rain God* 151ff; *Victuum* 13, 201; *Horseman* 259). By the same token, culinary terms can also have different and more complex functions, as we have already seen with *chile* in the context of sexually connoted puns (see above 170-71), and as *tortilla,* the most frequent of all the Spanish entries in the corpus, may further exemplify.

Tortilla, either on its own or in combinations like *tortilla de harina* or *tortillas duras,* appears in all the texts except for *Hunger, Rites,* and *Tattoo,* and is one of the most frequently repeated Spanish entries in *Alhambra, Barrio Boy* (more than forty times), *Buffalo, Louise,* and *Plum Pickers.* It is seldom used as a neutral term; most authors employ it as a token of Mexican identity that implies a value judgment. Acosta's *Buffalo* correlates *tortillas* most explicitly and most tangibly with Hispanic identity. When he tries to recover from a hash-wine-acid hangover in the kitchen of an Anglo stranger, he spots the reminder "Tortillas from Bishops" and the message "Jose, the pickles are hot" among other scotch-taped notes on the refrigerator (165). His reaction, which makes identity appear as a clearly fenced-off territory, lives up to Oedipa Maas's paranoia in Pynchon's *Crying of Lot 49*:

> But where does he get that *tortillas* shit? Jesus, isn't anything sacred anymore? And the *Jose*-bit? What is he up to? This is my territory, you pale-face sonofabitch! And does the "hot" on the pickles really mean *chile curtidos*? Is this another euphemism from the pussy-assed liberals? Do you really eat hot sauce? . . . Or are they merely being nice to me, their prisoner? Are they preparing for some giant put-on? (166)

Only *Alhambra* presents Mexican food in general, and *tortillas* in particular, throughout as cheap, inferior nourishment. *Tortillas* are food for cats and birds (52, 69, 71); a "sandwich of ham" offers "a welcome change from the tortillas and frijoles at home" (36); and the stomach of one of the central characters "seemed forever hungry, unfulfilled by beans and tortillas and chili" (176).[98] In the other texts, *tortillas* appear as inexpensive, but not for that reason inferior, food:

> They were more often in worse shape than we were, but they never failed to give us a bundle of tortillas duras which my grandma turned into chilaquiles after soaking them in water and frying them with chile. (*Louise* 35)

> . . . the flat, round tortilla bread was the only thing we had tasted of home in a long time. . . . I smiled and tasted Ismelda's fragrance in her warm tortilla bread. (*Tortuga* 64)

> On weekends the four of them went to nightclubs across the border, danced all night, and acted like the rich gringos who lived on the hill. At the end of every month the money they spent so lavishly was gone, and they were content to go to each others' houses and play casino after the evening supper of beans and tortillas. (*Rain God* 59)

---

98 Cf.: "I go home and it's good ol' beans staring at me right in the face . . . morning . . . noon and night . . . fried, boiled . . . mashed with cheese . . . you name it . . . but they're beans!" (*Victuum* 210)

Tortillas provide Antonio, the protagonist in *Ultima*, with a painful experience when he opens his lunch box at school: "My mother had packed a small jar of hot beans and some good, green chile wrapped in tortillas. When the other children saw my lunch they laughed and pointed again" (54). However, he himself does not see *tortillas* as a worthless dish. Mexican food, which in school separates him from the Anglo community, makes for happiness and togetherness at home: "The hot beans flavored with chicos and green chile were muy sabrosos. I was so hungry that I ate three whole tortillas. My mother was a good cook and we were happy as we ate" (39).

Ernesto Galarza, the author-narrator-protagonist of *Barrio Boy*, who otherwise often paints a primitivist picture of Mexican culture (see above 135-138), subverts cliché views of Mexican food as primitive and inferior. His minute description of how his aunt prepares *tortillas* transcends local color and converts a daily routine into an act of art, the women who make *tortillas* into artists:

> Doña Esther was already at the *comal*, making the fresh supply of tortillas for the day. She plucked small lumps, one by one, from the heap of corn dough she kept in a deep clay pot. She gave the lump a few squeezes to make a thick, round biscuit which she patted and pulled and clapped into a thin disk. The corncake grew larger and larger until it hung in loose ruffles around her hands. She spread her fingers wide to hold the thin, pale folds of dangling dough which looked as if they might drop off in pieces any moment. As she clapped she gave her wrists a half turn, making the tortilla tilt between each tat-tat of her palms. On each twist the tortilla seemed to slip loose but she would clamp it gently for another tat-tat. When the tortilla was thin and round and utterly floppy, she laid it on the comal. My aunt worked on the next tortilla as she turned those already on the griddle, nipping them by the edge with her fingernails and flipping them over fast. When they browned in spots, she nipped them again and dropped them into the *chiquihuite*, covering them with a napkin to keep them hot. (28)

The preparation of *tortillas* appears in various texts. Other authors are generally less elaborate about it than Galarza—Islas describes the making of *capirotada* at length (133)—, but also go beyond local coloring by describing it in affectionate, poetic, or ritualistic terms, and thus creating privileged moments. The emotionally marked language and the many adjectives that surround the Spanish term evoke in most cases happy moments of the past, the childhood of the protagonist, a world where Mexican values prevailed. The protagonist never prepares the *tortillas* her- or himself. They are always prepared by a woman. She may be the protagonist's niece:

> Fausto watched her place a large flour tortilla on the skillet. Then she removed the square vegetable grater from the nail above the breadbox. Carefully, without losing a shred, she grated a small block of jack cheese onto the middle of the tortilla. (*Tamazunchale* 54)

or his former lover:

> She was preparing breakfast for the two men, very carefully rolling out flour tortillas and cooking them on the griddle. "You eat your lousy bread and for them you make tortillas. You'll never learn." (*Leaving Home* 205)

In most texts, however, the male protagonist observes how an older member of his family—his aunt, his grandmother, or his mother—makes *tortillas:*

> . . . my old ma was busy at work making the tortillas at 5:00 A.M. . . . A shrill, foggy whistle woke us to the odors of crackling wood in the cast iron stove cooking the perfectly rounded, soft, warm tortillas. (*Buffalo* 72)

> I choose to recall some of the food tastes I acquired as a child and how they were prepared with so much love and taste by my abuela or mother. (*Louise* 52, cf. *Rain God* 132)

The use of *tortilla* in the corpus is striking for two reasons. First, this stereotypical token of Mexico is seldom presented from the outside. The authors do not opt for an anthropological presentation, but for a personal and intimate discourse. The intense and affectionate language that surrounds the word turns these scenes into privileged moments in the life of each protagonist.[99] On the other hand, the thematic coincidence, the repetition of similar scenes in various novels, converts these moments into a significant element of the Chicano experience. The question of whether the scenes described have any concrete autobiographical background becomes secondary in face of the statistical evidence. According to Deleuze and Guattari, every "minority text" has an exemplary, collective value (25); and in this case, the recurrence of strikingly similar privileged moments in different texts strengthens that exemplariness.

Maybe the most opulent culinary and verbal feast, which moreover includes a sideswipe at American food, can be found in *Plum Pickers*:

> Maíz. . . . Out of corn can come so many good things, tortillas, thin, round, suntoasted, and substantive. Tortillas have weight and substance. They are thin and heavy, not like those puffy white slices of spongy fluff called white bread. Lupe remembered her aged grandmother in Salpinango making tortillas solemnly, flap flap endlessly with her palms, pat pat with flying fingers, and then, on special occasions, turning tortillas into crisp fold-overs for tacos. Or rolled over a cheese or bean filling for enchiladas, thin and long and soft and rich and spicy with chile. And the masa from corn meal for tamales, ay ay ay, also for spe-

---

99 *Tortilla* is not the only Mexican food that helps to create privileged moments: "We had some tripitas, which I loved then and miss now" (*Louise* 46). The protagonist of *Leaving Home*, when he goes back to Mexico after years in the States, cries out: "this is coffee! Good coffee, how I missed it" (230). *Chile* appears in more than half of the novels analyzed, in *Alhambra* always in the Anglicized form *chili*, in *Buffalo* occasionally. It is often and stereotypically presented as an extremely spicy food that only a chosen few can handle (*Rain God* 36; *Cockroach* 37; *Buffalo* 75, 124, 140; *Louise* 104). It tends to be accompanied by qualifying adjectives or used in composite forms: *red*, *yellow*, or *green chile*, *chile peppers*, *chile relleno*, *chile pequín*, etc. In *Ultima* green and red chile appear repeatedly together, the latter almost always ritualistically accompanied by the Spanish term *ristra* and by intensifying adjectives: "The hot beans flavored with chicos and green chile were muy sabrosos . . . there is plenty of red chile for making ristras" (39). "Green chile was roasted and dried, and red chile was tied into colorful ristras" (47, cf. 131, 136).

cial feasts. Thick, fat, plump, and tender, flavored with hot spicy meat, tamales were wrapped in corn husks to be steamed long and lovingly in huge ollas. Those finger-licking foods that had filled her childhood days with happy joys brought a poignant tear of frustration to her eyes now and then. (*Plum Pickers* 123, cf. 68, 188)

The exuberant verbal celebration ends on a tone of resignation. Childhood has passed, acculturation has taken place. The memory of the *tortillas* prepared by the mother, the grandmother, another family member, or a lover, is a key element in the protagonists' longing for the closeness of the family, childhood happiness, and youth. Like the 'mother tongue' Spanish (see chapter 4), and characterized with the same range of adjectives ("soft," "warm," "tender"), *tortillas* form part of a subtext of nostalgia. And, again like the Spanish language, they are emblems of a paradise lost that the protagonists can only reconstruct momentarily, in a gathering of friends, in a Mexican restaurant, or on a trip to Mexico— while the authors reconstruct it through their texts. However regional the emblem, the process is universal: *se canta lo que se pierde.*

Stressing the personal and autobiographical aspects and their universal nature does not do away with the hierarchy between English- and Spanish-speaking America, nor with ethnocentric attitudes. The celebration of childhood happiness may reflect an authentic personal experience for the protagonists, the narrators, the authors, and for Chicano readers. But the very same aspects that signify their personal involvement may confirm stereotypes of Chicanos or Mexicans for readers who have grown up in a different cultural context. Reader response has a wider scope than the implied reader might suggest. Furthermore, as already mentioned in the context of Schleiermacher's lecture on tranlation, the borderline between the view from within and the view from without is thin. The cliché and the authentic do not always exclude each other but can overlap.

12. Spanish in the Chicano Novel after 1985: Four Women Writers

Chicano literary production did not come to a halt in 1985. Among the writers represented in the corpus who have published new works are Rudolfo Anaya, Sandra Cisneros, Lionel García, and Rolando Hinojosa. With *Becky and Her Friends* and *Los amigos de Becky*, the latter has once more written a novel in English and one in Spanish built on the same material. This time around though, the interrelation between the two novels is more intricate and cannot be reduced to a pattern of source and target as in the case of *Estampas* and *Valley*. Since I have already given ample coverage to Hinojosa's work, however, and since I am more interested in the evolution of the Chicano novel as a genre than in the overall production of particular authors, I have decided to draw on new voices to examine in what respects and to what extent their use of Spanish differs from that of the writers included in the 1967-1985 corpus. The four novels chosen for this purpose are:

> Estela Portillo Trambley: *Trini* (1986)
> Alma Luz Villanueva: *The Ultraviolet Sky* (1988)
> Mary Helen Ponce: *The Wedding* (1989)
> Ana Castillo: *Sapogonia* (1990)

Although this selection does not pretend to represent Chicano novel production between 1985 and 1990 as exhaustively as the corpus does for the earlier period, it counterpoints the corpus in more than one respect. None of the four authors is represented in the corpus and three of the texts are first novels. Furthermore, the dramatic increase in the publication of novels written by Mexican American women after 1985, allows me to compensate for the low representation of women authors in the corpus. By the same token, the four novels are auto-ethnographic texts in a double sense: They engage in dialogue not only with the white ethnographic master discourses but also with the male tradition within their own literature.

It is important to point out that the use of Spanish entries in the four texts is marked by continuity rather than change with respect to the earlier novels. The patterns of Spanish usage are—with the exception of the *songs* category in *Sapogonia*—statistically inconspicuous, they even repeat the strong showing of *tortilla* and *gringo* that appeared in the corpus. But continuity is not equivalent to invariability. *Trini, Wedding, Ultraviolet Sky,* and *Sapogonia* each contribute new facets to the use of Spanish in the Chicano novel in English, and my focus will be mainly on these new facets.

Two of the four novels correspond more closely than the other two to the stereotypical and hypothetical Chicano novel outlined in chapter three. Despite the fact that the central character is now female, and despite the differences of theme, setting, and style between the two texts, both *Trini* and *Wedding* are concerned with ethnic typicality, show a tendency towards ethnographic discourses, and depict a Chicana life set in the twentieth century, before the nineteen-sixties, with a strong impact of traditional values, family, and religion.

Estela Portillo Trambley: Trini

Texan author Estela Portillo Trambley is the first woman whose voice resounded in Chicano literature in the early seventies. Her play *The Day of the Swallows* was first published in 1971; in 1972 she won the Quinto Sol Award, and she is one of the two women represented in Bruce-Novoa's 1980 classic *Chicano Authors* (the other being Bernice Zamora). Whereas her earlier works are short stories and plays, *Trini* is her first novel.

Trini is a mestizo girl who grows up in Mexican Tarahumara country, moves to the city of Chihuahua, then to Juárez, crosses the American border illegally to give birth to one of her children in the United States and becomes, at the end of the novel, a resident of the United States. The novel has four thematic focuses:

- Life in rural Mexico and among the Tarahumara. This part bears a resemblance to the first part of *Barrio Boy* discourse and theme-wise, although the discourses are less ethnographic and more literary than those of Galarza's autobiography. The protagonist of this native setting is Sabochi, a Tarahumara leader whose exploits of cunning, visionary capacities and moral impeccability are reminiscent of the noble savage Chingachgook in Cooper's *The Last of the Mohicans*.

- Trini's American dream of a patch of land of her own in the United States comes true in the second part of the novel when, due to her endurance and the guidance of supernatural powers, she manages to cross the border, give birth to one of her children in the United States and gain possession of a piece of cultivable land there.

- The supernatural is tied to two characters. *El Enano*, a dwarf figure, appears in three different disguises—at the end of the novel as the old and dying owner of the land that Trini will inherit. The second protagonist in the context of the supernatural is Perla, a former prostitute, who is Trini's landlady in Juárez, and her benefactor by physical and metaphysical means.

- From childhood on, Trini's life is marked by her love for two men: Tonio, an incurable womanizer, whom she marries towards the end of the novel, and the highly idealized Sabochi, who is already married to a woman of his tribe. Faithful to the advice of Sabochi: "grow in silence," which she converts into a motto for her life, she suffers silently, takes what the two men are ready to give her and doesn't dare ask for more. Her only act of rebellion—apart from the realization of her North American dream—lies in her plan of eloping again with Sabochi at the end of the novel. Therefore, what Laverne González affirms in 1985 about Portillo Trambley's writing is only partially applicable to *Trini*:

Portillo Trambley's fiction is permeated by an uncompromising concern for the equality and liberation of women from the antiquated social norms of present-day society. It is a fiction in which women occupy the center of narrative attention and in which great care is taken to look at their motivation and behavior *from a feminist vantage point.* (317, emphasis added)

Spanish comes up in *Trini* from the very start. The loanword *gringo* and the toponym *Valverde* contribute a light touch of Spanish to the first paragraph, which ends:

She knew who he was, a gringo painter who had come to live among the Mexicans in Valverde. . . . He stood smiling down at her as he asked, "Waiting for me?"
His Spanish was soft and musical, almost like a native. (7)

This sample of fictitious Spanish and easily understandable Spanish elements—which repeats moreover the soft Spanish topos already encountered in the corpus—is misleading. In contrast to Lionel Garcia's *Leaving Home*, which introduces its Spanish-speaking setting in a similar way, *Trini* does not use secondary language elements in modest doses. With more than eight hundred entries—715 single words, 74 short entries, twenty long entries and one song—Spanish is prominently present in Portillo Trambley's novel. In addition, most Spanish entries are significantly more hermetic than their first specimen *gringo*; many of them are not translated, and among those that are, quite a few represent cases of what I have previously called *translational suspense:* a secondary language entry is not translated when it first appears in a text but only on one of its later appearances. This method is more frequent in *Trini* than in any of the other texts studied here.

When Trini leaves her village with her family, walking through the desert they meet an "old raramuri riding a mule leading two other pack mules" (46). As if the author expected her readers to know the word, *raramuri* is embedded in its context and in no way marked as a special term. It reappears twice shortly after it is first mentioned: "The old raramuri looked at them with suspicion," and "[t]he raramuri scrutinized each face" (47). *Raramuri*—not Spanish and not listed in Mexican or Chicano Spanish dictionaries either—is explained a couple of paragraphs later, when it still rings in the reader's mind, but as if it hadn't appeared before:

> "Is your village nearby, holy man?" José Mario asked. The old man was a raramuri—indicated by the three deep diagonal scars on his chest, signs of a mystical trial of indoctrination into a holy order among certain Tarahumara. (47)

In a similar way, *atole* appears six times and is thus already partially translated by context, before it is translated literally as "hot porridge" (163). *Arroyo* is mentioned several times, too, before it is translated in the parallel structured apposition "beyond the arroyo, past the river" (66). *Puta*, to give a final example of translational suspense in *Trini*, opens the second section of chapter fifteen. In the first section, Trini, pregnant with Sabochi's child after Tonio has left her for another woman, receives letters from Tonio, who wants to come back to her and marry her. She decides to give in to his pleas and meet him. "She knew she was going. She knew she had to tell him about Sabochi's baby" (175). The second section starts:

> "¡Puta!"
> Tonio hit Trini with the back of his hand. (175)

After hitting her and accusing her of loving Sabochi, Tonio leaves, and Trini's "thoughts [run] back to the morning when they had arrived . . ." (176). In this flashback, which constitutes one of the few interruptions of the chronological order of events in the novel, she reconstructs how she has met Tonio, eaten at a restaurant and gone to his house with him, where she has told him of her pregnancy. Tonio reacts angrily to this revelation and asks:

> "Do you still love him?"
> "Yes."
> He called her, "whore ..." (179)

In this manner we return to the word—this time in English—
and to the moment which opened the section, and the narration
continues from that point, but not without reintroducing Tonio's exclamation in Spanish:

> Now, in the darkness, as she lay alone with her child, she still
> felt the blow he had struck. She felt the knifing accusation. Puta!
> puta! puta! It rang in the darkness, but it rang untrue. (180)

The chapter is, as other parts of *Trini*, a bit too melodramatic
for my liking. In its structure and its use of the Spanish entry—which clearly is part of the structure—however, it is one
of the strongest parts of the novel.

Since not all the secondary language entries in *Trini* are
translated literally, Portillo Trambley adds, like Galarza in
Barrio Boy, a glossary of secondary language terms:

AUTHOR'S NOTE

In writing this novel I have attempted to impart some of
the flavor of the language used by the Tarahumaras, including a
number of vocabulary items of regional origin and use. In many
cases Tarahumara words were supplied by native informants, and
I have had to base my spelling solely on the pronunciation. Following are a few terms whose meaning might not be clear from
the context.

bule	a clay dipper or small bowl with a handle used as a cover for a water jug and as a dipper for drinking
cabaldura	saddlebag
garañones	wild horses
hilpa	a simple housedress made of coarse cotton; chemise
pitaya	flower of the carnation family, native to Mexico
revolijo	fish stew made with wine
salgazanos	thieves
sarso	large clay bowl that holds a whole cheese

The glossary represents, as the one in *Barrio Boy*, a traditional ethnographic discourse, a clear step towards the reader. At the same time, this glossary clearly differs from that in Galarza's autobiography. The note that precedes it adds a dimension that is missing in Galarza, who does not comment on his glossary at all. Portillo Trambley emphasizes the ethnographic aspect of the glossary; like an anthropologist, she affirms that she has had direct access to "native informants." By the same token, the word *flavor* points explicitly towards local color, towards *costumbrismo*. And the glossaries themselves differ, too. Galarza's is not complete either, but defines the larger part of the secondary language entries that appear in *Barrio Boy* and explains even such well known or transparent Hispanicisms as *gringo, maestro, respeto, tequila, revolucionario,* and *vámonos*. Portillo Trambley restricts herself to a handful of hermetic entries used by the Tarahumara—although not necessarily of Tarahumara origin; *cabaldura, garañones, revolijo* and *sarso*, at least, have an unmistakably Spanish etymology. Other native American words that appear in *Trini*, like *raramuri, huitoch,* or *tehueque* are not in the Glossary, and neither are the considerable number of Spanish or regional Spanish expressions that are left untranslated or only fuzzily defined by their context. Furthermore, some of the terms included in the glossary don't need definition anymore; the novel explains them sufficiently by context. The reader who can contain her or his urge to consult the glossary at the first mention of *hilpa*—which, to be sure, doesn't give much information (14)—will not know that a *hilpa* is "made of coarse cotton," but can gather from the contexts of its repeated appearance within a few pages that it is a piece of clothing that women put on by drawing over their head. It is the only garment that Trini puts on in the morning or takes off when she goes swimming, not only a 'housedress' as the glossary states, it seems, but the only clothing that Trini and her sister wear, in and outside the house (14, 19, 24, 25, 28). When Trini says later on in the novel, in her version of the Horatian topos *beatus ille*, that her *hilpa* was her "solitary garment in the hills of

Batopilas," she doesn't add any new connotations to the word, but only makes explicit what the earlier contexts have already made clear implicitly:

> Clothes multiply like people in a big city, she smiled as she mused. She remembered la hilpa which had been her solitary garment in the hills of Batopilas. Now there were stockings, shoes, undergarments, skirts, blouses, even a wrapper. She had to spend what she earned for clothes in an attempt to be modern, citified. (141)

The definition of the dish called *revolijo* is more detailed in the text than in the glossary, where it appears as "fish stew made with wine." In a scene that brings to mind similar ones in the corpus—although with other dishes like *tortillas, menudo* or *capirotada*—Trini assists in the preparation of *revolijo* one Christmas Eve, and we learn that it is a baked dish that contains *bacalao*, rum, "sweet bread, nuts, cheese, and raisins" (112). *Bacalao*, the Spanish term for "codfish" is the problem case in this list. The context doesn't give any hint as to what kind of food it is, and only by consulting a Spanish dictionary or the glossary, which defines *revolijo* as "fish stew," do monolingual readers get a more precise notion of its main ingredient. In the case of *revolijo* the context and the glossary complement each other; we could even say that the glossary doesn't contain a translation of *revolijo*—which is already explained in the text—as much as it contains one of *bacalao*.

The glossary added to *Trini* leaves the vast majority of the more than two hundred and fifty secondary language entries undefined. Whereas the monolingual reader of *Barrio Boy* can rely on the glossary; knows that she or he just needs to flip some pages to find secondary language entries explained, Portillo Trambley's glossary represents a mere ethnographic gesture, no real attempt at covering the rich secondary language vocabulary contained in her novel. The reader of *Trini* needs a Spanish dictionary in order to understand the secondary language entries, and even that will not always help:

Tía Pancha, austere virgin of thirty-three, stared down at the children. They knelt before her, looking straight up her nose.
"Buquis, inquesen! Pídanle a Dios gracias, y pidan que les ilumine el pensamiento."
Mouthing words, one on top of the other, the children did as they were told. They thanked God, asking Him to illuminate their thoughts. Buti fell on his haunches, then straightened up only to fall again. Trini's knees felt tender, not being used to kneeling for so long, while Lupita gave up altogether. (35)

Tía Pancha's intervention is standard Spanish, except for its first two words. *Buqui*—a Chicano Spanish expression for 'kid, child' which according to Santamaría stems from the Mexican province of Sinaloa—can only be found in specialized dictionaries; and not even specialized dictionaries will list *inquesen* as the non-standard imperative of *hincar*, 'to kneel.' Does this mean that Portillo has written her novel primarily with a bilingual readership in mind—for Mexican Americans only? The quotation just given proves convincingly that this is not the case. The entire contents of the Spanish sentence are repeated in the text that surrounds it. Pancha's admonition translates: "Children kneel down, thank God and ask him to illuminate your thoughts." All this is rendered in English, too. As a matter of fact, the children are already kneeling when Pancha asks them to do so, as if Portillo Trambley *didn't* expect her readers to understand the sentence in Spanish. While not all the other secondary language entries in *Trini* are as completely and literally translated as this one, even those that are left untranslated do not obstruct the understanding of the novel's argument. Thus, half of the long entries are religiously connoted, the other half are Mexican children's rhymes or fragments from Mexican songs. Among the fifteen different long entries, only the raramuri's phrase: "Habla derecho y seremos amigos" does not fit into one of these two categories. As in the novels of the corpus, the religious invocations are always pronounced by women. One of them and its thorough translation has just been dealt with, and three of them start out with the well known formula "Ave María": "Ave María, Madre de Dios," "Ave María ruega por nosotros" (58), and "Ave María, madre de Dios, bendita seas entre todas las mujeres" (210). Once they have read these two words, monolingual readers will know, or are supposed to know at least, what the Spanish entry is about, and may stop caring about the rest of it. Three additional religious *long entries* contain the word *Dios*, and of the only two which have to make do without either *Dios* or *Ave María*, one consists almost exclusively of *etymological pairs:* "Dos clases de gracia, actual y sacra- mental" (38). The last of the religiously connoted long entries, finally, also includes etymological pairs and is moreover sur- rounded by a context which leaves no doubt as to the gist of its contents: "She crossed herself and clasped her hands to her bosom. 'Bendita sea la Santísima Virgen' " (67).

Although monolingual readers may be left at odds as to the meaning of certain Spanish entries in *Trini*, and although the strong presence of Spanish may slow down their reading, they will nonetheless be perfectly able to follow the novel. That is not to say, however, that the Spanish entries in the novel are superfluous. They provide local color, they can leave the mo- nolingual reader—who can't assess them without making an effort at translation—intrigued about their contents, and they can fulfill other functions to boot, as the examples of *puta* and *raramuri* show, or the symbolic function of *hilpa* when Trini juxtaposes her life in the city to her rural childhood. And the fact that Spanish is foregrounded in *Trini* to a greater extent than in many other Chicano novels is, in itself, important.

Mary Helen Ponce: The Wedding

In contrast to *Trini*, which receives high scores for its use of Spanish, from single words to long entries, Mary Helen Ponce's *The Wedding* keeps itself inconspicuously in the middle or lower end of the rankings. *Wedding* makes for easy reading, and not only because it restricts its use of Spanish to homeopathic doses. The novel takes place in the late forties in

a small town in the Los Angeles area. It begins when the protagonist, eighteen-year-old Blanca Muñoz, starts going steady
with the pachuco gang leader Sammy the Cricket and ends
with the night of their wedding. It recounts the wedding prepa-
rations, Blanca's work plucking turkeys on a poultry farm, the
Saturday night dances, and the ensuing brawls between *Los
Tacones*, Cricket's gang, and the *Planchados*, their enemies.
Spanish language elements in *Wedding* restrict themselves
to single words and short entries. The longest entry is in the
form of a fragment of a song and is four words long: "Mam-
bo, que rico es" (175). The other short entries are, to give the
possibility of a comparison with, for example, Tía Pancha's
sentence in *Trini* quoted above, the three names *El Gato Cor-
tez, El Pan Tostado* and *La Más Popular* and the phrases or
fragments: "A mí los Philip Morris" (137), "Ay, ay, ay"
(186), "Ay, Dios" and "Ay, sí" (116), "gracias, muchas gracias" (152), "m'ijita" (70), "muy bonitos" (68), "Sí, muy"
(137) and "Sí, m'ijita" (115). While the names are frequently
repeated, the other short entries all appear just once.
    Much more than in *Trini*, Spanish is present in *Wedding*
for the mere flavor of it. Spanish entries are short, easily
understandable in general—*americana, barrio, chile, señorita,
señor, señora, tamal, tequila, tortilla, vino*, etc.—, and the
more hermetic ones tend to be readily translated or explained,
the English term often even preceding the Spanish one:

> The Wedding Breakfast, or el almuerzo, as it was popularly
> called. . . . (115)

> . . . azares, orange blossoms made of wax, the traditional head-
> piece worn by most Mexican-American brides. It was a sign of
> purity. (89)

> "I gotta pee," whispered Petey to Blanca as he edged around the
> damaged cushions. "I gotta makes chi." (112)

> "Lucy! This thing is squashing my tetas. I got my tits up to my
> chin almost. . . ." (86)

One of the few entries left without literal translation is a
swearword, following what might be termed a tradition in the
Chicano novel. Father Ranger is the village priest who—as the
priest in *Leaving Home*, although less dedicated to alcohol and
more to jazz—gives an outside view of the Mexican American
society depicted. He uses a Spanish term when Blanca and
Cricket visit him unexpectedly. The context leaves no doubt
that it can hardly be a term of endearment:

> Father Ranger recovered his composure, slid behind the desk,
> pulled open the middle drawer, selected a gold pen and began to
> fill out the marriage forms. Cabrones, he thought, as his shaking
> fingers fought to control the pen. Cabrones. (107)[100]

Does *Wedding* have less of everything in comparison with
Trini as far as Spanish entries are concerned? This is not the
case. The setting facilitates the inclusion of Pachuco Spanish
terms, and with *bato, carnala, esa, ese, nel, orale, simón,* and
yesca, Ponce's novel contains more of them than any other
text of the corpus. The pachuco setting may also be responsible for the few—however modest—attempts at a more genuine
type of code switching than what Portillo Trambley's novel
offers. Single word entries in *Trini* are mainly nouns, and the
few verbal forms are independent syntactic units, like *basta*,
or *ándale*. The list of the Spanish entries in *Wedding* consists
mainly of nouns, too, but includes nevertheless a few tokens
that do not fit that pattern. Included are articles, the conjunction *y*, and the verbal form *es*—functional elements that don't

---

100 Galván and Teschner define *cabrón* rather prosaically: "Cabrón.
     m. husband deceived by an adulterous wife; (general term of in-
     sult, usually vulg.: son of a bitch, bastard, etc.)." Polkinhorn et
     al. provide a more detailed and more succulent definition: "CA-
     BRON-A (*m.* and *f.n., adj., excl.*) *sm* [standard meaning]: a buck;
     he-goat; nanny goat; a cuckold; unfaithful wife; pimp. *nsm* [non-
     standard meaning]: Something like son-of-a-bitch; sometimes used
     affectionately (*El es muy cabroncito;* he's a cute son-of-a-bitch.
     Está cabrón; that's wild, groovy. *Es muy cabrón, ese bato;* that
     guy is a real stud. *¡Orale, cabrón!* Hey, mother-fucker! *¡Ay, ca-
     brón!* Ouch! used to express pain."

carry any semantic weight, but need complementing, and Ponce complements them with English:

> From the first, Blanca hated the job at los turkeys.   (15)

> Es one-way!   (156)

Paradoxically enough, while they are semantically unessential, *los* and *es*—precisely because they operate on the syntactical level—foreground the language switch more radically than inserted nouns would. For obvious reasons, their effect will be mitigated if they are frequently repeated within a novel—in *Wedding* they are not—or if the reader is already familiar with Southwest code switching.

The use of incomplete Spanish entries in *Wedding* can also be observed on the level of *short entries*. In *Trini*, the *short entries* are noun compounds, names, or short, but *complete* phrases. In *Wedding*, two among the twelve *short entries* are syntactical *fragments*: "A mí los" and "sí, muy." They both occur when "on the Friday before the wedding, Blanca's mother and some neighbor women . . . cook the food" (136). *Mole*, the name of the main dish, may create confusion with monolingual readers because of its various English homonyms. The detailed description of its preparation can be seen as Ponce's contribution to the topos of Mexican American recipes in Chicano novels. Once *mole* is ready, the women take a break. One of them lights a hand-rolled cigarette and inhales:

> "Ummmmm."
> "Bueno?"
> "Sí, muy good."
> "I like los Camels."
> "A mí los Philip Morris."
> "They gives cupones?"
> "Sí! I'm going to buy a radio!"
> "Eees too much money!"
> "And lots of cupones!"   (137)

Bueno, *cupones* and *sí* correspond to the pattern that *Trini* shows in the use of its secondary language entries. Combinations of English and Spanish, however, as in the sequence "*Sí, muy* good" / "I like *los* Camels" / "*A mí los* Philip Morris," never occur in Portillo Trambley's text. As in the case of the *single words* mentioned above—and the Spanish article *los* attributed to "Camels" here—the two *short entries* do not contain any nouns, but are complemented by an English adjective in one case and by a trade name in the other. More—and more radical—intrasentential code switches than in *Wedding* can be found in Abelardo Delgado's *Louise.*

The conversation between the women evokes the language of Hispanics in the Southwest. The local color provided by the Spanish entries is enhanced by nonstandard English—a recurring feature in the direct speech passages of *Wedding*—and by trade names, which in Ponce's novel compete with the Spanish entries in providing local color—maybe "temporal color" is a more appropriate expression in the case of these internationally known brand names that place the novel time-wise rather than geographically. Their list includes cosmetics like Max Factor pancake makeup, Tangee Real Hot Red lipstick (6), or Toni Home Permanent (96); candy like Juicy Fruit (22, etc.) or Milk Duds (24, 75); drinks like Kool Aid (68, 148), Jim Beam (43), or Hill & Hill (8, etc.); cigarettes like Camel (22, etc.), Lucky Strike (7, etc.), or Kool (183f); and cars like Chevy, 44 Ford, or Mercury (171). No other Chicano novel I know of uses trade names to the same extent.

Ponce adds yet another kind of "secondary language entry" or "local color" marker. Her novel is replete with names of stars from the film and music business. John Wayne, Humphrey Bogart (22), Ava Gardner (131), Hedy Lamarr (42), Duke Ellington (50), and Ella Fitzgerald (54) are just a few of them. The only Mexican star who appears among them is the only one who is negatively connoted: "Damn, Blanca thought, all I needs is for Jorge Negrete to sing one of his songs . . . and I'm back in Mexico!" (68). The English-speaking American movie stars are the idols of Blanca and her friends, and the jazz greats come in because Father Ranger "particularly liked music played by Negroes" (106). Film actors appear in several other Chicano novels, too, but only *Buffalo*—with an avid moviegoer as protagonist—includes them with a frequency comparable to *Wedding*. *Wedding* presents a picture of a social group and its values. The quotation above, for example, shows how the first electronic mass medium, radio, is a status symbol that not everyone can afford yet, and how the coupon system is used as a marketing strategy. Descriptive discourses outline the picture of Chicano families and Pachuco gangs; trade names, names of stars, and Spanish language entries add color to it by joining their evocative forces. And they are complemented by humor, a fourth element adding to the picture. While Portillo Trambley couples ethnographic discourses with pathos, Ponce couples them with humor, local color humor mostly. In doing so, she chooses a discourse that traditionally tends to belittle its subject matter or to relegate it to the realm of a colonized object. To late twentieth-century readers Blanca's dreams of the "best wedding in the barrio" (199) may appear naive or even ridiculous, especially with the kind of bridegroom she has chosen, and they will hardly be astonished when Blanca's great expectations are not met. The author leaves no doubt, however, as to who is to blame if Blanca's dreams fail.

Mary Helen Ponce persuasively counterpoises the effect that the local color discourses may have on her readers. The surface discourse of her novel is plain *costumbrismo*, a kind of *American Graffiti*, with car races, pachuco gang feuds, and a lot of local color humor. But the contents work surreptitiously against this surface. Although *Wedding* is far from being a tragedy, it has an underlying tragic subtext. Ponce drives home her point that Blanca, hard as she may try, is inescapably trapped by the machismo that surrounds her—in Mexican American culture as well as among Pachucos—and trapped, too, by her situation as a second-class citizen of the United States who has to spend her childhood summers picking fruit and who is educationally deprived. Blanca, caught between Mexican traditions, Pachuco values, and the American dreams presented to her in Hollywood movies, may choose as her wedding gown "a 'colonial' style dress, then the current rage, similar to that worn by Scarlett O'Hara in 'Gone With the Wind,' " (80) but she will never be a southern belle.

Alma Luz Villanueva: The Ultraviolet Sky

The protagonists of *Wedding* drink Kool Aid, Jim Beam, and Hill & Hill. The protagonists of *Trini* drink liquor or *aguardiente* (40, 161, 169, etc.), *chicha* (48, 74), milk (25), *pochote* milk (10), mint tea (31), and tequila (153, 230). The protagonists of *Ultraviolet Sky* drink a lot of coffee and tea but also brandy (38, 56, etc.), champagne (48, 136, 239), chardonnay (50ff, 239), chablis (102, 146f), colombard (108, 350), margaritas (98, 356), petite sirah (156, 343), pinot noir (25), retsina (73), sake (54), *Sangre de Toro* (24, 26, 29, etc.), sangría (54f), and zinfandel (85, 184). The list of the drinks imbibed in Villanueva's novel is a representative indicator of a basic difference between *Ultraviolet Sky* and most texts of the corpus.

Wedding and *Trini* both have a female protagonist of Mexican background and are both set in the forties, one mainly in rural Mexico, the other one in small town California. The protagonist of *Ultraviolet Sky* is also a Mexican American woman, and this is far from being irrelevant, but—compared to Blanca or Trini—she is, time- and culture-wise, less distant from a late twentieth-century middle-class readership in the United States—or in Europe, for that matter. Rosa Luján is a teacher and an artist, with "a couple of paintings in the Oakland Museum and the San Francisco Museum of Modern Art" (264). The title of the novel alludes to the sky on one of her paintings-in-progress, which accompanies her through all the novel, and for which she cannot find the appropriate color. Rosa, to sketch out the argument very briefly, leaves her husband Julio, her son, and her home near San Francisco and moves to a cabin in the Sierra Madre mountains. When she gets pregnant unexpectedly, she decides to give birth at home, in her cabin. And just when the author has lulled you into expecting a natural and wholesome birth under the auspices of the Mexican goddess Quetzalpetlatl and a Native American midwife, she abruptly shifts gears and takes you, for the last seventy pages, on a tumultuous ride.

Rosa's friends—to come back to the change of perspective in the depiction of a Mexican American protagonist—are not blue collar workers nor pachucos, and even though she has a Yaqui grandmother and consciously integrates Native American traditions and values into her life and thoughts, she never "believed and lived by Indian ways, Indian rhythms of the blood" in the same way as Trini's father and aunt did (*Trini* 133). Furthermore, in contrast to *Trini*, *Wedding*, and the texts of the corpus that place themselves in the vicinity of the *Bildungsroman*, the protagonist of *Ultraviolet Sky* is an adult from the very start of the novel, her childhood and upbringing are only present in the form of short flashbacks, which evoke in concentrated form some of the themes that are dealt with more extensively in other Chicano novels:

> . . . and somewhere deep inside she was still a Spanish-speaking Mexican kid from a San Francisco barrio, one of the places the tourists didn't linger in; and for that reason—poverty, an inarticulateness in the face of White Authority, or an irresistible urge (still) to scream FUCK YOU ALL, shame of the poverty, defiance of the poverty, the desire to embrace everyone, the inability to embrace everyone, the knowledge that they were poor, that they spoke Spanish, that they were Mexican, that they were different (from what?), that Mexican people lived only here or here or here, drove her crazy (still)—and for that reason she didn't see herself as a regular teacher, but as an escapee, and a woman-escapee, not too popular. In war she'd be raped, the final humiliation, and wasn't this war, she mused—am I not continually waiting for My Rapist, isn't the Earth continually struggling to survive Man? (41)

Rosa is no longer poor, and ethnic typicality is not the chief constituent of *Ultraviolet Sky*. Villanueva does not present her readers with the image of a woman who is underprivileged, exploited, and poverty-stricken because she is Mexican Amer-

ican. Rosa is an utterly privileged human being. She spends
her time painting and teaching, listens to good music on her
stereo, goes out a lot, is surrounded by good-looking men and
women who are all talented artists, and all the men she falls
for also fall for her. When she separates from her husband and
moves to the cabin, she has to work part time to keep herself
afloat. But this does not convert her into a working class woman, let alone a wetback. *Ultraviolet Sky* does not live up to the
expectation of those readers and critics who postulate that
"minority" writing has to radically foreground the power
structure between colonizer and colonized, between the center
and the margin, and that only discourses that speak of poverty,
pain, and resistance are appropriate for marginalized writers
(cf. Perreault 134). There *is* a power struggle going on in
Ultraviolet Sky, a very fierce one, moreover, cruel and at the
same time subtle, and more than once described in terms of
warfare; but the borders in this struggle are not the ones that
prevail in the novels of the corpus. The main bone of contention is between Rosa and her husband Julio, two Mexican
Americans. Social class and ethnic group, the traditionally
dominant categories of the power struggle in the Chicano novel are overlapped—overlapped, not overlayed, and certainly
not replaced—by the focus on gender. This shift in perspective
entails a movement of particularization and one of generalization. On the one hand, the incessant power games between Rosa and Julio transfer the struggle *into* the ethnic group; on the
other hand, the struggle transcends the ethnic group and the
United States, as the last lines of the quotation above, and
some of the quotations still to come, show. The way in which
Villanueva approaches the themes of childbearing, childbirth,
and abortion may be the most obvious example of how her
novel subverts the discourses of the male dominated literary
tradition established by her Chicano colleagues and by mainstream writers. Both groups tend to create distance by choos-
ing either idealistic or ironic discourses for the treatment of
this theme, if they treat it at all. Rosa's abundant use of
offensive language and her and other people's comments on it

all through the novel may be mentioned as another example of how Villanueva subverts gender stereotypes.

Emphasis on the issue of gender is not the only reason why the Mexican American identity of the protagonists is less stressed, or stressed differently, in *Ultraviolet Sky* than in other Chicano novels. Another element that contributes to the shift in perspective is the author's refusal to define her protagonist solely as a Mexican American. When Julio asks her whether she already has thought of a name for their baby, Rosa says:

> "I call her a Native Person. She's a mestizo, a mixed-blood. That's what a Mexican really is—a mestizo. We're all mestizos."
> Julio laughed. "How's that?"
> "She'll be a Native Person of the Earth, that's what. If we're going to survive into the next century, we're all going to have to be Native People. . . . (247)

While the novels of the corpus tend to accentuate Mexican American specifics and the narrator of *Clemente* talks of:

> . . . the Spaniard who, in getting hot for the Mexican, created the mestizo and sealed his own doom. (48, cf. 29)

Ultraviolet Sky presents Mexican culture, and all of humanity, as a mestizo culture. This attitude may be a reflection on the North American pluralism debate of the 1980s, but it also enters into dialogue with and subverts the discourses predominant in the earlier Chicano novel production. *Ultraviolet Sky* is not the only novel that does this, nor is the corpus a monolithic unit as far as the representation of Mexican American culture, values, and characters is concerned. The implicit dialogue with and subversion of earlier models is already present in the corpus; *Rain God, Tamazunchale, Mango Street*, and *Hunger* are maybe the most salient examples. By the same token, Acosta and Hinojosa have accentuated the mixed and open nature of Mexican American civilization in their novels long before *Ultraviolet Sky*; Ricardo Sánchez has celebrated it

in his poetry; and *Alhambra* introduces the *mestizo* in terms
which are not very far removed from those of *Ultraviolet Sky:*

> . . . his Spanish ancestors married (a euphemism?) American
> Indians to form the North American version of the New World
> mestizo. The new race forged of Old World and New. A promise
> of what the future had to bring if the earth's people were to live
> in peace. (181)

This propagation of mestizo culture is the rare exception in
Candelaria's novel, whose protagonist and narrator tend to
single out ethnic and racial differences, as I have already
shown, and as wording like: "[t]he new race forged" also insinuates. The protagonist of *Ultraviolet Sky,* however, while
she has strong ties to her Mexican background, rejecting some
of its traditions and values, and cherishing others, is someone
whose cultural identity is not solely defined by the ethnic
group she belongs to by birth. The word *mestizo* only appears
three times in Villanueva's text—the three times contained in
the quotation above. But in no other Chicano novel that I
know of is there so much of an overall strategy to construct a
"multicultural" and "multiethnic" protagonist—a *mestiza* not
only by birth, but also by choice. The variety of wines from
different countries and different continents mentioned in the
novel are one sample of this strategy. The semantic field of
food offers a similarly various list, from feta cheese (69),
marshmallows (91), and paella (24 etc.), to quiche (265f,
German pancakes (242), and won-ton (108). A third list, not
entirely unrelated to the first two, could be compiled with different restaurants, from a Greek taverna to a Japanese restaurant, a flamenco place, and a country-style bar; and yet
another list with different music styles. Rosa is very fond of
flamenco, but also fancies Peruvian flute music (58), Joni
Mitchell (60), Renaissance music (77), Brazilian jazz (155),
Bach (248), Chopin (193), and Villa-Lobos (278). The
reproduction of these lists within one paragraph and stripped
of their contexts, might lead to the impression that *Ultraviolet
Sky* is either dominated entirely by stylish music, fancy food

and fine wines or that the novel advocates an "everything goes" arbitrariness, that cultural identity, in other words, is entirely inventable or entirely a matter of choice. Both impressions would be wrong. First, the elements that appear here in concentrated form, lose part of their impact when they are distributed over almost four hundred pages; and secondly, Rosa is very clearly conditioned by her background and upbringing. The lists are illuminating nonetheless, because they present us with an abundance of cultural markers that are in no way Chicano-specific, but that could represent the preferences of many an artist or teacher in the United States or Europe. In this, *Ultraviolet Sky* marks a clear contrast to *Trini* and *Wedding*, as well as to the corpus. The list of trade names and movie stars in *Wedding* is impressive, too, but all its tokens conform to the group depicted. Arturo Islas's *Rain God*, to give a further example, subverts former Chicano narrative discourses in various ways, but does so without taking the focus away from a specifically Mexican American setting. Miguel Chico, the narrator of Islas's novel, is an academic, but we learn very little about his university life; he concentrates on depicting his childhood, his family, his relatives, thus remaining in a setting dominated by traditional Mexican American values.

It might be argued that the cultural markers which surround Rosa are very specific for a Californian artist of the late seventies, that she is portrayed with no less ethnographic fidelity than the central characters of *Trini, Wedding, Ultima,* or *Barrio Boy*. I would agree with that, but I would also stress that the degree of mimesis in the depiction of the protagonist is not of primary importance for my argument. Two other factors are much more essential: For one thing, the change in the literary discourse as such; for another, the fact that a middle class European or non-Chicano U.S. American reader can no longer place her- or himself at an ethnographic distance to the protagonists of the novel.

Rosa cannot place herself at an ethnographic distance to a middle class European any longer. Quite early on in the novel, she has dinner in a Spanish restaurant and is approached by a "strikingly handsome, young man" (28). Vis-à-vis Rosa and Flora—the flamenco dancer who owns the restaurant and whose name indicates her closeness to the protagonist—, Rolf, a German sculptor, defines himself by using one of the top scoring Spanish entries in the corpus:

> Your dancing was quite beautiful, and very moving. I'm a gringo —isn't that what you say here? A gringo from Berlin, and this place of yours makes me feel at home. . . . I don't mind this word 'gringo'—you must call me this so that I may really feel at home, here. (33)

Though Flora and Rosa burst out laughing, Rolf's words do not merely have a comic function. They correspond to an overall scheme of *Ultraviolet Sky* by showing that cultural identity is complex and often ambiguous rather than absolute and fixed and that it depends, moreover, on the context. Rolf, as a German who has been to Spain, identifies with flamenco when he is in America. His use of *gringo* is complex, as well. While the term is generally applied to North Americans, he asks two U.S. citizens to call him *gringo*. Since they both are Hispanics, however, his reversal is not without logic, and since he is "blonde, with the bluest of eyes" (28), he may have been called *gringo* while in Spain, and therefore, being called *gringo* in San Francisco makes him feel closer to home. A term, which appears all through the corpus denoting *otherness*, thus becomes a term of identification. And Villanueva does not stop here.

Rosa immediately likes Rolf, but reacts very strongly and very negatively to his nationality

> Would I make love to him if I weren't with Julio? she asked herself. I think so. It feels like I certainly want to, though his being German—Hitler, concentration camps, his blondeness—disturbs me. (35)

Although her stereotype of what being German means keeps haunting her (49), and although she repeatedly dreams that she died as a young girl in a concentration camp (57), Rosa has to revise her image of Germany later on in the novel, not only because she ends up making love to Rolf, but also because she learns that one of her grandmothers was German. When she writes about this to Rolf, he—who has signed one of his earlier letters with "amor, El Gringo" (199)—writes back: "I like it . . . that you're German. Does that make you a Gringo, as well?" (275) Rolf's question is never answered explicitly, but Villanueva leaves no doubt that Rosa assumes the German in her as well as the *gringo*. This does not mean that all ethnic differences are smoothed over or that the protagonist, once she has realized that she is part *gringo*, now includes all of humanity in an egalitarian meta-ethnic embrace. She still has her preferences and is still marked to some extent by ethnocentric attitudes and stereotypes, as becomes plain when she works as a waitress and attends a group of what looks like WASP customers:

> Three men and their wives. A little over middle age, a little over-weight, and a little too white. Rosa's white people phobia loomed into view. I wonder if they're German or English, like me? she reminded herself. But unlike me, they aren't Mexican, or Yaqui. Her guard went back up. (356)

Significantly enough, Rolf has been described as "light-skinned, *but tanned*" (28, my emphasis) when he approached Rosa at the flamenco place.

Villanueva clearly defines her protagonist as a Mexican American but she equally clearly puts less stress on Rosa's *otherness* than the novels of the corpus, *Trini* and *Wedding*. Or, to put it differently, she stresses Rosa's *otherness*, but also her *sameness*. The only text of the corpus that goes beyond *Ultraviolet Sky* in the protagonist's identification with a white middle-class readership is *Hunger*, Richard Rodriguez's story of how his Hispanic childhood is replaced by his public identity as an English-speaking American intellectual. Rodriguez describes this process in terms of loss and gain, of one culture *re-placing* the other, of Ricardo becoming Richard:

Only when I was able to think of myself as an American, no longer an alien in *gringo* society, could I seek the rights and opportunities necessary for full public individuality. The social and political advantages I enjoy as a man result from the day that I came to believe that my name, indeed, is *Rich-heard Road-ree-guess.* (27)

Rosa Luján shares little of Richard Rodriguez's preoccupations, and never considers changing her name to *Rose.* The mechanism at work in *Ultraviolet Sky* is not replacement, but rather integration, however partial, however conflictive. And while *gringo* tends to be used in the corpus as a swearword or to denote *otherness*—and loses these connotations for the protagonist of *Hunger*—Villanueva converts it into a many-sided, complex, and ambiguous signifier.

The complexity of *gringo* is in no way representative for the general use of Spanish in *Ultraviolet Sky.* Spanish entries occur about as frequently as in *Leaving Home,* less frequently than in *Mango Street,* and most of them are used straightforwardly, simply and conventionally, giving rise to no syntactic irregularities and having mainly an evocative function. There are some geographical and personal names in Spanish; the list of international dishes above could be extended by a dozen Mexican culinary terms; and nine of about fifteen letters in the novel end with a greeting formula in Spanish, although Spanish is never used in the letters as such—with the exception of *flamenco* and *Sangre de Toro* in one of them, and *Sierra Madres* in another. Finally, Spanish is sometimes used between Julio and Rosa when they are making love and also enters into the game with some of her other lovers.

The two most frequently appearing terms by far, both with about twenty occurrences, are *flamenco*—which among the corpus texts emerges only a couple of times in the novels of Acosta (*Buffalo* 56, 123, *Cockroach* 199)—and *tortilla,* which is very frequent in the texts of the corpus. *Tortilla* is one of the few terms in *Ultraviolet Sky* that have a connotative richness comparable to that of *gringo.* It first appears, positively connoted, as part of a breakfast her husband has prepared for

Rosa. They both know that they will make love after eating and the description of the dish couldn't be more explicit or exuberant in its sexual symbolism:

> The omelette was neatly folded in half full of hot, spicy chorizo, sliced raw onion on the side like she loved it, a wet, green jalapeño pepper which she never tried to resist, and a folded tortilla to one side dripped with butter. (19)

Trini and *Wedding* also connote the term *tortilla* positively. Cricket's mother—living under circumstances quite different from Rosa's—"took pride in her wheat flour tortillas. . . . and liked to cook them for her sons" (*Wedding* 30-31, cf. 74); and when Trini gets homesick for Mexico in the United States, her mind "spill[s] over with hunger for the brazen colors of her own world. The smell of cooking beans, the slap of tortillas" (188). Portillo Trambley and Ponce leave it at that, and in Ana Castillo's *Sapogonia*, the fourth Chicana novel included here, *tortilla* is touched on very lightly. It appears twice, once in a description of North American stereotypes of Mexicans, the other time, with more positive connotations, at a gathering of young artists (18). Villanueva, in contrast, has *tortilla* pass through a process of enrichment. After breakfast and after making love, Rosa lies alone on her bed and thinks about *tortillas* in a more traditional Mexican husband-wife arrangement than hers. Her thoughts, which develop into a general reflection on gender and language, shed new light on all the male protagonists in the texts of the corpus who treasure the memory of their mothers or grandmothers making *tortillas:*

> . . . For some reason she thought of her aunt Maria who dutifully made tortillas every morning for her overweight husband as he sat waiting, impatient if not regal. And the tortillas must be hot or she would jump up to warm them if displeasure crossed his face after the third or fourth one.
> Rosa had to admit it, Mexican Men had always turned her off, them and their fucking tortillas made by their mothers, their grandmothers, and finally their slavelike wives. Yet when Julio had spoken Spanish in her ear the first time they'd made love, she felt herself drop into an old and necessary part of herself as though his words were linked to an intimacy she'd forgotten.

The words spoken to her as a child, her first words: *mesa, leche, hambre, por qué*: her first language. And at the same time she knew she had to watch it because he reached her there, and she'd forget her own warning and repeat the words, *"Te quiero,"* without a thought to safety. Her own safety. Because it was inevitable, always it seemed inevitable that the overweight Mexican Man demanding a hot tortilla would appear (not woman enough for this, not woman enough for that, not a proper woman anyway). However, Julio made a mistake in the scheme of things—he made love to her exactly as she needed to be made love to. (21-22)

Rosa coincides with Tía Cuca in considering Spanish "the language of love and romance" (*Rain God* 142, cf. above 40) but is from the start wary of this attitude: "she knew she had to watch it." Shortly after the passage just quoted, when Julio has left the house "detached, businesslike," Spanish is evaluated in slightly different terms:

There was a note on the table in Spanish, "Querida . . ." It made her cry again, and she hated him as much as last night. "Querida, my ass," Rosa hissed and tore the paper into pieces to dispel her stupidity. (23)

She now judges differently the fact that her husband, unlike traditional Mexican men, has made breakfast for her: ". . . he heats me a tortilla but he sure doesn't let me forget it" (22). When she begins working on her paintings, the image of the tortilla is once more redefined and then becomes part of a feminist manifesto, the outspokenness of which would be unthinkable in *Trini* or *Wedding*. The passage also shows that Villanueva has not chosen the name of her protagonist accidentally:

Rosa felt like painting a disintegrating, bleeding tortilla with overweight vultures surrounding it. And then she laughed because what she'd started was destined to be beautiful; a black, lace shawl suspended in a lilac sky. . . .
    The bleeding tortilla was feminine, the black shawl was feminine, the Earth was feminine, and everything that was feminine, she felt, was in danger of being destroyed by the masculine. She included herself. Tears came to her eyes but they

didn't fall. Rosa was intent on completing at least one black flower. One black rose. (23)

Tortilla reappears several times more in *Ultraviolet Sky*, sometimes it is neutrally or positively connoted (85, 87, 190f); at other times negatively. When Julio spends a weekend at her cabin, she tells him about her perception of the Mexican Man and the uneven standards in Mexican society: ". . . men have moments of freedom, release, women count the tortillas and the children. Men have affairs, women become whores" (243, cf. 369). On the following night, Julio and Rosa act out the stereotypes of the Mexican Man and La Gran Puta in their verbal and sexual intercourse (244f); easing the tensions between them for a time, but not resolving them.

Most of the Spanish entries in *Ultraviolet Sky* evoke local color in fairly conventional ways. *Gringo* and *tortilla,* however, through their use in different contexts and with differing and contradictory connotations, create a tension that Villanueva leaves be without trying to smooth over or eliminate. *Puta* 'whore,' could be mentioned as a third example of this strategy. Since *puta, gringo,* and *tortilla* all occur very frequently in the corpus, too, and since *Rain God* is the only other novel that uses strategies of semantic enrichment of Spanish entries to an extent comparable to *Ultraviolet Sky* (see above 161-64), Villanueva undermines the generally more uniform use of these words in the corpus—and in society. By the same token, her presentation of some Spanish entries as complex signifiers is part of her more comprehensive strategy to represent reality as complex—though not in a complex way. Villanueva refuses to advocate easy solutions, to represent cultural identity along clear-cut lines, to make use of an unequivocal symbolism, to paint in black and white.

Toward the very end of *Ultraviolet Sky*, Rosa realizes that she will never be able to see, let alone represent, the appropriate color of the sky she has been trying to paint for so long.

. . . I'll never be able to see it. I can only witness what it does. The way it births us, the way it kills us, came to Rosa's mind.

Yes, the way it births us, the way it kills us, *the ultraviolet light,*
like love.
"Like Germany killed me, and a German birthed me,"
Rosa said to whomever was listening. "Like love. Like the ultraviolet sky that I fear so much, that I love so much. God-fucking-
damnit!" (378)

Ana Castillo: Sapogonia

> *Sapogonia is a distinct place in the Americas where all mestizos
> reside, regardless of nationality, individual racial composition,
> or legal residential status—or, perhaps, because of all of these.*
> (5)

The emphasis on mestizo culture seems to have become a
topos in Chicana writing in the late 1980s. It occurs not only
in *Ultraviolet Sky* and in the first sentence of the prologue to
Sapogonia, but also in the subtitle of Gloria Anzaldúa's collection of essays and poetry *Borderlands / La Frontera: The New
Mestiza* (1987). But whereas the tag *mestiza* on Anzaldúa's
title page points at the core of her book, Ana Castillo—in
opening her prologue—evokes one of the many facets of her
novel rather than its prime issue. At the core of *Sapogonia* we
do not find *mestizaje*, but a fatal attraction of sorts and male
megalomania.

Ana Castillo's second novel after her collections of poetry
and her epistolary novel *The Mixquiahuala Letters* (1986)
shows some striking analogies with *Ultraviolet Sky*, over and
above the propagation of mestizo culture. Both texts set out—
as does *Trini*—with a short chapter that represents a very late
instant in the novel's chronology and then fall back to a rather
chronological treatment of time interspersed with flashbacks.
Both *Ultraviolet Sky* and *Sapogonia* are set among artists. In
both of them, the female protagonist relates to Indian
goddesses—another topos they share with Anzaldúa's *Borderlands* and with *Trini*—, experiences a birth with complications,
and has to suffer her lover's fits of jealousy at a party. Both
texts foreground the question of gender at least as much as the

question of ethnicity, and in both of them, flamenco is the most prominent music style. For all these affinities, the two novels are by no means identical. *Sapogonia* may well be the most literary novel ever written by a Chicana or Chicano. It is permeated by literature, and not only because of its subtitle—*(An Anti-Romance in 3/8 Meter)*—the added chapter mottoes by Anaïs Nin (17) and Feodor Dostoyevsky (180), or the uncommon definition of the term *anti-hero* that precedes it. It also goes beyond *Louise, Plum Pickers, Rain God,* and *Tamazunchale,* and is at least on a par with Hinojosa's texts, in its use of metafictional comments, changing narrative perspective and narrator, explicit and implicit literary quotation. Finally, and not least importantly, the caliber of its protagonists Pastora Velásquez Aké and Máximo Madrigal contributes further to its literariness. Many of the protagonists of the corpus are, as paradigmatic Chicanos, ethnographically distant from their readers, and those of *Hunger* and *Ultraviolet Sky* share with a lot of readers their condition as middle-class Americans. Pastora and Máximo, on the other hand, while versed in both these parts, offer readers less possibility for identification or relegation because their literary nature, the fact that they are fictional constructs, is made more obvious, and more explicit, than in other Chicano novels.

Máximo Madrigal—names are as telling in Castillo's novel as in *Ultraviolet Sky*—grows up on his grandfather's ranch in Sapogonia, a fictional Latin American country. He becomes an indifferent university student, leaves his country for Paris "because the unknown and unventured were inherently more attractive than the boredom in what was already secured" (32), sells vegetables in a Parisian market, moves to Madrid where he meets his father, who teaches him to play the flamenco guitar and to weld and then sends him off to the United States. Max plays the guitar in a Spanish restaurant in New York, works as a waiter in California, enrolls in a school of performing arts in Chicago, and joins a theater group for one production, until Laura, the daughter of a museum director, "nurture[s him] into a respected artist" (135)—a sculptor—and

becomes his first wife. When Laura divorces him, he goes to
see his mother in Sapogonia and learns that his grandparents
have been killed. He spends a gothic night at their now devas-
tated ranch, haunted and protected by the ghost of his grandmother. Back in Chicago, he meets Maritza, an extremely
sexy and extremely rich woman who "likes to be in the lime-
light." He decides to get emotionally involved with her—"That
was the kind of woman I needed" (237)—and ends up marry-
ing her.

Unlike many other Chicano novels, a summary of the protagonist's life in no way summarizes the contents of Castillo's
book—the way in which Máximo is presented and the image
he promotes of himself are as crucial to the understanding of
the novel. Readers of *Sapogonia* are presented with an artist
whose talents in many different fields are repeatedly recognized by the people around him, but whose own assessment of
himself exceeds even his most benevolent critics. "[A]ware
of" his "unusual talents" (127), he intends "to follow in the
footsteps of Dalí and Picasso" (298), and feels that he has
"inherited" "the true gift of the musician" (134). He makes
himself known to his readership as a connoisseur of Shakespeare (49f), "very good at cards," (52) an excellent cook
(212, 240), and a versatile dancer (260). He claims all the ex-
celling roles in the novel for himself and leaves little breathing
space for the other characters. He is the main narrator in either first or third person and cannot suppress an occasional
wink to the reader either. His presence is so imposing, that in
those few instances in which the narrative voice belongs to a
narrator who judges him from a distance, we are left bewil-
dered about the origin of that voice and suspect some kind of
plot on behalf of Máximo's, who must have twisted the narrator's arm and forced her to say, for instance: "It might be
argued that Máximo didn't respect women; but in his own paradoxical way, he did. Surely he did" (174). Furthermore, his
omnipresence is not without contradictions. Thus he is presented throughout as elitist, arrogant, and incapable of feeling

becomes a spokesperson of the underprivileged in his country, a role that hardly ties in with his character.

The female protagonist of Castillo's novel is presented as a morally integer and coherent spokesperson of the underprivileged. Pastora Velásquez Aké, Máximo's main antagonist, and —alongside his mother and grandmother—the most important woman in his life, is a Mexican American singer whose political commitment brings to mind Joan Baez. In contrast to Máximo, Pastora does not crave stardom, feels ill at ease when she has to talk in public, doesn't like to talk much anyway, and gives preference to her cause, her message, rather than to promoting herself. Her solidarity with the underprivileged even costs her two years of jail. Her life story is much less spectacularly rendered than Máximo's, although her rescue work for illegal immigrants and her time in jail add some zest to it. Apart from that, the most apparent changes in her life are the birth of her child and her marriage. She does the same kind of job from the beginning practically to the end of the novel, again in contrast to the male protagonist.

The central relationship in *Sapogonia* is the one between Máximo and Pastora, a relationship which consists mainly of sexual encounters, and which he doesn't hestitate to compare to couples like Diego Rivera and Frida Kahlo, Virginia and Leonard Woolf (295), or Salvador Dalí and Gala (171), while she is much more down to earth about it: "when are you going to end this pathos driven by superficiality" (161). Whereas his feelings take on the form of an obsession, her feelings towards him, and what exactly it is in him that attracts her, remain unclear, and so does the chemistry of their relationship, in spite of the various attempts at pinning it down. Castillo gives the clearest clue to her protagonist couple's real identity in the epilogue to *Sapogonia*, which starts as an idyllic scene with Pastora as a caring mother and wife and then presents us with one of the few assessments of the fatal attraction that dominates the novel from Pastora's perspective. Pastora—at least she still seems to be the narrator—goes on to define herself:

> Pastora was celluloid, the chanteuse of the silver screen of silent films, and larger than life. She was all the heroines who had impassioned young men in adolescent novels. . . . (311)

Pastora and Máximo, because he also refuses to come to be merely a mimetically depicted human being, are constructed of and around literature. Besides the fact that Máximo tries to affect the manners and mannerisms of a dandy, and besides the explicit mentioning of literary authors, characters, and works, from *Don Quijote* (17) to *Tess of the D'Urbervilles* (47), and from Borges, Shakespeare, and Plato (49) to Rodolfo Usigli (117), *Sapogonia* also includes more hidden types of intertextuality. The night Máximo spends at the ranch of his dead grandparents follows the model of a gothic tale, and, on the level of vocabulary, the Spanish word of Arawakan origin *guayaba*, which has one indistinct showing in the corpus (*Barrio Boy* 6, see above 138-39), appears twice in the context of Máximo's fictional native country, both times connected to scent: "the aroma of guayaba trees" (218), and "the guayaba-scented garden" (285). I take it that this is a more than accidental coincidence with the title of Gabriel García Márquez's collection of talks with Plinio Apuleyo Mendoza, *El olor de la guayaba*, in which the Columbian author talks of the scent of the guava as a token from his mother country, a scent he misses when he is abroad, and to which he has to return from time to time.

Pastora defines herself not only as a heroine of novels, but also as the "chanteuse of the silver screen." The fatal attraction between her and Máximo is not only literature, but also "celluloid," and—as in the case of literature—the connection to film becomes clear long before Pastora spells it out.

> Pastora's resistance to Máximo Madrigal held itself in the acute differences inherent to their genders. Each was a prima donna, a matador, fearless with the kind of bravado inherent in those whose motives are heightened in the face of danger before a crowd. (110)

Apart from all its semantic and symbolic charge, the Spanish word *matador* may point out an intertextual reference to Pedro Almodóvar's movie by the same name, which in its depiction of an excruciating relationship is not without similarities to *Sapogonia*. And this is by no means the only reference to film in Castillo's novel. Max's feat of "conducting" Wagner's entire *Ring des Nibelungen* in a couple of hours, while it is playing on the radio, may allude to a similar scene in the screen adaptation of William Styron's *Sophie's Choice*. Implicit allusions of this kind are backed up by explicit references to film. Pastora is not only defined as "celluloid," but is more than once compared to the Mexican actress María Félix, and to other movie protagonists, most insistently by Max:

> We made love half-clothed, rested, talked, disrobed completely, and made love again. I was dazed with remembrances of *La Generala*, the haughtiness of a cursed woman who would castrate a man and let him live. I told Pastora that she had traces of María Félix, not the way she looked in *La Generala*, but earlier. So many films raced through my mind that the night was heightened by the illusory romance of cinema, of fable and myth. Had she seen *In the Realm of the Senses?* How would she feel, knowing as she tightened the sash around my neck, that she was receiving the last of my energies, my semen surging into her body, hoping against mortality as I gasped my last breath? (305)

The imposing images of film, and the fact that he has never been able to really conquer Pastora, lead Max to stab Pastora with a pair of scissors in the climactic scene that opens and ends the novel—or does this murder only occur during one of his nightmares? Apart from literature, film, and supernatural occurrences, dream is a fourth important referential layer in this multilayered text and a chief agent in producing an ambiguity that differs from the ambiguity of *Ultraviolet Sky*. While Villanueva accentuates the complex nature of cultural identity to a greater degree than Castillo, and uses some words as ambiguous signifiers, ambiguity becomes part of the *plot* in *Sapogonia*. Does Max kill Pastora or not? Is he a talented artist or is he a fraud? Is he affected by paranoia or does Pastora really perform voodoo against him? Castillo leaves these questions as unanswered as Pynchon does with similar ones in his *Crying of Lot 49.* She may at times present more evidence for one of two possibilities, but gives readers at the same time just enough leeway not to discard the second one entirely.

If we take the mere number of Spanish entries as a measure, *Sapogonia* is way below *Trini* and only slightly above *Wedding* in its use of Spanish. If we take into consideration the length of Spanish entries, however, the different ways in which they are applied, the use of fictitious Spanish, and the inclusion of comments on the Spanish language, the picture changes, and *Sapogonia* becomes one of the Chicana—and Chicano—novels in which Spanish is most conspicuously and most variously present. Most of the techniques found in other novels can be found in *Sapogonia*, too. In order to avoid excessive repetition, I will restrict my analysis to a few strategies which are less—or not at all—present in other novels.

Characterization is one function of Spanish entries in *Sapogonia*. Max's second wife Maritza opportunistically adapts to a changed socio-political paradigm in the United States by pretending to be of Hispanic origin. Max's friend Miguel says: "Of course, you're Latina *now*, Maritza! It's cool to be Hispanic, whatever that means!" (254). It is not astonishing therefore, that her Spanish vocabulary is much restricted to the commonplace high impact term *coño* (256, 257, 262). Adolfo Zaragoza, another character, is the only one who uses the formula *mi amigo* (259, 262).

Máximo, who perceives of gender-relations very much in terms of warfare, uses Spanish as a weapon towards his first wife Laura, when she discloses to him that:

> . . . I don't care if you don't want children yet, Max. My body can't wait until you're ready!"
> "Cómo chingan estas mujeres," he muttered, not looking up, but the sounds of the unknown language caused her to shrink and she went to the bedroom to watch t.v. (170)

Máximo uses this strategy—an insider pun from which the monolingual reader as well as Laura are excluded—not only in Spanish, but also in French:

> . . . Hilda spoke in a tone that grated against Máximo's nerves, as he took it all as hypocrisy. He couldn't believe she meant she would like the idea of an attractive woman working in the same place as Máximo.
> "Autre femme plus ravissante que vous?" He smiled at Hilda and put an arm around her tight waist. She almost blushed, so flattered was she by his unexpected charm. Max had begun to prepare his lamb for the slaughter. (81-82)

There is one category of Spanish entries in which *Sapogonia* decidedly surpasses other Chicano novels. No other text of the corpus comes anywhere near Castillo's novel in its use of *songs*. The first of these *songs* is a fandango sung by Pío de la Costurera, Max's father (56), when the two first meet as cellmates in a Madrid jail. The narrator informs us that the four metrically very regular stanzas are an "old fandango," an "old cante," but refuses to provide any information about its contents. Each of the stanzas is an independent unit, but they all —and with increasing cruelty—deal with unrequited love. This foreshadows the clash between Pastora and Max in a manner which brings to mind the use of blues verses in *Rayuela* by Julio Cortázar, to whom *The Mixquiahuala Letters*, Castillo's first novel, is dedicated. *Mixquiahuala Letters* is also indebted to *Rayuela* structurally: both novels offer the reader a choice as to the order of reading the text (on the use of blues verses in *Rayuela*, cf. my essay "Mestizaje," 40-41).

Sapogonia brings in flamenco lyrics as a variation of the excruciating gender antagonism that later on will be acted out in the novel. Mexican songs, e.g., those of José Alfredo Jiménez, could perfectly fulfill the same function, but, significantly, Castillo opts for a European tradition. The virtual absence of the term *flamenco*, and of flamenco as a theme, in the Chicano novel before 1985 and its very strong representation in *Ultraviolet Sky* and *Sapogonia*, two more recent Chicana novels, might be interpreted as a sign that, while weight is taken away from Mexican American traditions and cultural stereotypes, another Hispanic cultural manifestation becomes central and is treated, at least in *Sapogonia*, somewhat stereotypically. While he works with the theater group, Max ineffectively tries to convince the director to stage a play by the Spanish author García Lorca rather than one by the Mexican playwright Usigli, which they are rehearsing. After the failure of the production, he states his case in the following terms, attacking the stereotype depiction of Mexicans by North Americans:

> . . . if any cultural figure was going to gain prominence among the American status quo, it was not going to be someone like Rudolfo Usigli. . . . the North American public culturally could only relate to Latinos insofar as their roots lie in Spain. Yes, the Spanish Civil War, the great battle against fascism; castenets, toreadors in tight pants, women with thorned roses between their teeth. But bring up our amigos just south of the border, conjuring images of gritty, snotnosed children; women in dust-covered skirts squatting before a griddle over hot stones, patting the crude dough between their dark palms for the meal of tortillas; and their men, loathsome bandit types, with beady black eyes and those wretched bodies, tough like those of desert mules—and they wrinkle their nose as if someone had just passed air. (117-118)

While Max is not successful in convincing his director, he seems to have convinced his author at least to some extent. Castillo brings in García Lorca, as we shall soon see, and flamenco. And while her novel thematizes and subverts North American stereotypes of Mexicans, it links flamenco in Spain to delinquency, drinking and gambling, thus repeating a stereotype view of flamenco that is well established in peninsular Spanish literature (cf. Grande 425-465)

The second *song* in *Sapogonia* occurs at the end of a chapter in which Máximo, as a first person narrator, tells how his grandfather raped and then married a Mayan virgin,[101] how the second child of that marriage went to the hills to fight the government and how a ballad was written for him. The ballad

---

101   Castillo seems to underscore the fictional character of the country of Sapogonia by having its Mayans speak Quechua (106, cf. 196).

"Mestizo Mireles," a Sapogonian *corrido* of sorts, consists of five metrically very irregular *romance* quatrains and is similar in tone to the *corrido* fragment quoted in *Horseman* (above 139-40). In contrast to Villarreal, however, Castillo once more does not provide any translation, but retakes the narration, and at the same time ends the chapter, with two sentences, a change of narrator, and a wink to the reader:

> That's all that I remember of it, but you get the idea. Máximo put down his guitar and wondered why you didn't turn to the next page. (108)

This ending moves in two opposite directions. The guitar enhances the illusion of orality of Máximo's tale while the remark to the reader destroys that illusion and emphasizes at the same time Max's fictional constitution. Moreover, the last sentence contains an implicit comment on the preceding twenty-one lines in Spanish. The long untranslated ballad may well cause a reader to hesitate before turning to the next page. Castillo thus foregrounds the fictional character of her text as well as the Spanish language entry.

The remaining two *songs* in *Sapogonia* are not songs at all, but two fragments from a book of poems which Max reads on a Chicago bus terminal. I would like to concentrate on one of them:

> It was a book of poems by García Lorca. Inside there was an inscription: "To Hilda on your birthday. . . . The year in which the dedication was inscribed was the same that Max had had sex with a girl for the first time.
>
> Sí, tu niñez ya fábula de fuentes.
> El tren y la mujer que llena el cielo
> Tu soledad esquiva en los hoteles
> y tu máscara pura de otro signo
>
> "¡Pastora! ¡No se te vaya a olvidar tu mochila!" The woman's voice broke his concentration and Max instinctively turned about, hearing the familiar Spanish and curious to see who spoke it. (84)

Again, the narrator does not make any gesture towards translation, and again, Lorca's verses establish a dialogue with Castillo's text, this time more complex and intense than in the case of the flamenco lyrics. The first line is like a direct comment on Max's evocation of his younger years: "Yes, your childhood already a fable of fountains" (my translation). The word *train* in the second line as well as the loneliness in hotels mentioned in the third one can be placed into the context of Max's life as a refugee. The "pure mask of another sign" summoned forth in the last line may be read as an allusion to the masquerade that will mark the relationship between Máximo and Pastora. The four verses are the opening lines of the poem "Tu infancia en Menton" from the collection *Poeta en Nueva York*. In contrast to the ballad of "Mestizo Mireles," this time the author does not give her readers the benefit of a pause before they turn to the next page, but continues in Spanish after the inserted verses. The woman who is addressed in Spanish is Pastora, and—unless it is our habit to skip all the secondary language passages—we see the two protagonists, who don't know each other yet, cross each other's path without meeting, as characters sometimes cross the stage without talking to one another and without meeting in García Lorca's play *Así que pasen cinco años*. Since *Sapogonia* is not strictly chronologically structured, we are in the privileged position to already have knowledge of the coming liaison between Pastora and Máximo, while they are still excluded from that knowledge.

Max continues waiting for his bus, observing the people around him, and reading *Poeta en Nueva York*. Some lines from "Fábula y rueda de los tres amigos" interact with his surroundings in a similar way as "Tu infancia en Menton" does with his relationship to Pastora (86). He then witnesses how a dark complexioned stranger is approached by immigration officials, asks himself in a "flash of bravado" if he should intervene and warn the man, but continues reading. The officials arrest the stranger and chase another one "as if they were after a vicious criminal, determined to take him in and see justice carried out." A third excerpt from Lorca's poetry follows, which also engages in dialogue with the scene observed by Máximo and with Máximo's attitude. But unlike the two previous Lorca quotations, this one is rendered in an English version, almost as if it were a translation of the earlier fragments in Spanish, which it is not:

> I will not see it!
> Tell the moon to come
> for I do not want to see the blood
> of Ignacio on the sand.
> I will not see it!
> . . . .

The strategy of alternating between Spanish and English stanzas is not new in *Sapogonia*. Already the fandango lyrics cited above were preceded by a fandango stanza of sorts in English (55). Here, Castillo creates the impression that the two fragments in Spanish and the one in English belong to the same collection, or the same poem even. The fragment in English, however, does not stem from *Poeta en Nueva York* but from García Lorca's *Llanto por Ignacio Sánchez Mejías*. It makes monolingual readers aware of the dialogue going on between the poem and the surrounding prose, may thus increase their interest in the fragments in Spanish and cause a feeling of missing something for not knowing that language. It may even lead them to read an English translation of *Poeta en Nueva York*. Once more we get the impression that "the master of the game" (*Mixquiahuala* 6) is looking over Ana Castillo's shoulder: Julio Cortázar.

After the verses from *Llanto por Ignacio Sánchez Mejías*, the chapter set in the Chicago bus terminal, which is—as other sections of *Sapogonia*—highly reminiscent of cinema, ends as follows:

> It was time for Max to board the bus. He double-checked his ticket and watched the bus driver as he changed the sign over the windshield to one that read a series of stops, the final one being Los Angeles. (87)

We may read this just as plain information. Or we may, fore-warned by the amount of poetry and Spanish that the chapter contains, and by the fact that Castillo started out as a poet, read it as a more lyric and more symbolic discourse. If we do so, the last two words suddenly are no longer just the signifier for a Californian city, but become affected by their Spanish meaning as they do in the collection of poems *Sobre los ánge-les* by Lorca's friend Rafael Alberti.

Let me, to finish my analysis of *Sapogonia*, return to the second line of the first excerpt from a García Lorca poem: "El tren y la mujer que llena el cielo." The verse already prefig-ures the ending of the novel or, which amounts to the same, the ending of *Sapogonia* is a variation of Lorca's verse "The train and the woman who fills the sky." Because one of the last paragraphs of the epilogue, the last one in which Máximo is mentioned explicitly, ends:

> . . . if he suggested an ungodly hour, an abandoned building, a car parked beneath the elevated tracks so that at the precise moment the train sped above, their moans would not be heard, he managed to have her without prelude or pretext. (311)

The passage is somewhat puzzling, because, while Pastora's attitude toward Máximo has only been very indeterminately defined, she clearly is far from being an "easy prey" for him, as these unexpected lines might suggest. They just don't seem to fit into the picture—or they fit into the picture as little and as much as her lover for a one-chapter stand, who has "the looks of the all-American hero, the contemporary Hollywood movie star, Aryan, well built" (167). Or maybe *Hollywood* is the keyword, maybe the picture makes sense if we convert it into a motion picture, if we pay heed, in other words, to the already quoted passage which defines Pastora as "celluloid," as a heroine of films and novels, and which Castillo places im-mediately after she has Pastora evoke her lovemaking "be-neath the elevated tracks." The train speeding above and the couple making love not only take up a literary image intro-duced many pages before in a fragment from a García Lorca poem, but allude to the topos of trains in Hollywood movies, and, maybe, more concretely, to Liza Minnelli, screaming at the top of her lungs under a railroad bridge in *Cabaret*, "at the precise moment the train sped above," and then moaning and panting in what appears to be an act of compensation for the act of love with the Michael York character that never takes place.

The plurivalent imagery and the references to film and literature give Ana Castillo's *Sapogonia* a lyric density in spite of the not at all lyric argument, and create a complex, ambiguous, and multilayered symbolism.

Cabaret is not the only movie that uses the image of the train with sexual undertones or as a cinematographic euphemism. And a second image that almost invariably appears in this context is that of the *tunnel*. The last line of *Sapogonia*, therefore, which reads:

> She was the dark tunnel through which you passed and began your first memory of this world. (312)

also goes beyond its surface function as a feminist statement. As a promising direction for further investigation, I suggest: *North by Northwest*. For those who speak Spanish, *62 podría ser un modelo para armar*.

13. By Way of Conclusion: A Response to Reed Way Dasenbrock

> Virtually every other critic working in this field has seen misunderstanding or unintelligibility as the danger to be avoided at all costs. I argue, in contrast, that intelligibility cannot be made the sole criterion in our understanding and evaluation of multicultural texts. Ready intelligibility is not always what the writer is striving for; it therefore cannot be what the critic always demands. (Dasenbrock 11)

I assume my argumentation so far has shown that easy readability is not what I am looking for in a literary text. I agree with the quintessential suggestion in Reed Way Dasenbrock's article on "Intelligibility and Meaningfulness in Multicultural Literature in English." Nevertheless, I have two points of contention with him:

> Difficulties in a text cannot simply be attacked as destroying the "universality" of a work or celebrated as establishing its "localism," as closing the text to outsiders. The critic needs to decide whether unintelligibility exists merely for its own sake or for the sake of the work the reader must do to make the text intelligible. *Writers accommodate themselves to their readers' horizons as much as they can; where they honestly cannot, the reader must take over.* (18, emphasis added)

Did Blake or Melville, did Stein or Joyce "honestly accommodate themselves to their readers' horizon as much as they could?" Does Pynchon? Why should we require intelligibility from the authors of "New Literatures" if we celebrate at the same time the cryptic texts of consecrated and canonized writers? Why should a reading process that—even with the help of the *Iliad*, an old street map and an old phone book of Dublin, and dictionaries for most languages of the Western World—may not lead to more than a partial understanding, be regarded as a challenge, while the need for a Spanish or Maori dictionary in order to look up some words in a "multicultural text" is rejected as an undue imposition? And why should the use of foreign language entries be regarded as an asset in *The Waste Land* and in the *Cantos* but as a drawback in multicultural texts? I have not yet found a good book—if I may use such an outdated concept—that did not impose some difficulties on me, make me go some way towards it. I cannot share the underlying supposition contained in the emphasized sentence, namely, that authors must strive to accommodate themselves to their readers' horizons, must make the text move instead of the reader, to put it in Schleiermacher's terms, and can only impose difficulties on them if there is no other way out. This claim is all the more striking since Dasenbrock himself states that "meaning and meaningfulness are not entirely functions of intelligibility" (16), and comments repeatedly on the positive aspects of the learning process that unintelligible words—or well-known words in new contexts, *ghost* in M.H. Kingston's *The Woman Warrior*, for example—may lead to. The quotation is not in line with the rest of his article, and looks almost like an apologetic gesture towards those critics who, as he himself says, see "misunderstanding or unintelligibility as the danger to be avoided at all costs," who fear that multicultural texts might lose their "universal" potential if they include "unintelligible localisms" (11).

My second point of dispute is closely linked to the first one. But whereas there Dasenbrock is too moderate for my liking, here he is too radical. In regard to *Ultima*, the Chicano example in the four texts he analyzes (the others are Narayan's *The Painter of Signs*, Kingston's *The Woman Warrior*, and Ihimaera's *Tangi*), he comes to the conclusion that:

> the voyage of the reader through the book mirrors Antonio's experience. No one translates for Antonio, no one cushions his transition into English. He is thrown into the school world of English and forced to find his way in it. By the end, he is moving toward becoming someone who could write the book in which he appears. In the same way, though less violently, the reader is thrown into a world of Spanish without translation or cushioning, and even the monolingual reader moves toward a functional bilin-

gualism, an ability to understand the world of the novel. Antonio moves toward being able to write the novel; the reader moves toward being able to read it. (16)

I agree with most points in that argument, and all the more so, since the last sentence quoted fits Schleiermacher's concept of translation as nicely as his phraseology. *Ultima* is, with an average of about two entries per page, one of the texts that use Spanish most frequently. Moreover, it includes *hermetic* Spanish and leaves some Spanish entries untranslated. It makes the monolingual reader move, in other words. That move, however, is considerably smaller than Dasenbrock suggests. Monolingual readers of *Ultima* may encounter difficulties and experience a learning process during which they become familiar with certain Spanish words and expressions. Nevertheless, Dasenbrock's statement that the reader of *Ultima* is "thrown into a world of Spanish without translation or cushioning," is inaccurate. Even the most monolingual of monolingual readers can read and enjoy *Ultima* without the help of a dictionary. There are a few insider puns in Spanish, like *a la veca* mentioned above (168-169), which exclude her or him from the full picture, but Anaya's overall strategy works in the opposite direction, is a careful and masterful attempt at not shutting monolingual readers out in spite of the relatively frequent use of Spanish. I would go even further and argue that Anaya uses Spanish in most cases with the monolingual reader in mind and not with the bilingual one. Paradoxical as it may sound, the bilingual reader loses from knowing Spanish, while the monolingual reader wins from not knowing it: in contrast to Dasenbrock's affirmation, literal translation abounds in *Ultima* and many Spanish entries are contextually "cushioned." From the standpoint of a bilingual reader, many of the translations in Anaya's novel seem unmotivated and slow the novel down unnecessarily. Furthermore, there are passages which use an increased dose of Spanish and seem nonetheless intended for a non-Hispanophone readership in the first place, forming a counterpoint to the Spanish *insider puns* for bilingual readers:

The house was quiet, and I was in the mist of some dream when I heard the owl cry its warning. I was up instantly, looking through the small window at the dark figure that ran madly towards the house. He hurled himself at the door and began pounding. "¡Márez!" he shouted, "¡Márez! ¡Andale, hombre!" I was frightened, but I recognized the voice. It was Jasón's father. "¡Un momento!" I heard my father call. He fumbled with the farol. "¡Andale, hombre, andale!" Chávez cried pitifully, "mataron a mi hermano—" "Ya vengo—" My father opened the door and the frightened man burst in. In the kitchen I heard my mother moan, "Ave María Purísima, mis hijos—" She had not heard Chávez's last words, and so she assumed the aviso was one that brought bad news about her sons. "Chávez, ¿qué pasa?" My father held the trembling man. "¡Mi hermano, mi hermano!" Chávez sobbed, "He has killed my brother!" "¿Pero qué dices, hombre?" my father exclaimed. He pulled Chávez into the hall and held up the farol. The light cast by the farol revealed the wild, frightened eyes of Chávez. (14)

Monolingual readers know from the beginning that something dreadful is going on. But they are kept in suspense about what exactly has happened till they read the clarifying "He has killed my brother." For bilingual readers, on the other hand, who understand "mataron a mi hermano," the suspense does not work, and neither does the "translational suspense" that the term *farol* maintains up to the metonymic contextual translation "the light cast by the farol." By the same token, the explanation that Antonio's mother "had not heard Chávez's last words, and so she assumed the aviso was one that brought bad news about her sons," is redundant for a Hispanophone audience. For a reader who does not know Spanish, the passage builds up and releases various tensions, while the bilingual reader is left with an impression of needless redundancy and excessive repetition. The foreign language may disorient monolingual readers and make them feel excluded; they may even deplore the fact that they don't know Spanish. But their disorientation functions as an element in creating suspense; if they knew Spanish, the text would not be half as intriguing. And if the use of Spanish decreases substantially after its eye-catching appearance in the passage quoted, this technique, which we have encountered in the same text before (see above 114), further confirms that the monolingual reader of Anaya's novel is not "thrown into a world of Spanish without translation or cushioning," but guided through it with utter carefulness.

The attempt at bringing the Spanish language entries to the monolingual reader is not restricted to *Ultima*, but can be observed throughout the corpus, as well as in the four Chicana novels analyzed in chapter 12. Most other texts make the reader move even less than *Ultima*. And the few that are more demanding do not pose great problems to a monolingual reader either. The four *songs* in *Sapogonia*, for example, offer an additional layer of symbolic references, but they do not carry the gist of the argument, and besides, Castillo's novel includes enough layers in the primary language to keep monolingual readers intrigued, too. *Louise*, to give a second example, is maybe the most difficult of the texts as far as Spanish entries are concerned. It offers the least help or translation to an English monolingual reader for the great number of Spanish entries and includes passages like:

> —This bato would always pester me. Me cantaba por chinga-zos. I would ignore him. I told him, sí hombre, tú ganas. Ya estuvo, and would walk away. One day I was all dressed up at a party with two or three girls when again he asked me to go out y darnos en la madre. Yo le contesté, Pos' aquí está suave, pa' que vamos pa' fuera y le puse dos cabronazos y lo senté. He had a lot of friends and they soon jumped me. My friend Felipe tried to get me out of the mess. Someone le aterrizó un patadón and that brought all his brothers and cuñados into the act. Se armó la bronca. Felipe y yo left very quietly. (112f)

Louise may disorient the readers, and may make them move towards Spanish more than any other text, but even *Louise* never reaches the point of making the reader who is not familiar with Spanish lose the gist of the argument.

What is striking in the Chicano novels in English is neither the use of Spanish nor the translation of these Spanish entries,

but the *extent* to which Spanish is translated and "translated."
Many Spanish entries are defined two or three times over, and
translation is not only used for *hermetic* entries, but also for
many *loanwords* and *etymological pairs*. The texts I have
analyzed show the following salient features as far as the accessibility of the Spanish entries is concerned:

- Most Spanish entries are easily understandable for monolingual readers. Many of them are *loanwords, clichés*, or
  etymological pairs; most of them are single words or *short
  entries*. Except for some Spanish poems or songs, they do
  not exceed the length of a sentence.
- Spanish entries in the corpus show a high degree of literal
  translation.
- There are few *hermetic entries*, and only a very small
  number of them *remain* hermetic to a monolingual reader,
  are translated neither contextually nor literally.
- Translation is not used economically; Spanish entries are
  overdefined rather than underdefined.
- The frequency of Spanish entries in a text is seldom an indicator of the difficulties in understanding that the work
  imposes. By the same token, some of the stylistically most
  convincing instances of undermining existing stereotypes
  through Spanish language elements occur in *Mango Street*
  and *Rain God*, novels which otherwise use Spanish sparingly. *Barrio Boy*, the text which uses Spanish most frequently, hardly does so in any innovative way and imposes
  no difficulties on readers not familiar with Spanish. The
  fact that Galarza's text is an autobiography and not a novel
  has certainly its share in this.
- Spanish is used mainly mimetically, as a token of the
  Spanish-speaking community portrayed. The use of Spanish in the corpus is generally closer to the use of foreign
  language elements in Hemingway's *For Whom the Bell
  Tolls* and to the local color and *costumbrismo* traditions
  than to the bilingual or multilingual strategies employed in,
  say, Julio Cortázar's *Rayuela*, Julián Ríos's *Larva*, James
  Joyce's *Ulysses*, or Vladimir Nabokov's *Pale Fire*.

The texts analyzed here provide ample "translation" and "cushioning" for the monolingual reader, and the inclusion of other Chicano novels in English published so far would not change that panorama in any considerable way. The Chicano novels published between the late sixties and the mid-eighties, offsprings of the Chicano movement (except maybe for *Tattoo*), and often marketed as "revolutionary literature," are—on the level of language—very reluctant to use experimental techniques and to be subversive. Some of the early texts are politically outspoken (*Buffalo, Cockroach, Plum Pickers*); *Mango Street* and *Tamazunchale* are two lyric novels that undermine stereotype concepts of *otherness* in very subtle ways. There are instances of subverting mainstream discourses in various texts, above all in *Mango Street, Rain God, Louise*—and in *Ultraviolet Sky* and *Sapogonia* as far as the more recent novels are concerned. But generally, the discourses and registers employed work in the opposite direction, make the texts converge on the Anglo American readership.

All in all, and with the exceptions mentioned, the authors that manifest themselves in the texts seem more concerned with writing "proper English" than with using English, "the one distinctive common weapon bequeathed to them by the colonizers" (Thorpe 346), in an inventive or "revolutionary" way. They use it as a trustworthy means of communication and seem hesitant to tamper around with it, to subvert it. This kind of restriction is not present in the Chicano novels in Spanish of the same period, which employ bilingual techniques and code switching more radically. Like their protagonists, who have adapted to the Anglo American society, the authors of the texts of the corpus tend to adapt stylistically to what is considered "literary English"—as if they, as "Hispanics" and as "minority writers," had to prove to the "mainstream" public that they are capable of writing a competent English prose. This might lead to the hypothesis that inventive language in literature is restricted to native speakers, which would also explain the greater inventiveness of those Chicano novelists who write in Spanish. Stein and Joyce, then, could undermine

English because they never had to adapt to it as their second language. The hypothesis, tempting as it may sound, does not hold up to closer scrutiny. For one thing, it fails to account for Nabokov's stylistic audacity; for another, Joyce was not as daring and subversive from the start. And many of the texts of the corpus are first novels and thus thematically and stylistically much closer to a *Portrait of the Artist as a Young Man* than to an *Iliad*.

Unlike some of their colleagues who write in Spanish, writers of Chicano novels in English seem to shy at exploring the considerable leeway that exists between a monolingual and a bilingual work. However subversive their texts may be in other respects, their use of bilingual techniques doesn't break much fresh ground. If *For Whom the Bell Tolls* were included in the corpus, it would come to the fore as one of the texts that applies bilingual strategies most daringly. But novels do not stand or fall by their use of bilingual techniques. And in our times, I would rather be stranded on a deserted island in the company of *Buffalo, Louise, Mango Street, Rain God, Sapogonia, Tamazunchale,* or *Ultraviolet Sky,* than with Hemingway's classic.

Statistics

14. Semantic Fields

(single words in the 1967-1985 corpus)

List of Symbols

The number that precedes each word indicates the number of texts in which that word appears.

  &   Appears more than a dozen times in a text.

&& Appears more than two dozen times.

  !   Deviates from the spelling in the *Diccionario de la lengua española (DRAE)*.

 @   Mexican Spanish Term (appears in Santamaría and not in *DRAE*, or with different connotations).

 #   Pachuco Term (appears in Barker, Blanco, Galván, or Polkinhorn)

 %   South American other than Mexican (Morínigo).

 *   Is not listed in any dictionary or not with the connotations it has in the corpus

14.1 Terms of Address

7 adiós (1&)
4 amigo (1&)
1 cálmate
3 carnal # (1&)
1 carnala #
7 comadre
1 cómo
7 compadre (2&)
1 compañero
3 corazón (1&)
2 cuándo
3 cuñado
1 chamaco
1 changa
3 chango
2 chavala
1 chavalo #
1 chica
1 chilpayate @
2 chula @
1 dame
1 despedida
1 dispénseme
9 don (4&&)
4 doña (2&, 1&&)
1 entiendes
1 éntrale
1 epa
2 esa #
3 ese # (1&&)
1 feíto
1 flaco
1 gordita
6 gracias
1 guapa
1 guapo
1 güela !
1 güelita !
1 habla
1 hermana
5 hermano
1 hija
1 hijada !

2 hijito
5 hijo
1 hola
5 hombre (1&)
1 jefa #
5 jefe #
1 jefita #
2 madrina
2 maestro (1&&)
8 mamá (2&)
3 mamacita
1 mano #
1 mija ! &
2 mijita ! (1&)
1 mijo !
2 mira
2 mocosa
1 mocosito
1 momentito
2 momento
1 muchacha
5 muchacho (1&)
1 mujer &
1 negra
1 negrito
1 negro
1 niña &
2 niño
2 órale #
1 oye
2 padre
1 padrecito
6 papá (3&)
1 papacito
1 perdón
1 permiso
1 prima
4 primo (1&)
1 probrecito !
4 qué
1 querida
1 quién
1 rata #

1 sabes
1 salud
2 saludo
10 señor (2&, 2&&)
8 señora (2&, 1&&)
5 señorita (1&)
1 señorito
6 sí (1&)
1 suerte
1 tata
5 tía (1&&)
7 tío (2&)
6 vámonos
2 vamos
2 vente
1 vete
5 vieja #
3 viejo #
1 voy

14.2 High Impact Terms

1 ajúa !
1 arre
1 asqueroso
6 ay (2&)
1 babosa
2 baboso
2 basta
1 bravo
1 bruto
2 bueno
8 cabrón (1&)
1 cabrona @
1 cabroncito
7 caca
1 caramba
1 cochar #
1 cochina
1 cochinita
1 cojones
1 condenado
1 cuaco @
1 cuchara ? %
1 cuebole ! #
1 cuidado
2 culo
1 chi @
4 chichi @
1 chifletera #
1 chihuahua @
1 chinga
1 chinga'o !
3 chingada (1&)
2 chingado
1 chingao !
1 chingaso !
1 chingazo
1 chingo
2 chingón
4 desgraciado
4 diablo
1 dios
1 fundillo @
1 hay

2 híjola ! #
1 idiota
1 imbécil
1 jesús
1 jodido
1 joto @
7 loco
3 malcriado
1 maldición
3 maldito
1 maleducado
2 mamasota #
1 marrana
1 marranín
2 marrano
1 mentiroso
1 mentira
3 mierda
1 mondado @
1 necio
1 olé
1 peda #
1 pedo @
2 pendeja
6 pendejo
3 pinche @
1 placa #
7 puta
4 puto (1&)
1 quico #
2 tapado @
1 tonta
1 tontera
1 tontito
2 tonto
2 verga
2 viva (1&)

14.3 Ethnographic Terms

6 abrazo	1 calconomía	2 choza
1 acacia	1 caliche	1 destiladero
1 acequia	1 calzón	1 diligencia
9 adobe (1&, 1&&)	1 camada	1 duende
1 afición	1 camioneta	1 ejido
3 alameda	2 campo	2 embarcadero @
3 alamo	1 canasto	1 encomienda
1 alboroto	1 cancel	1 enganche @
1 alcancía	1 canción	1 espíritu
1 aleluya	1 candil&	1 fandango
1 alpaca &	1 cántaro	1 farol
1 altiplano	7 cantina (2&)	1 feo
1 armadillo	1 carbón	1 feria
1 armario	1 carbonato	6 fiesta
1 arañas	1 carretilla	2 flamenco
4 arroyo (1&&)	1 casita	1 formal
1 asistencia	5 centavo (1&)	1 fuerte
1 atajo	1 cerro	1 gallina
1 atenciones	1 cervecería	2 gallo
2 autoridades (1&)	1 cobija	1 gobierno
1 avenida	1 coca	1 graza !
1 aviso	3 colonia	1 grillo
2 baile	2 comal	4 grito
1 bajío	1 conquista	1 guamúchil @
1 banderilla	1 condor	1 guaripa @
1 barranca	1 consultorio	1 guayín @
9 barrio (1&, 1&&)	1 corcholata #	2 guerrilla (1&)
1 bola @	8 corral (2&&)	2 hacendado
1 bolero	1 corrida	3 hacienda (1&, 1&&)
1 botica	3 corrido	1 huacal
1 bravura	1 coyote @	7 huarache (1&)
3 bronco @	5 cucaracha	1 huerta
1 buey	1 cucuyo	2 jacal
1 bule	4 cuento	1 jaripeo @
6 burro (2&)	1 culebra	1 jarro
1 cabalgada	1 cumbia	1 juzga'o !
1 caballo	1 chaleco	1 lagarto
1 cabrito	1 chamisa !	1 lana @
1 cábula	1 chamizal	1 lazo
1 cachucha	1 charreada @	1 liana
1 cajón	2 chicote	1 loma
1 calabaza	1 chiquihuite @	1 loro
1 calabozo	1 chirona	1 lucha

2 llama
2 llano (1&)
5 llorona @ (1&)
1 macizo
3 machete (1&)
3 machismo
7 macho
1 malinche @
1 mamey
3 mañana
1 manantial
2 mandado
1 manta
2 mantilla
1 manzanita
7 mariachi
1 marina *
2 mercado
1 merengue
2 mesa (1&)
1 mesilla
1 mesón
2 mesquite @
3 metate
2 milpa (1&)
1 misa
1 mitote
1 mixto (tren)
2 mochila (1&)
1 mojonera
1 molcajete
2 molino
1 molote @ (moño)
1 montaña
2 monte
1 morral
1 mosquito
2 mula
1 nagua
1 nocturna
1 nogal
2 nopal
1 nopalera
2 novena
1 ocote
1 ocotillo
2 olla

1 oso
1 palo
1 paloma
1 palomilla @
2 panadería
1 pañal
1 pantalón
1 pañuelo
1 pastura &
1 paternostro !
6 patio (1&)
1 pedregal
2 peonada
1 perro
1 pésame
1 peseta
3 peso (1&)
1 petaca
5 petate
3 piñata
1 piñon
1 piojo
1 pistola
1 pizarra
1 pizarrín
1 platanar
1 plática
4 plaza (1&&)
1 polvo
3 poncho
1 portal
2 posada
1 postigo
1 prepa *
1 presa
1 presidio @
1 pretil @ &&
6 pueblo (1&&)
1 puesto
1 puro
1 ranchito
4 rancho
2 reata @ (1&)
1 relámpago
1 remuda @
1 respeto
1 revolución

3 río
1 ristra
1 rodeo
1 sala
1 sanctuario !
3 sarape (1&, 1&&)
1 secundaria
1 sentimiento
3 serape !
2 sierra
2 siesta
2 sinvergüenza
6 sombrero
1 sota *
1 taco @ (polaina)
1 tango
1 tapanco &
1 tardiada ! @
1 tienda
1 tiendita
1 tina
1 tirante
1 tocoloche ! @
1 tortillería
2 tostón
1 trabajo
1 tranca
1 trenza
1 tristeza
2 vecindad (1&)
1 vela
1 velo
2 velorio
1 vereda
2 vergüenza
1 víbora
1 virgen
1 yesca #

14.4 Culinary Terms

2 aguardiente
1 albóndiga
1 alimento
1 anís
2 antojito @
3 atole (1&)
1 avena
1 barbacoa
1 barreteada !
1 birote @
1 birria @ (carne)
1 bizcochito
1 botana @
1 botella
1 buñuelo
4 burrito @
2 café
2 camote
1 canela
3 capirotada
1 caramelo
2 carnitas @
2 cruda #
1 crudo #
1 chico @
1 chicha
2 chicharrón @
1 chilaquile @
9 chile (1&)
(2 chili)
1 chilindrina @
2 chirimoya
1 chocolate
1 chopo @
4 chorizo
1 churro
1 elote
3 empanada
6 enchilada
1 enhierbado @
1 epasote !
1 fideo
4 frijol (1&)

1 frijolito
1 garbanzo
1 gaseosa
1 guacamole
1 guayaba
1 helote !
1 hielito
3 huevo
1 jalapeño @
1 jitomate @
2 jocoque @
1 jerez
1 larga *
1 leche
1 machito @
2 maguey
1 maíz
2 mango
1 manteca
1 manzanilla
1 margarita *
1 marihuana !
4 marijuana #
3 masa
7 menudo @
1 mescal !
1 mezcal
1 mojo @
1 mollete @
1 morisqueta @
1 morsilla !
2 mota #
1 nieve
2 orégano
1 oshá *
1 pambazo @
1 pandulce #
2 panocha @
2 papaya
1 peyote @
1 picadillo
1 pilón
1 piloncillo @

1 pinole @
1 pirulí
2 pisto @
2 plátano
1 polvorón
1 ponche
3 posole ! @
2 pozole
3 pulque
2 pinto (adj.)
1 punto
2 quesadilla
1 raspada
2 sal
2 salsa
1 sangría
1 sopaipilla %
1 sotol
1 surtido
6 taco @
1 taquito
8 tamal
1 tamalada
1 tamarinda !
1 tamarindo
1 tatema @
7 tequila (1&&)
1 tlacollo ! @
1 toronjil
1 torta
1 torteando
15 tortilla (3&, 1&&)
1 tostada
1 tripa
1 tripita
2 tuna
1 vino
1 yerbabuena

14.5 Groups of People

1 abuela &	1 contador * &	3 gringa @
3 abuelita (&)	1 contratista	12 gringo @ (3&, 1&&)
2 abuelito	2 conquistador	1 gringuita @
3 abuelo	1 coronel	1 guardia
1 administrador	1 criatura	1 gucho ! @
2 aficionado	1 cuarterona	3 güera # (1&&)
1 alambrista #	1 cuate	1 güerita #
1 alcaide	1 cubano	1 güero # &
1 alcalde	1 cumplidor	1 hechicera
4 americano	6 curandera (1&)	1 guerrillero
8 anglo (3&)	2 charro (1&)	2 hidalgo
2 arriero (1&)	1 chicana	1 hispano &
2 arrimado	2 chicanito	1 huasteca @
1 azteca	8 chicano (4&, 1&&)	1 huertista *
1 bandido	1 chinita	1 india
1 bastardo *	2 chinito	2 indio (1&)
1 bato	1 chola #	2 inglés
3 bolillo #	2 cholo #	1 inglesa
3 borracho	5 chota @	1 inocente
5 bracero #	1 descamisado	1 jalcocotecano * &
2 bruja (1&)	1 desperado	1 jinete &&
2 caballero	1 director	1 judío
3 cacique	1 Dorados @ &	1 julia @
2 californio	1 enamorado	2 jura #
2 camarada	1 enbrujado !	1 ladrón
1 camello #	1 enganchado @	1 lavaplatos
1 camotero	1 enganchador @	1 licenciado
6 campesino	1 entremetido	1 limosnero
1 cantinera	1 escamado	1 llanero
1 capataz	1 escribano	1 machetero
1 capitalista	4 familia	1 maderista *
2 capitán	1 fanático	1 marchante
1 caporal	2 federales * (1&)	1 mariguano @
1 carbonero	2 gabacha #	1 marijuano !
1 carrancista *	1 gabachito #	1 marinero *
2 católico	1 gabacho # &	1 matador
1 cervecero	3 gachupín @	1 mayate #
1 colero @	1 gachupina @	1 mazatleco
1 comanchero *	1 gambusino @	1 médica
1 compatriota	3 general	2 mejicano
1 comunista	1 gente	1 merolico @
1 concuño	1 gerente	1 mestiza
1 conductor @	1 gobernador	4 mestizo

3 mexicano
1 minero
1 mojado # &
1 monjita
1 moreno
1 morisco
2 mozo
1 nana
1 nayarita
1 necesitado
1 norteamericana
1 norteamericano
1 norteño
2 novia
1 novio
5 pachuco @ (1&)
4 padrino
1 paisano
1 panadera
1 pansón !
2 panzón
1 pastor
3 patrón (1&&)
2 patrona
1 patroncita
1 pelado
1 pelón
3 peón (1&&)
2 perico
1 picador
2 pobre
2 pobrecito
1 pobretería
1 pochito @
3 pocho @
3 policía
4 político
1 porfirista @
1 pozolera @
1 preguntón
3 ranchera
2 rancherita
4 ranchero
6 raza #
1 revolucionario
2 rico
1 rinche #

1 rojo
1 ruca #
1 ruka #
1 ruquito #
2 rurales& @ (1&, 1&&)
2 soldadera
2 soldado
1 surumato #
1 taquillera
1 tarahumara @
1 tejano
1 torero
1 tortillera
2 tuerto
2 turista
1 vagabundo
4 vaquero
1 varillero @ &
3 vato (2&)
1 vecina
2 vendido #
2 veterano
2 villista @
3 viejita
1 viejito
1 virulo #

15. Frequency

(1967-1985 corpus)

The descending row to the left indicates in how many texts the listed terms occur. The number of texts in which a given term occurs more than a dozen times is added in parentheses. Spelling variants (*bato, vato*) are not counted separately. Personal or geographical names (*Pancho Villa, Tenochtitlán, México*) and currencies (*centavo*) are not included.

If accents are not counted as distinctive markers, forty-five of the sixty words that occur in five and more texts appear in *Webster's*, still thirty-seven of them in the considerably smaller "American College Edition" of the *American Heritage Dictionary* (*AHD*), which might correspond better to the actual North American usage of English. *Abrazo, campesino, cucaracha, jefe, mexicano, muchacho, petate,* and *pachuco* appear in *Webster's*, but not in *AHD, cabrón, caca, chota, comadre* (in contrast to *compadre*), *curandera, gracias, hijo, Llorona, menudo, pendejo, puta, raza, sí, tía, tío,* and *vámonos* in neither of the two dictionaries. The fact that a Spanish word does not appear in a dictionary of American English does not necessarily mean that it is *hermetic. Raza* is close enough to its etymological pair *race* and *Gracias, sí,* and *vámonos* can be counted as *clichés.*

	Address	Impact	Ethnographic	Culinary	Groups	Others	
15				tortilla (4)			
14							
13							
12						gringo (4)	
11				chile (1)			
10	señor (4)		barrio (2)				
9	don (4)		adobe (2)			anglo (3)	
8	señora (3) mamá (2)	cabrón (1)	corral (2)		tamal	chicano (5)	
7	compadre (2) tío (2) comadre adiós (1)	ay (2) caca loco puta	cantina (2) huarache (1) macho mariachi		menudo tequila (1)		
6	papá (3) gracias sí (1) vámonos	pendejo	burro (2) fiesta patio (1) sarape (2) sombrero abrazo pueblo (1)		enchilada taco	campesino curandera (1) raza	
5	hombre (1) hermano hijo jefe muchacho (1) señorita (1) tía (1) vieja	Ave María Purísima (1)	cucaracha Llorona (1) petate		marihuana	bracero chota pachuco	
4	amigo (1) doña (3) primo (1)	chichi chingado diablo desgraciado puto (1) Virgen de Guadalupe	arroyo (1) cuento plaza (1) rancho grito		burrito chorizo frijol (1)	americano familia mestizo padrino político ranchero vaquero vato	qué

	Address	Impact	Ethnographic	Culinary	Groups	Others
3	carnal (1)	chingada (1)	álamo	atole (1)	abuelita (1)	muerte
	chango	malcriado	alameda	capirotada	abuelo	
	corazón (1)	maldito	bronco	empanada	bolillo	
	mamacita	mierda	colonia	huevo	borracho	
	buenos días	pinche	corrido	masa	cacique	
	buenas noches	hacienda (2)	pulque		gachupín	
	qué pasó	ay Dios	machete (1)		gringa	
	se habla es-	palo blanco	machismo		güera (1)	
	pañol	viva la ra-	mañana		patrón (1)	
		za (1)	metate		pocho	
			piñata		policía	
			poncho		peón (1)	
			río		ranchera	
			Segundo Barrio	viejita		

Entries which are not listed above but appear more than a dozen times in one text (most of the ethnographic terms listed occur in Barrio Boy*):*

Address	Impact	Ethnographic	Culinary	Groups	Others
ese	viva	alpaca		abuela	
maestro		autoridades		arriero	
mija		candil		bruja	
mijita		guerrilla		contador	
		llano		charro	
		mesa		Dorados	
		milpa		federales	
		mochila		gabacho	
		pastura		güero	
		pretil		hispano	
		reata		indio	
		tapanco		jalcocotecano	
		vecindad		jinete	
				mojado	
				rurales	
				varillero	

Entries that appear more than two *dozen times in a text*

Address	Impact	Ethnographic	Culinary	Groups	Others
don (4)		adobe	tequila	chicano	
doña		arroyo	tortilla	gringo	
ese		barrio		güera	
maestro		corral (2)		jinete	
señor (2)		hacienda		patrón	
señora		plaza		peón	
tía		pretil		rurales	
		pueblo			
		sarape			

16. The Texts

(expanded corpus)

The statistic tables have to be taken with a grain of salt. While secondary language elements can be counted exactly, their understandability for a nonnative speaker cannot be assessed in absolute terms, and neither can the degree of translation. By the same token, the cumulative index in 16.8 represents no absolute classification but depends up to a certain point on the weighing of each individual factor.

The texts are listed in descending order, those including most Spanish entries, the most hermetic Spanish, or that offer least translation, are on top. The four Chicana novels analized in chapter 12 are printed in boldface. Given the low frequency of Spanish entries in *Leaving Home*, *Mango Street* and *Tattoo*, the statistic results are of little significance as far as these three texts are concerned. The following page numbers have been used for the calculations: *Alhambra* 185, *Barrio Boy* 266, *Buffalo* 189, *Clemente* 148, *Cockroach* 248, *Horseman* 398, *Hunger* 193, *Leaving Home* 249, *Louise* 124, *Mango Street* 96, *Plum Pickers* 196, *Rain God* 178, *Rites* 106, *Sapogonia* 307, *Tamazunchale* 98, *Tattoo* 341, *Tortuga* 197, *Trini* 238, *Ultima* 232, *Ultraviolet Sky* 373, *Victuum* 345, *Wedding* 195.

16.1 Single Words

(sorted on different words per page)

	different words	different words per page	absolute number of words	absolute number per page	repetition average
Louise	224	1.81	389	3.14	1.74
Barrio Boy	284	1.07	1600	6.02	5.63
Tamazunchale	95	0.97	237	2.42	2.49
Clemente	139	0.94	323	2.18	2.32
Trini	190	0.80	715	3.00	3.76
Plum Pickers	137	0.70	440	2.24	3.21
Ultima	117	0.50	348	1.50	2.97
Alhambra	86	0.46	177	0.96	2.06
Cockroach	112	0.45	394	1.59	3.52
Sapogonia	112	0.36	285	0.93	2.54
Wedding	68	0.35	270	1.38	3.97
Horseman	134	0.34	675	1.70	5.04
Rites	35	0.33	66	0.62	1.89
Buffalo	58	0.31	103	0.54	1.78
Valley	31	0.31	240	2.40	7.74
Victuum	94	0.27	600	1.74	6.38
Rain God	40	0.22	64	0.36	1.60
Hunger	38	0.20	126	0.65	3.32
Tortuga	36	0.18	88	0.44	2.44
Mango Street	15	0.16	21	0.22	1.40
Ultraviolet Sky	47	0.13	160	0.43	3.40
Leaving Home	30	0.12	46	0.18	1.53
Tattoo	3	0.01	16	0.05	5.33
Total Number:	2130		7388		
Average Number:		0.48		1.51	3.46

16.2 Short Entries

(sorted on different entries per page)

	different	different per page	absolute	absolute per page
Louise	109	0.88	119	0.96
Clemente	73	0.49	82	0.55
Barrio Boy	102	0.38	173	0.65
Tamazunchale	35	0.36	36	0.37
Plum Pickers	68	0.35	79	0.40
Ultima	80	0.34	120	0.52
Rites	29	0.27	30	0.28
Trini	51	0.21	74	0.31
Alhambra	38	0.21	45	0.24
Sapogonia	5	0.19	113	0.37
Cockroach	38	0.15	50	0.20
Victuum	50	0.14	74	0.21
Buffalo	24	0.13	25	0.13
Ultraviolet Sky	27	0.07	57	0.15
Rain God	12	0.07	13	0.07
Horseman	24	0.06	42	0.11
Valley	24	0.06	24	0.06
Wedding	12	0.06	32	0.16
Hunger	10	0.05	10	0.05
Leaving Home	10	0.04	10	0.04
Mango Street	2	0.02	2	0.02
Tortuga	4	0.02	6	0.03
Tattoo	0	0	0	0
Total Number:	827		1216	
Average Number:		0.20		0.26

16.3 Long Entries and Songs
(sorted on long entries per page)

	long entries	per page	songs
Louise	53	0.43	0
Clemente	48	0.32	0
Trini	20	0.08	1
Ultima	18	0.08	1
Barrio Boy	19	0.07	1
Sapogonia	16	0.05	4
Plum Pickers	8	0.04	2
Alhambra	6	0.03	0
Cockroach	7	0.03	2
Buffalo	5	0.03	0
Tamazunchale	2	0.02	0
Victuum	5	0.01	1
Ultraviolet Sky	3	0.01	0
Valley	1	0.01	0
Hunger	1	0.01	0
Tortuga	1	0.01	2
Leaving Home	1	0.00	0
Mango Street	0	0	0
Rites	0	0	1
Rain God	0	0	0
Tattoo	0	0	0
Horseman	0	0	1
Wedding	0	0	0

Total Number: 214   16
Average Number: 0.05

16.4 Hermetic Entries
(out of a sample of 30 entries)

Trini	17
Rites	15
Louise	14
Wedding	13
Leaving Home	12
Barrio Boy	12
Sapogonia	12
Rain God	11
Ultraviolet Sky	11
Buffalo	10
Clemente	10
Tortuga	10
Valley	10
Alhambra	9
Victuum	9
Cockroach	8
Ultima	8
Tamazunchale	8
Mango Street	8 (extrapolated)
Horseman	8
Hunger	7
Plum Pickers	6
Tattoo	n/a

Average Number: 10

16.5 Translation

(out of a sample of ten entries; listed in ascending order)

Each sample entry was given 0 (no translation at all), 1 (partial translation, translation by context), or 2 points (full translation, explanation)

Clemente	7
Cockroach	9
Tamazunchale	9
Sapogonia	9
Buffalo	10
Tortuga	10
Alhambra	10
Louise	10
Rites	10
Ultima	11
Trini	11
Ultraviolet Sky	12
Plum Pickers	12
Victuum	12
Hunger	12
Horseman	14
Wedding	15
Rain God	17
Leaving Home	19
Valley	19
Barrio Boy	22 (additional translation in Glossary)
Mango Street	n/a
Tattoo	n/a

16.6 Language as a Theme
(sorted on occurrences per page)

	occurrences	per page
Hunger	54	0.28
Clemente	27	0.18
Barrio Boy	38	0.14
Sapogonia	43	0.14
Rites	14	0.13
Louise	15	0.12
Mango Street	9	0.09
Valley	9	0.09
Rain God	13	0.07
Tamazunchale	5	0.05
Plum Pickers	10	0.05
Cockroach	12	0.05
Leaving Home	11	0.04
Buffalo	8	0.04
Trini	7	0.03
Alhambra	4	0.02
Victuum	7	0.02
Horseman	7	0.02
Ultima	4	0.02
Ultraviolet Sky	5	0.01
Tortuga	2	0.01
Tattoo	1	0.00
Wedding	0	0

| **Total Number:** | 305 | |
| **Average Number:** | 13 | 0.07 |

16.7 Fictitious Spanish
(sorted on occurrences per page)

	occurrences	per page
Rain God	14	0.08
Alhambra	13	0.07
Sapogonia	14	0.05
Leaving Home	5	0.02
Clemente	3	0.02
Louise	3	0.02
Tamazunchale	2	0.02
Victuum	6	0.02
Barrio Boy	3	0.01
Horseman	2	0.01
Trini	2	0.01
Ultima	2	0.01
Hunger	1	0.01
Buffalo	1	0.01
Cockroach	1	0.00
Ultraviolet Sky	1	0.00
Wedding	0	0
Plum Pickers	0	0
Tattoo	0	0
Rites	0	0
Total Number:	73	
Average Number:	3	0.01

16.8 Cumulative Classification

This classification, an attempt at an overall assessment of the use of Spanish, is based on a cumulative index of tables 16.1-16.7. It lists, in descending order, the twelve texts that use Spanish most frequently, include the most hermetic Spanish entries, and translate them least.

1. *Louise*
2. *Barrio Boy*
3. *Clemente*
4. **Trini**
5. **Sapogonia**
6. *Tamazunchale*
7. *Plum Pickers*
8. *Ultima*
9. *Rites*
10. *Cockroach*
11. *Alhambra*
12. *Buffalo*

Bibliography

The Corpus

Acosta, Oscar Zeta. *The Autobiography of a Brown Buffalo.* San Francisco: Straight Arrow Books, 1972.

———. *The Revolt of the Cockroach People.* San Francisco: Straight Arrow Books, 1973.

Anaya, Rudolfo. *Bless Me, Ultima.* Berkeley: Tonatiuh-Quinto Sol, 1972.

———. *Tortuga.* Berkeley: Justa, 1979.

Arias, Ron. *The Road to Tamazunchale.* 1975. 3rd ed. Tempe, AZ: Bilingual / Bilingüe, 1987.

Barrio, Raymond. *The Plum Plum Pickers.* 1969. Binghamton, NY: Bilingual / Bilingüe, 1984.

Candelaria, Nash. *Memories of the Alhambra.* Palo Alto: Cibola, 1977.

Cisneros, Sandra. *The House on Mango Street.* Houston: Arte Público, 1985.

Delgado, Abelardo. *Letters to Louise.* Berkeley: Tonatiuh-Quinto Sol, 1982.

Galarza, Ernesto. *Barrio Boy.* Notre Dame: U of Notre Dame P, 1971.

Garcia, Lionel. *Leaving Home.* Houston: Arte Público, 1985.

Hinojosa, Rolando. *Rites and Witnesses.* Houston: Arte Público, 1982.

———. *The Valley.* Ypsilanti, MI: Bilingual / Bilingüe, 1983.

Islas, Arturo. *The Rain God: A Desert Tale.* Palo Alto: Alexandrian, 1984.

Rios, Isabella. *Victuum.* Ventura: Diana Etna Inc., 1976.

Rodriguez, Richard. *Hunger of Memory: The Education of Richard Rodriguez.* 1982. New York: Bantam, 1983.

Salas, Floyd. *Tattoo the Wicked Cross.* New York: Grove, 1967.

Villarreal, José Antonio. *Clemente Chacón: A Novel.* Binghamton, NY: Bilingual / Bilingüe, 1984.

———. *The Fifth Horseman.* 1974. Binghamton, NY: Bilingual / Bilingüe, 1984.

Other Chicano Novels Mentioned

Anaya, Rudolfo. *A Chicano in China.* Albuquerque: U of New Mexico P, 1986.

———. *Heart of Aztlán.* Berkeley: Justa, 1976.

———. *The Legend of La Llorona.* Berkeley: Tonatiuh-Quinto Sol, 1984.

———. *Segne mich Ultima*. Trans. Horst Tonn. Frankfurt am Main: Nexus Verlag, 1984.

Brito, Aristeo. *El diablo en Texas*. Tucson: Peregrinos, 1976.

Candelaria, Nash. *Inheritance of Strangers*. Binghamton, NY: Bilingual / Bilingüe, 1985.

———. *Not by the Sword*. Ypsilanti, MI: Bilingual / Bilingüe, 1982.

Castillo, Ana. *The Mixquiahuala Letters*. Binghamton, NY: Bilingual / Bilingüe, 1986.

———. *Sapogonia*. Tempe, AZ: Bilingual / Bilingüe, 1990.

Chávez, Denise. *The Last of the Menu Girls*. Houston: Arte Público, 1986.

Cota-Cárdenas, Margarita. *Puppet*. Austin, TX: Relámpago Books, 1985.

Elizondo, Sergio. *Muerte en una estrella*. México, D.F.: Tinta Negra, 1984.

Garcia, Lionel. *Hardscrub*. Houston: Arte Público, 1989.

———. *A Shroud in the Family*. Houston: Arte Público, 1987.

Hinojosa, Rolando. *Dear Rafe*. Houston: Arte Público, 1985.

———. *Partners in Crime: A Rafe Buenrostro Mystery*. Houston: Arte Público, 1985.

———. *Becky and Her Friends*. Houston: Arte Público, 1990.

———. *Estampas del Valle y otras obras*. Berkeley: Justa, 1973.

———. *Klail City y sus alrededores*. La Habana: Casa de Las Américas, 1976. Republished as *Generaciones y semblanzas*. Bilingual edition. Trans. Rosaura Sánchez. Berkeley, CA: Justa, 1977.

———. *Claros varones de Belken*. Bilingual edition. Trans. Julia Cruz. Tempe, AZ: Bilingual / Bilingüe, 1986.

———. *Los amigos de Becky*. Houston: Arte Público, 1991.

———. *Mi querido Rafa*. Houston: Arte Público, 1981.

Méndez, Miguel. *Peregrinos de Aztlán*. Berkeley: Justa, 1974.

———. *El sueño de Santa María de las Piedras*. Guadalajara, Jalisco: EDUG, 1986.

Morales, Alejandro. *Caras viejas y vino nuevo*. México, D.F.: Joaquín Mortiz, 1975.

———. *La verdad sin voz*. México, D.F.: Joaquín Mortiz, 1979.

———. *Reto en el paraíso*. Ypsilanti, MI: Bilingual / Bilingüe, 1983.

Pineda, Cecile. *Face*. New York: Penguin, 1985.

———. *Frieze*. New York: Penguin, 1986.

Ponce, Mary Helen. *The Wedding*. Houston: Arte Público, 1989.

Portillo Trambley, Estela. *Trini*. Binghamton, NY: Bilingual / Bilingüe, 1986.

Rivera, Tomás. *. . . Y no se lo tragó la tierra*. Berkeley: Justa, 1977.

Romero, Orlando. *Nambé—Year One*. Berkeley: Tonatiuh-Quinto Sol, 1976.

Salas, Floyd. *Lay My Body on the Line.* Berkeley: Y'Bird, 1978.
——. *What Now My Love.* New York: Grove, 1969.
Torres-Metzgar, Joseph V. *Below the Summit.* Berkeley: Tonatiuh-Quinto Sol, 1976.
Valdés, Gina. *There Are No Madmen Here.* San Diego, CA: Maize, 1981.
Vasquez, Richard. *Chicano.* Garden City, NY: Doubleday, 1970.
Villanueva, Alma Luz. *The Ultraviolet Sky.* Tempe, AZ: Bilingual, 1988.
Villarreal, José Antonio. *Pocho.* Garden City, NY: Doubleday, 1959.
Villaseñor, Edmund. *Macho!* New York: Bantam, 1973.

Other Literature Mentioned

450 años del pueblo chicano / 450 Years of Chicano History in Pictures. Albuquerque, NM: Chicano Communications Center, 1976.

Acuña, Rodolfo. *Occupied America: A History of Chicanos.* 2nd ed. New York: Harper & Row, 1981.
Akers, John C. "From Translation to Rewriting: Rolando Hinojosa's *The Valley.*" *The Americas Review* 21.1 (1993): 91-102.
Alberti, Rafael. *Sobre los ángeles.* Madrid: Cátedra, 1984.
Alurista. "Cultural Nationalism and Chicano Literature: 1965-75." Bardeleben et al. 41-52.
——. *Floricanto en Aztlán.* Los Angeles: Chicano Studies Center, University of California, 1976.
Alurista. *Return: Poems Collected and New.* Ypsilanti, MI: Bilingual / Bilingüe, 1982.
——. *Spik in Glyph.* Houston, TX: Arte Público, 1981.
Anzaldúa, Gloria. *Borderlands / La Frontera: The New Mestiza.* San Francisco: Aunt Lute Books, 1987.
Arciniega, Tomás A. "The Myth of the Compensatory Education Model in the Education of Chicanos." O. de la Garza et al. 173-83.
Arguedas, José María. *El zorro de arriba y el zorro de abajo.* Ed. Eve-Marie Fell. Colección Archivos 14. Madrid: CSIC, 1990.
Arrabal, Fernando. *Pic-Nic. El triciclo. El laberinto.* Madrid: Cátedra, 1986.
Ayala, Francisco. *La imagen de España: continuidad y cambio en la sociedad española.* Madrid: Alianza, 1986.

Baker, Houston A., Jr., ed. *Three American Literatures: Essays in Chicano, Native American, and Asian-American Literature for Teachers of American Literature.* New York: MLA, 1982.

Bakhtin, Mikhail. "Discourse in the Novel." *The Dialogic Imagination: Four Essays by M.M. Bakhtin.* Ed. Michael Holquist. Trans. M. Holquist and Emerson Caryl. Austin: U of Texas P, 1981. 259-422.

"Banned Books Week Hits Home With UNM Professor." *New Mexico Daily Lobo* 24 Sept. 1986: 6.

Bardeleben, Renate von, Dietrich Briesemeister, and Juan Bruce-Novoa, eds. *Missions in Conflict: Essays on U.S.-Mexican Relations and Chicano Culture.* Tübingen: Gunter Narr, 1986.

Barker, George C. *Pachuco: An American-Spanish Argot and Its Social Functions in Tucson, Arizona.* Tucson: U of Arizona P, 1979.

Beddow, Michael. *The Fiction of Humanity: Studies in the Bildungsroman from Wieland to Thomas Mann.* Cambridge: Cambridge UP, 1982.

Benjamin, Walter. "Die Aufgabe des Übersetzers." *Illuminationen: Ausgewählte Schriften.* Frankfurt: Suhrkamp, 1980. 50-62.

———. "The Task of the Translator." *Illuminations.* Trans. Harry Zohn. Glasgow: Collins, 1973. 69-82.

Berkhofer, Robert. *The White Man's Indian: Images of the American Indian from Columbus to the Present.* New York: Vintage, 1979.

Binder, Wolfgang. *Anglos Are Weird People for Me: Interviews with Chicanos and Puerto Ricans.* Materialien 12. Berlin: John F. Kennedy-Institut für Nordamerikastudien, 1979.

———. "Mothers and Grandmothers: Acts of Mythification and Remembrance in Chicano Poetry." Bardeleben et al. 133-43.

Blanco, Antonio S. *La lengua española en la historia de California: contribución a su estudio.* Madrid: Cultura Hispánica, 1971.

Booth, Wayne C. *The Rhetoric of Fiction.* 2nd ed. Chicago: U of Chicago P, 1983.

Bruce-Novoa, Juan. *Chicano Authors: Inquiry by Interview.* Austin: U of Texas P, 1980.

———. *Chicano Poetry: A Response to Chaos.* Austin: U of Texas P, 1982.

Bus, Heiner. "The Presence of Native Americans in Chicano Literature." *International Studies in Honor of Tomás Rivera.* Ed. Julián Olivares. Spec. issue of *Revista Chicano-Riqueña* 13.3-4 (1985): 148-62.

Calderón, Héctor. "History as Subtext in Contemporary Chicano Narrative: The Examples of Rivera and Anaya." Symposium on "Vision and Representation of History in the Cultural Production of Hispanics in the United States." Centre Interdisciplinaire de Recherches Nord-Américaines, Université Paris VII. Paris, 12 and 13 May 1987.

——. "On the Uses of Chronicle, Biography and Sketch in Rolando Hinojosa's *Generaciones y Semblanzas*." J. D. Saldívar, *Hinojosa Reader* 133-42.

——. "The Rain God: A Desert Tale. By Arturo Islas." Rev. *Revista Chicano Riqueña* 12.2 (1985): 68-70.

Calvo Buezas, Tomás. *Los más pobres en el país más rico: clase, raza y etnia en el movimiento campesino chicano.* Madrid: Encuentro, 1981.

Canonica-de Rochemonteix, Elvezio. *El poliglotismo en el teatro de Lope de Vega.* Kassel: Edition Reichenberger, 1991.

Cazemajou, Jean. "*Hunger of Memory* (1982) de Richard Rodriguez: La parole et le verbe." *Le facteur réligieux en Amérique du Nord. Nº5: Religion et groupes ethniques au Canada et aux Etats Unis.* Ed. Jean Béranger. Talence: M.S.H.A., 1984. 147-65.

Cela, Camilo José. *Cristo versus Arizona.* Barcelona: Seix Barral, 1988.

——. *Mazurca para dos muertos.* Barcelona: Seix Barral, 1983.

Cervantes, Miguel de. *Los trabajos de Persiles y Segismunda.* Ed. Juan Bautista Avalle-Arce. Madrid: Castalia, 1969.

Cockroft, James D. *Outlaws in the Promised Land: Mexican Immigrant Workers and America's Future.* New York: Grove, 1986.

Colón, Cristóbal. *Diario de a bordo.* Madrid: Generales Anaya, 1985.

Cooper, James Fenimore. *The Last of the Mohicans.* 1826. New York: New American Library, 1962.

Cortázar, Julio. *Rayuela.* Buenos Aires: Sudamericana, 1968.

Cruz, Sor Juana Inés de la. *Inundación Castálida.* 1689. Madrid: Castalia, 1982.

Dasenbrock, Reed Way. "Intelligibility and Meaningfulness in Multicultural Literature in English." *PMLA* 102.1 (1987): 10-19.

Deleuze, Gilles, and Felix Guattari. *Kafka. Für eine kleine Literatur.* Trans. Burkhart Kroeber. Frankfurt: Suhrkamp, 1976.

Delgado, Abelardo. *Bajo el sol de Aztlán: 25 soles de Abelardo.* El Paso, TX: Barrio, 1973.

——. *Chicano: 25 Pieces of a Chicano Mind.* Denver, CO: Barrio, 1969.

——. *It's Cold: 52 Cold-Thought Poems of Abelardo.* Salt Lake City, UT: Barrio, 1974.

de Man, Paul. " 'Conclusions': Walter Benjamin's 'The Task of the Translator.' " *The Resistance to Theory.* Theory and History of Literature 33. Minneapolis: U of Minnesota P, 1986. 73-105.

Durán, Richard P., ed. *Latino Language and Communicative Behavior.* Norwood, NJ: ABLEX, 1981.

Eger, Ernestina N. *A Bibliography of Criticism of Contemporary Chicano Literature*. Chicano Studies Library Publication Series No. 5. Berkeley: Chicano Studies Library, University of California, 1982.

——. "A Selected Bibliography of Criticism of the Chicano Novel." Lattin, *Contemporary Chicano Fiction* 316-31.

Ehrlich, Elizabeth. "Should English-Only Be the Law of the Land?: A Controverial Campaign Led by S.I. Hayakawa Will Be Put to a Big Test in California's Election." *Business Week* 10 Nov. 1986: 62.

Ehrlich, Paul R. Assisted by Loy Bilderback and Anne H. Ehrlich. *The Golden Door: International Migration, Mexico, and the United States*. N.p.: Wideview, 1981.

Eliot, Thomas Stearns. *The Waste Land*. Ed. Valerie Eliot. 1922. New York: Harcourt Brace Jovanovich, 1971.

"English Plus: English Plus Information Clearinghouse, Statement of Purpose." *American Studies Newsletter* 22 (Sept. 1990): 38.

Fabian, Johannes. *Time and the Other: How Anthropology Makes Its Objects*. New York: Columbia UP, 1983.

Faulkner, William. *The Hamlet: A Novel of the Snopes Family*. 1940. New York: Vintage-Random House, 1956.

Fernández-Shaw, Carlos M. *Presencia española en los Estados Unidos*. Madrid: Cultura Hispánica, 1972.

Forster, Leonard. *The Poet's Tongues: Multilingualism in Literature*. London: Cambridge, 1970.

Galván, Roberto A., and Richard V. Teschner. *El diccionario del español chicano: The Dictionary of Chicano Spanish*. Lincolnwood, IL: National Textbook Company, 1985.

García, Eugene E., Francisco A. Lomelí, and Isidro D. Ortiz, eds. *Chicano Studies: A Multidisciplinary Approach*. New York: Teachers College, 1984.

García Lorca, Federico. *Así que pasen cinco años*. Ed. E. F. Granell. Madrid: Taurus, 1981.

——. *Poeta en Nueva York. Tierra y luna*. Ed. Eutimio Martín. Barcelona: Ariel, 1981.

——. "Llanto por Ignacio Sánchez Mejías." *Obras Completas I*. Madrid: Aguilar, 1977. 551-58.

García Márquez, Gabriel, and Plinio Apuleyo Mendoza. *El olor de la guayaba: conversaciones con Plinio Apuleyo Mendoza*. Barcelona: Bruguera, 1982.

García Yebra, Valentín. *Teoría y práctica de la traducción*. Madrid: Gredos, 1982. 2 vols.

Gil, Carlos B. "Galarza, Ernesto." Martínez and Lomelí 441-48.

Glazer, Sarah. "Bilingual Education: Does It Work?" *American Studies Newsletter* 22 (Sept. 1990): 28-33.

González, Laverne. "Portillo Trambley, Estela." Martínez and Lomelí 316-22.

Gonzales-Berry, Erlinda. "Chicano Literature in Spanish: Roots and Content." Diss. U of New Mexico 1978.

———. "*Estampas del Valle*: From *Costumbrismo* to Self-Reflecting Literature." Lattin, *Contemporary Chicano Fiction* 149-61.

Goethe, Johann Wolfgang von. "Chronik von Goethes Leben." Compiled by Franz Götting. *Registerband*. Vol. 18 of *Sämtliche Werke*. Zürich: Ex Libris, 1979. 435-540.

———. "Übersetzungen." *Sämtliche Werke*. Vol. 3. Zürich: Ex Libris, 1979. 554-57.

Grande, Félix. *Memoria del flamenco*. Madrid: Espasa-Calpe, 1979.

Güiraldes, Ricardo. *Don Segundo Sombra*. 1926. Madrid: Cátedra, 1985.

Hayakawa, S. I. "English Should Be the Only Language: Bilingualism in America." *American Studies Newsletter* 22 (Sept. 1989): 34-37.

Hemingway, Ernest. *For Whom the Bell Tolls*. London: Grafton, 1976.

Herms, Dieter. "Die Literatur des Chicano Movement: Identitätssuche, Kulturkonflikt und Protest." Ostendorf, *Amerikanische Ghettoliteratur* 293-322.

Hernández, José. *Martín Fierro*. 1872-79. Barcelona: Bruguera, 1975.

Hernández-Chávez, Eduardo, Andrew D. Cohen, and Anthony F. Beltramo, eds. *El Lenguaje de los Chicanos: Regional and Social Characteristics Used by Mexican Americans*. Arlington, VA: CAL, 1975.

Hinojosa, Rolando. "A Voice of One's Own." J.D. Saldívar, *Hinojosa Reader* 11-17.

Iser, Wolfgang. *The Implied Reader: Patterns of Communication in Prose Fiction from Bunyan to Beckett*. Baltimore: Johns Hopkins UP, 1974.

Isernhagen, Hartwig. "Anthropological Narrative and the Structure of North American (auto-)biography." Ed. Udo Fries. *SPELL* 3 (1987): 221-33.

———. "Nationale Geschichte und Internationale Kultur: Zur Problematik neuer englischsprachiger Literaturen (am Beispiel Albert Wendt)." *Anglistentag 1983 Konstanz: Vorträge*. Ed. J. Schläger. Giessen: Hoffman, 1984. 405-21.

Jiménez, Francisco. "Chicano Literature: Sources and Themes." *Bilingual Review / Revista Bilingüe* 1 (1974): 4-15.
———, ed. *The Identification and Analysis of Chicano Literature.* New York: Bilingual / Bilingüe, 1979.
Joyce, James. *Ulysses.* 1922. Harmondsworth: Penguin, 1971.

Kanellos, Nicolás, and Claudio Esteva-Fabregat, eds. *Handbook of Hispanic Cultures in the United States.* Vol. 4. Houston: Arte Público, 1993.
Keller, Gary D. "How Chicano Authors Use Bilingual Techniques for Literary Effect." García et al. 171-92.
———. "The Literary Strategems Available to the Bilingual Chicano Writer." Jiménez, *Identification* 263-316.

Lattin, Vernon E., ed. *Contemporary Chicano Fiction: A Critical Survey.* Binghamton, NY: Bilingual / Bilingüe, 1986.
———. "Contemporary Chicano Novel, 1959-1979." Martínez and Lomelí 184-97
Leal, Luis. *Aztlán y México. Perfiles literarios e históricos.* Binghamton: Bilingual / Bilingüe, 1985.
———, ed. *A Decade of Chicano Literature (1970-1979): Critical Essays and Bibliography.* Santa Bárbara: La Causa, 1982.
———. "History and Memory in *Estampas del Valle.*" J. D. Saldívar, *Hinojosa Reader* 101-08.
———. "Mexican American Literature: A Historical Perspective." *Revista Chicano Riqueña* 1.1 (1973): 32-44.
———. "Narrativa Chicana: Viejas y nuevas tendencias." *Aztlán y México* 111-20.
Leal, Luis, and Pepe Barrón. "Chicano Literature: An Overview." Baker 9-32
Le Guin, Ursula K. "Bryn Mawr Commencement Address (1986)." *Dancing at the Edge of the World.* New York: Grove, 1989. 147-60.
Lipski, John M. *Linguistic Aspects of Spanish-English Language Switching.* Special Studies 25. Tempe: Arizona State University, Center for Latin American Studies, 1985.
———. "Spanish-English Language Switching in Speech and Literature: Theories and Models." *The Bilingual Review/La Revista Bilingüe* 9.3 (1982): 191-212.
Lomelí, Francisco. "Novel." Leal, *Decade* 29-40
Lomelí, Francisco, and Donaldo Urioste. *Chicano Perspectives in Literature.* Albuquerque: Pajarito, 1976.
Lope Blanch, Juan M. *Léxico indígena en el español de México.* 2ª ed. México: El Colegio de México, 1979.

Lyon, Ted. " 'Loss of Innocence' in Chicano Prose." Jiménez, *Identification* 254-62.

Machado, Antonio. *Poesía y prosa*. Madrid: Espasa-Calpe, 1989. 4 vols.

Mackey, William F., and Jacob Ornstein, eds. *The Bilingual Education Movement: Essays on Its Progress*. Studies in Language and Linguistics 1977-78. El Paso: Texas Western, 1977.

Márquez, Antonio. "A Discordant Image: The Mexican in American Literature." *Minority Voices* 5.1-2 (1981): 41-51.

——. "Literatura Chicanesca: The View from Without." Unpublished ms. 1985.

——. "Richard Rodriguez' *Hunger of Memory* and the Poetics of Experience." *Arizona Quarterly* (1983): 130-41.

Martín-Santos, Luis. *Tiempo de silencio*. Barcelona: Seix Barral, 1986.

Martínez, Julio A., and Francisco A. Lomelí, eds. *Chicano Literature: A Reference Guide*. Westport, CT: Greenwood, 1985.

Mejías, Hugo A. *Préstamos de lenguas indígenas en el español americano del siglo XVII*. México, D.F.: Universidad Nacional Autónoma de México, 1980.

Meléndez, Teresa. "Hinojosa-Smith, Rolando." Martínez and Lomelí 229-44

Mencken, H. L. *The American Language: An Inquiry into the Development of English in the United States*. 4th ed. New York: Knopf, 1941.

Mirandé, Alfredo. *The Chicano Experience: An Alternative Perspective*. Notre Dame: U of Notre Dame P, 1985.

Morínigo, Marcos A. *Diccionario de americanismos*. Barcelona: Muchnik, 1985.

Mounin, Georges. *Les problèmes théoriques de la traduction*. Paris: Gallimard, 1963.

Nabokov, Vladimir. *Pale Fire*. New York: Putnam's, 1962.

Namias, June. *First Generation, in the Words of Twentieth-Century American Immigrants*. Introd. by Robert Coles. Boston: Beacon, 1978.

Nervo, Amado. *Obras completas*. Volume II. Madrid: Aguilar, 1952.

O. de la Garza, Rudolph, Z. Anthony Kruszewski, and Tomás A. Arciniega, eds. *Chicanos and Native Americans: The Territorial Minorities*. Englewood Cliffs, NJ: Prentice-Hall, 1973.

Ong, Walter J., intro. "On Saying We and Us to Literature." Baker 3-7.

Ornstein, Jacob. "Sociolinguistics and New Perspectives in the Study of Southwest Spanish." *Studies in Language and Linguistics 1969-70*. Ed. Ralph W. Ewton and Jacob Ornstein. El Paso: Texas Western, 1970. 127-84.

Ortega, Adolfo. "Of Social Politics and Poetry: A Chicano Perspective." *Latin American Literary Review* 5.10 (1977): 32-41.

Ortega y Gasset, José. *Miseria y esplendor de la traducción / Elend und Glanz der Übersetzung*. Übersetzt von Gustav Kilpper. Ebenhausen bei München: Edition Langewiesche-Brandt, 1957.

Ostendorf, Berndt, ed. *Amerikanische Ghettoliteratur: Zur Literatur ethnischer, marginaler und unterdrückter Gruppen in Amerika*. Darmstadt: Wissenschaftliche Buchgesellschaft, 1983.

——. "Einleitung." Ostendorf, *Amerikanische Ghettoliteratur* 1-26.

Paz, Octavio. *El laberinto de la soledad; Posdata; Vuelta a El laberinto de la soledad*. 1950-1979. México: Fondo de Cultura Económica, 1981.

Peñalosa, Fernando. "Some Issues in Chicano Sociolinguistics." Durán 3-18.

Penfield, Joyce, and Jacob L. Ornstein-Galicia. "Chicano Literature: Self Portrait." *Chicano English: An Ethnic Contact Dialect*. Amsterdam and Philadelphia: John Benjamins, 1985. 85-94.

Pérez Galdós, Benito. *Fortunata y Jacinta: dos historias de casadas*. Madrid: Cátedra, 1983. 2 vols.

Perreault, Jeanne. "New Dreaming: Joy Harjo, Wendy Rose, Leslie Marmon Silko." *Deferring a Dream: Literary Subversions of the American Columbiad*. Ed. Gert Buelens and Ernst Rudin. ICSELL. Basel: Birkhäuser, 1993. 120-36.

Pettit, Arthur G. *Images of the Mexican-American in Fiction and Film*. Ed. Dennis E. Showalter. College Station, TX: Texas A&M UP, 1980.

Polkinhorn, Harry, Alfredo Velasco, and Mal Lambert. *El libro del caló: Pachuco Slang Dictionary*. San Diego: Atticus, 1983.

Pratt, Mary Louise. "Arts of the Contact Zone." *Profession (MLA)* (1991): 33-40.

Pynchon, Thomas. *The Crying of Lot 49*. 1965. London: Pan Books, 1979.

Real Academia Española. *Diccionario de la lengua española*. 20th ed. Madrid: Espasa-Calpe, 1984. 2 vols.

Ríos, Julián. *Larva: Babel de una noche de San Juan*. Barcelona: del Mall, 1984.

Robinson, Cecil. *Mexico and the Hispanic Southwest in American Literature*. Tucson: U of Arizona P, 1977.

Rodríguez-Luis, Julio. *Hermenéutica y praxis del indigenismo: la novela indigenista de Clorinda Matto a José María Arguedas.* México, D.F.: Fondo de Cultura Económica, 1980.

Rodríguez del Pino, Salvador. *La novela chicana escrita en español: cinco autores comprometidos.* Ypsilanti, MI: Bilingual / Bilingüe, 1982.

Rudin, Ernst. "Don Quijote y un torero en un castillo de naipes: Bilingüismo literario, *Camino Real* de Williams y *Zaya* de Sánchez Mejías." *Literatura y bilingüismo. Homenaje a Pere Ramírez.* problemata literaria 15. Kassel: Reichenberger, 1993. 407-26.

——. "*The Fifth Horseman:* a He-male Revision of the Mexican Revolution)." Symposium on "Vision and Representation of History in the Cultural Production of Hispanics in the United States." Centre Interdisciplinaire de Recherches Nord-Américaines, Université Paris VII. Paris, 12 and 13 May 1987.

——. "Hard English and Soft Spanish: Language as a Theme in the Chicano Novel in English 1969-1985." *Gender, Self, and Society: Proceedings of the IV International Conference on the Hispanic Cultures of the United States.* Ed. Renate von Bardeleben. Frankfurt: Peter Lang, 1993. 395-410.

——. "Mestizaje cultural en forma de Rayuela." *500 Jahre Mestizaje in Sprache, Literatur und Kultur.* Ed. Sonja M. Steckbauer and Kristin A. Müller. Bibliotheca Hispano-Lusa 2. Salzburg: Institut für Romanistik der Universität Salzburg, 1993. 27-43.

——. "Se canta lo que se pierde: lengua española, discurso autobiográfico y tortillas mejicanas en la novela chicana escrita en inglés." *Versants* 21 (1992): 89-102.

Saldívar, José David, ed. *The Rolando Hinojosa Reader: Essays Historical and Critical.* Spec. issue of *Revista Chicano-Riqueña* 12.3-4 (1984).

——. "Rolando Hinojosa's *Klail City Death Trip*: A Critical Introduction." J. D. Saldívar, *Hinojosa Reader* 44-63.

Saldívar, Ramón. "A Dialectic of Difference: Toward a Theory of the Chicano Novel." Lattin, *Contemporary Chicano Fiction* 13-31.

Sánchez, Marta. "Hispanic- and Anglo-American Discourse in Edward Rivera's *Family Installments.*" *American Literary History* 1.4 (1989): 853-71.

Sánchez, Ricardo. *Amsterdam Cantos y Poemas Pistos.* Austin, TX: Place of Herons, 1981.

——. *Milhuas Blues and Gritos Norteños.* Milwaukee, WI: The Spanish-Speaking Outreach Institute, 1980.

——. *Selected Poems.* Houston, TX: Arte Público, 1985.

Santamaría, Francisco J. *Diccionario de Mejicanismos.* 4ª ed. corregida y aumentada. México, D.F.: Porrúa, 1983.

"Say It in English." *Newsweek* 20 Feb. 1989, 32-33.

Schleiermacher, Friedrich. "Ueber die verschiedenen Methoden des Uebersetzens." *Abhandlungen der philosophischen Klasse der Königlich-Preußischen Akademie der Wissenschaften aus den Jahren 1812-1813.* Berlin: Realschul-Buchhandlung, 1816. 143-72.

Smollet, Tobias. *The Expedition of Humphry Clinker.* 1771.

Sollors, Werner. *Beyond Ethnicity: Consent and Descent in American Culture.* New York: Oxford UP, 1986.

Steiner, George. *After Babel: Aspects of Language and Translation.* London: Oxford UP, 1975.

Swales, Martin. *The German Bildungsroman from Wieland to Hesse.* Princeton: Princeton UP, 1978.

Tatum, Charles M. *Chicano Literature.* TUSAS 433. Boston: Twayne, 1982.

——. "Contemporary Chicano Prose Fiction: A Chronicle of Misery." *Latin American Literary Review* 1 (1973): 7-17.

——. *A Selected and Annotated Bibliography of Chicano Studies.* Lincoln, NE: Society of Spanish and Spanish-American Studies, 1979.

Thorpe, Michael. "Literatures of Rehabilitation." *English Studies* 64 (1983): 345-60.

Todorov, Tzvetan. *La Conquête de l'Amérique.* Paris: Editions du Seuil, 1982.

——. *Mikhaïl Bakhtine: le principe dialogique.* Paris: Editions du Seuil, 1981.

Tonn, Horst. *Zeitgenössische Chicano-Erzählliteratur in englischer Sprache: Autobiographie und Roman.* Mainzer Studien zur Amerikanistik 22. Frankfurt: Peter Lang, 1988.

Trujillo, David F. "Memories of the Alhambra, by Nash Candelaria." Rev. *De Colores* 5.1&2 (1980): 130-32.

Valdés-Fallis, Guadalupe. "Code-Switching in Bilingual Chicano Poetry." *Hispania* 59 (1976): 877-86.

——. "The Sociolinguistics of Chicano Literature: Towards an Analysis of the Role and Function of Language Alternation in Contemporary Bilingual Poetry." *Point of Contact / Punto de Contacto* 1.4 (1977): 30-39.

Valdez, Luis. *Early Works: Actos, Bernabé and Pensamiento Serpentino.* Houston: Arte Público, 1990.

Valdez, Luis, and Stan Steiner, eds. *Aztlán: An Anthology of Mexican-American Literature.* New York: Knopf, 1972.

Wiget, Andrew. "English First: A Comment." *MLA Newsletter* Summer 1987: 13-14.

Ybarra Frausto, Tomás. "The Chicano Movement and the Emergence of a Chicano Poetic Consciousness." *New Scholar* 6 (1977): 81-109.

Zamora Munné, Juan Clemente. *Indigenismos en la lengua de los conquistadores.* San Juan de Puerto Rico: Universidad de Puerto Rico, 1976.

General Index

Index of Spanish Entries